The Immersive Internet

The Immersive Internet

Reflections on the Entangling of the Virtual with Society, Politics, and the Economy

Edited by

Robin Teigland
Stockholm School of Economics, Sweden

and

Dominic Power
Uppsala University, Sweden

First published 2013 by
PALGRAVE MACMILLAN

Palgrave Macmillan in the UK is an imprint of Macmillan Publishers Limited, registered in England, company number 785998, of Houndmills, Basingstoke, Hampshire RG21 6XS.

Palgrave Macmillan in the US is a division of St Martin's Press LLC, 175 Fifth Avenue, New York, NY 10010.

Palgrave Macmillan is the global academic imprint of the above companies and has companies and representatives throughout the world.

Palgrave® and Macmillan® are registered trademarks in the United States, the United Kingdom, Europe and other countries.

ISBN 978–1–137–28301–6

This book is printed on paper suitable for recycling and made from fully managed and sustained forest sources. Logging, pulping and manufacturing processes are expected to conform to the environmental regulations of the country of origin.

A catalogue record for this book is available from the British Library.

A catalog record for this book is available from the Library of Congress.

10   9   8   7   6   5   4   3   2   1
22 21 20 19 18 17 16 15 14 13

Contents

Figures and Tables

Figures

Tables

Preface and Acknowledgments

Although the book in your hands or on your screen is all about the promises and challenges of the internet, avatars, and virtual spaces, the idea for the book started with a gathering of eight people around a table in the small mountainside village of Can Serrat overlooking Barcelona in September 2010. We were there as part of the Nordic Virtual Worlds Network (NVWN) project planning and writing workshop; the NVWN project was a two-year international, interdisciplinary project co-funded by Nordic Innovation that investigated entrepreneurship and innovation through virtual worlds and the 3D internet (more information on the NVWN project and its deliverables can be found at www.nordicworlds.net). We met physically in what to us at the time seemed a relatively remote retreat, as we hoped it would provide the opportunity to interact with each other and immerse ourselves in the project without the usual distractions from our workplaces or homes: in order to exchange ideas and get things done we needed to carve out a temporary proximate and immersive space.

While each member came with his or her own views and experiences related to the Immersive Internet, a curiosity as to how this emerging phenomenon was going to impact our lives united the group. We discussed at length how the virtual might become entangled with all aspects of society, politics, and the economy on both local and international levels. Since one of the primary deliverables for the NVWN project was an edited volume, the idea for the book began to take form and has gradually evolved into what you are now reading.

As such, we would very much like to acknowledge the financial support from Nordic Innovation and in particular Nordic Innovation Advisor Hans Christian Bjørne. In addition, we would like to thank the NVWN project members and their respective institutions for their support: Elia Giovacchini and Göran Lindqvist of the Center for Strategy and Competitiveness at the Stockholm School of Economics, Sweden; Eilif Trondsen of Strategic Business Insights, USA; Bjørn-Tore Flåten, Jan Inge Jenssen, and Erik Arntsen of Agder Research at the University of Agder, Norway; Linda Björg Árnadóttir of the Iceland Academy of the Arts, Iceland; Lisbeth Frölunde and Sisse Siggaard Jensen of Roskilde University, Denmark; Titiana Moldovan, Matti Näsi, and Antti

Ainamo of the University of Turku, Finland; Christian Björkman and Per Jonasson of MindArk AB, Sweden; Ulf Berlin of Silver Design, Sweden; and Riku Mäkelä of TEKES, Finland.

We would like to thank all the contributors to this book and hope that you find their reflections on the Immersive Internet as stimulating and thought-provoking as we did.

Dominic Power and Robin Teigland
Summer 2012

Contributors

Antti Ainamo is Adjunct Professor at the School of Economics and at the School of Arts, Design and Architecture at Aalto University, Finland, as well as Guest Professor at the Umeå School of Business, Sweden. His publications include articles in the *Scandinavian Journal of Management*, *Human Relations*, *Research in the Sociology of Organizations*, *Organization Science*, *Supply Chain Management*, and *Business Strategy Review*. His current research interests include design, fashion, mountain-climbing, and other phenomena related to temporary and cooperative forms of organizing and university management cooperation.

Smiljana Antonijević is Assistant Professor of Culture and Technology at Roskilde University, Denmark and a researcher at the e-Humanities Group of the Royal Netherlands Academy of Arts and Sciences, the Netherlands. In addition to a PhD in communication/new media studies from the University of Minnesota-Twin Cities, she holds BA degrees in social anthropology and music and an MA degree in social anthropology. Her research and teaching interests intersect the areas of communication, culture, and technology while her publications focus on issues such as scholarly collaboration in virtual environments (forthcoming), digital humanities (2012), e-research (2011), trust in online interaction (2009), non-verbal communication in digital environments (2008), psychological aspects of blogging (2008), digital rhetoric (2008), and new media use in the state of crisis (2004). For more details, please see www.smiljana.org.

James Barrett is an Adjunct at HUMlab and a PhD Candidate in the Department of Language Studies at Umeå University, Sweden. His PhD thesis is titled 'Narrative Freedom: Techniques for the Control of Reading in Four Works of Digital Literature'. He has published internationally on virtual worlds, transcultural narrative, and pedagogy. His present research interests include augmented reality, virtual spaces, avatars, reading, and narrative.

Tom Boellstorff is Professor in the Department of Anthropology at the University of California, Irvine, USA, and he was Editor-in-Chief of *American Anthropologist*, the flagship journal of the American Anthropological Association, from 2007 to 2012. He is the author of many articles. Books include *The Gay Archipelago* (2005); *A Coincidence of Desires* (2007); and *Coming of Age in Second Life* (2008). He is also the co-author of *Ethnography and Virtual Worlds: A Handbook of Method* (2012). With Bill Maurer, he is the series editor for the *Princeton Studies in Culture and Technology*.

Cynthia Calongne is Professor and Chair of Emerging Media at Colorado Technical University, CTU Doctoral, USA, and is the co-editor and co-author of *Identity, Learning and Support in Virtual Worlds*. She was a Grand Prize Winner in the Federal Virtual World Challenge for the Mars Expedition Strategy Challenge. Her current research integrates virtual worlds, education, intelligent agents, and game design. Highlights from more than 100 of her conference presentations are available at http://www.slideshare.net/lyrlobo/presentations.

Edward Castronova is Professor of Telecommunications and Cognitive Science, Indiana University, USA. He has a PhD in economics from the University of Wisconsin and is a founder of scholarly online game studies and an expert on the societies of virtual worlds. Among his academic publications on these topics are two books: *Synthetic Worlds* (2005) and *Exodus to the Virtual World* (2007). He teaches graduate and undergraduate courses on the design of games, the game industry, and the management of virtual societies, and, outside his academic work, he makes regular appearances in mainstream media (*60 Minutes*, the *New York Times*, and *The Economist*), gives keynotes at major conferences (Austin Game Conference, Digital Games Research Association Conference, Interactive Software Federation of Europe), and consults for business (McKinsey, Vivendi, Forrester).

Stefano Consiglio is Full Professor of Organization Studies at the University of Napoli Federico II, Italy, where he currently teaches on organization theory and human resources topics. His research interests are mainly focused on organizational design of private and public enterprises and on human resource management topics.

Alicia B. Corts is a PhD Candidate in the Department of Theatre and Film Studies at the University of Georgia, USA. Her dissertation, 'What

Dreams May Come: Ritual Performance as Legitimization of Gendered Individual and Community Identity in Virtual Environments', focuses on performances of birth, marriage, and death in Second Life. She is also a lead researcher on the Kutiyattam Project, a working theater created in Second Life with the intent of making this ancient Indian theatrical form more accessible to Asian theater students.

William N. Dilla is the Union Pacific/Charles B. Handy Associate Professor of Accounting at Iowa State University, USA. His research focuses on information display effects on accounting judgments, accounting-related issues in virtual worlds, and judgment and decision-making in auditing. He received his PhD from the University of Texas at Austin and his MBA from Syracuse University. He has published articles in the *Accounting Review, Decision Sciences, Organizational Behavior and Human Decision Processes, Auditing: A Journal of Practice and Theory, Journal of Information Systems,* and *International Journal of Accounting Information Systems.*

Denise Doyle is an Artist Researcher and Senior Lecturer in Digital Media at the University of Wolverhampton and PhD Co-supervisor at the SMARTlab Research Institute at University College Dublin, Ireland. With a background in fine art painting and digital media, she has published widely on the subject of the virtual and the imaginary, the experience of the avatar body in virtual worlds and game spaces, and the use of virtual worlds for creative practice. Recent publications include 'Transitional Spaces: Consciousness, Imagination, and the Avatar-Mediated Experience' in *Video Game Play and Consciousness* (2012), edited by Jayne Gackenbach, and 'Hybrid Worlds, Hybrid Practices, and the Enchantment of Place' in a special issue of *Acta Academiae Artium Vilnensis* (2012) published in Lithuania. Her current research interests include virtual worlds, art-sci dialogues, interactive film, philosophies of the imagination, practice-based research methods, and digital narratives.

Inger-Marie Falgren Christensen is an e-learning consultant at the University of Southern Denmark, Denmark. Her current responsibilities are teacher training in the fields of e-learning and e-learning platforms, planning and conducting of projects that explore the learning potential of virtual learning environments, and idea development with and pedagogical support of teachers in relation to the application of e-learning. In 2008, she completed an online master's program on ICT and learning offered by a network of Danish universities, and her master's thesis focused on the competence development of teachers within the field of e-learning. She has an MA degree in English, international studies, and communication and was employed as a teacher and in the function of technical and IT-pedagogical support at Tietgen Business College in Odense, Denmark, from 1995 to 2008.

Andrew Forney is a doctoral student in computer science at the University of California, Los Angeles, USA, with an emphasis on artificial intelligence. He received his BS from Loyola Marymount University in computer science, psychology, and pure mathematics. His interests include the application of a multidisciplinary perspective to the study of virtual environments.

Richard Gilbert is Professor of Psychology at Loyola Marymount University in Los Angeles, California, where he directs the PROSE (Psychological Research on Synthetic Environments) Project (www.proseproject. info). He is also the founder of Loyola Marymount Virtual University (LMVU) in Second Life and Co-chair of the Psychology of Immersive Environments (PIE) working group of the Immersive Education Initiative. He received his BA in psychology from Princeton University and his PhD in clinical psychology from the University of California, Los Angeles.

Chuck Hamilton is the IBM Smart Play Framework and Social Learning Leader at IBM's Center for Advanced Learning, and he is also Associate Professor at the Master's of Digital Media Program in Vancouver, Canada. Prior posts include Virtual Learning and New Media Lead for IBM's 3D Internet Group and leader of a program called IBM@PLAY.

Andrew Harrison is a PhD student at Iowa State University, USA, studying management information systems. His research interests include technology-mediated fraud and deception, social media and virtual worlds, e-commerce, and knowledge management. He has presented and published work at the Americas Conference on Information Systems and the Hawaii International Conference on Systems Science.

Jonny Holmström is Professor of Informatics at Umeå University, Sweden. His research program examines how organizations innovate with IT, in particular the processes through which technological artifacts co-evolve with social contexts. Currently, he is investigating how organizations in the process industry develop sustainable competitive advantages through the mindful use of IT and how media organizations make use of a heterogeneous media portfolio. His work cuts across information systems studies, organization studies, communication studies, and science and technology studies and has been published in leading journals, such as *European Journal of Information Systems, Journal of the AIS*, and *The Information Society*. He serves on the editorial board for *European Journal of Information Systems* and *Information and Organization*.

Isto Huvila is Associate Professor in the Department of ALM at Uppsala University, Sweden, and his interests focus on the management and organization of what we know and how we know in different contexts ranging from social media to more traditional arenas of learning and working. He has published on virtual worlds, knowledge organization, and information and archival management in articles such as the 'Participatory Archive', 'Social Capital in Second Life', and 'The Politics of Boundary Objects: Hegemonic Interventions and the Making of a Document'.

Steve Mahaley is Director of Learning Innovations for Duke Corporate Education, Ltd, USA. He is an explorer at the intersection of new technologies and education design, and his current areas of interest include game-based learning, virtual worlds, enabling global teams, network-based design, mobile learning technologies, and advances in learning theory. He has published in the *Chief Learning Officer Magazine* and presented at a variety of human resource, learning technology, and serious games conferences in the US, Europe, and Africa.

Gianluigi Mangia is Associate Professor of Organization Studies at the University of Naples Federico II, Italy. He obtained his PhD in organization theory and management from the Università del Molise, and he is a visiting researcher at the London School of Economics, Warwick University, and Cardiff University. In his academic research, he has deeply investigated the knowledge management domain, with a particular emphasis on project teams.

Andrew Marunchak joined the University of Hertfordshire, UK, as an academic staff member in 2007, during which time he worked in the School of Computer Science and was responsible for the creation of interactive 3D environments for learning and teaching. Since that time, he has worked at the Learning and Teaching Institute as the Lead

3D Educational Technologist, and, as of 2011, he is a member of the Centre for Online Distance Learning. He participated in two European Commission projects designed to determine how new technologies are able to facilitate communication and learning. He is also the owner of VirtualAutonomy.com, an online community designed for sharing 3D environments.

Rhonda McEwen is Assistant Professor at the Institute of Communication, Culture, and Information Technology at the University of Toronto in Mississauga, Canada. She holds an MBA in information technology from City University in London, UK, an MSc in telecommunications from the University of Colorado, and a PhD in information from the University of Toronto. Her research and teaching center around information practices involving new media technologies, with an emphasis on mobile and tablet applications, social media design, and youth. She has designed and researched digital communications media for 15 years, both in companies providing services and in management consulting to those companies. She is currently researching sensory information processing.

Brian E. Mennecke is Associate Professor of Management Information Systems at Iowa State University, USA. His research interests include collaboration and collaborative systems, social media and virtual worlds, embodiment and perceptions of space, security systems and biometrics, mobile and electronic commerce, and spatial technologies. He has previously published a book on mobile commerce and articles in academic and practitioner journals such as *Management Information Systems Quarterly*, *Decision Sciences Journal*, *International Journal of Human-Computer Studies*, *Journal of Management Information Systems*, *Organizational Behavior and Human Decision Processing*, *Journal of Information Privacy and Security*, and *the Journal of Digital Forensics, Security & Law*.

Riccardo Mercurio is Full Professor of Organization Studies at the University of Napoli Federico II, Italy, where he currently teaches organization theory. He has an MBA from IMD, Switzerland, and he has been a visiting scholar at York University, UK. He has deeply investigated the public utilities domain with a particular emphasis on transport and logistic systems.

Tony O'Driscoll is Executive Director at Duke Corporate Education, USA. His focus is on working with clients to develop and implement strategies that enable organizations to realize the full potential of their most valuable asset: people. His current research focuses on how emerging technologies are rapidly disrupting existing industry structures and business models. His publications include articles in *Management Information Sciences Quarterly*, *Journal of Management Information*, *Harvard Business Review*, and *Chief Learning Officer Magazine*, among others.

Rick Oller is an artist and software designer who specializes in education, media, and collaborative systems and has a master's in academic technology from Marlboro College, USA. He is Chief Technology Officer of Noosphere Media LLC in New York City, Director of Technology at Chief Media LLC in New York City, and a founding member of the Wild Learning Consortium in Vermont, USA. He has been both a student and a teacher in virtual worlds, and his current research and interests are directed towards cognitive science, complexity, cyborgs, virtual worlds, human–computer interaction, and the digital humanities.

Dominic Power is Professor of Economic Geography at Uppsala University, Sweden. As a geographer, he is particularly interested in new types of spaces and how technologies shape and mediate our relationship to space. His research primarily focuses on the geographical foundations of business competencies and competitiveness and on the economic geography of contemporary economic change, with a specific focus on cultural and creative industries. He is a leading international expert in the area of creativity and culture-based industries, innovation and public policy, and regional industrial competitiveness. He has published over 70 articles, books, and reports on these topics and has lectured at major scientific and policy conferences.

Peggy Sheehy has been a pioneer in virtual worlds and games in education since 2005. She currently serves as Instructional Technologist in Suffern Middle School in the Ramapo Central School District in New York, USA. Her latest project, WoW in School, serves as an exemplar for using commercial video games to support learning in the classroom.

Cristina Stefanelli has a background in architecture and urban planning, and she has worked for several years at the Research Lab in Architecture Design at the University IUAV of Venice, Italy. From 2000 onwards, she became increasingly involved in the field of technology-enhanced learning and was involved in national and EU projects focused on teaching and learning technologies and virtual mobility.

Her work during this time was largely related to EU projects, including European R&D projects funded under the R&D Framework Programmes and the EC's Lifelong Learning Programme. In 2011, she started working at International Projects, R&D Office of FOR.COM in Rome. Currently, she holds the position of Project Manager, works with EC-supported projects across the educational and technical domains, and explores the learning potential of virtual worlds and openness in education.

Andrew Stricker is a distributed learning architect for the Air University, USA, and helps to design, develop, and implement advanced and emerging learning technology innovations in US Air Force educational and professional military programs. He has served for 28 years as an Air Force officer and scientist in the learning sciences and human factors engineering. He has supported 12 research grants and written dozens of publications. His research focuses on modeling adaptive expertise and the design of learning technologies.

Tuukka Tammi works as Senior Researcher at the National Institute for Health and Welfare (THL) in Helsinki, Finland. He has also acted as Chair of the Finnish Society for Alcohol and Drug Research. His current research activities deal with addiction policies, drug users, addiction treatment systems, and the regulation of gambling.

Robin Teigland is Associate Professor at the Center for Strategy and Competitiveness at the Stockholm School of Economics (SSE), Sweden, the caretaker of SSE's virtual campus, and Adjunct Professor at the University of Agder, Norway. Her research interests include how the Immersive Internet and social media impact the creation and diffusion of knowledge in social networks and the subsequent impact of these knowledge flows on organizational and regional competitive advantage. She has published numerous articles and chapters in leading international journals and publications, and she has participated in numerous EU and regional projects and as a reviewer for the US and Swiss National Science Foundations. She currently leads the Nordic Virtual Worlds Network (NVWN, www.nordicworlds.net), which resulted from a two-year international project investigating innovation and entrepreneurship through VWs and the 3D internet financed by the Nordic Innovation Center. More information is at www.knowledgenetworking.org.

Francisco Gerardo Toledo Ramírez is a PhD Candidate in media studies at the Faculty of Information and Media Studies at the University of Western Ontario, Canada, and Professor/Researcher of the Semiotics of Design Research Area in the Department of Evaluation of Design at the Metropolitan Autonomous University in México. His master's thesis was titled 'Visuality, Transdiscipline, Aesthetics and New Media: A Visual Essay'. In addition to several journal publications, he has published an e-book: *El dibujo como proceso de configuración para la enseñanza del diseño de la comunicación gráfica (Drawing as a Process of Configuration for Teaching Design of Graphic Communication)*, which was the 1999 winner of the category 'Textbook and Innovative Didactic Material in the UAM-AZC'. His current research interests include virtual world aesthetics, digital humanities, new media design and information, synthetic worlds, and immersive technologies and human computer interaction. He is also a visual communication designer and a visual and media artist.

Maria Laura Toraldo is a visiting doctoral researcher at the Warwick Business School, UK, and a doctoral researcher in the Department of Management, University Federico II of Naples, Italy. She gained a master's in organization of culture and the arts in the Department of Economics, University of Bologna, Italy, and her current research interests are in unpaid forms of labor and affective labor, the field of festivals and cultural industries, and critical management studies.

Anthony M. Townsend is Associate Professor of Management Information Systems at Iowa State University, USA. He has published in *MIS Quarterly, Information Systems Research*, and *Communications of the ACM* as well as in a number of other management and MIS journals. His research focuses on virtual teams and group processes as well as on the socio-technical interface of people and technology. He has also trained in theater with the Performance Group and performed professional opera.

Barry Wellman is the S.D. Clark Professor of Sociology and Director of NetLab at the University of Toronto, Canada. He founded the International Network for Social Network Analysis (INSNA) in 1976. A member of the Royal Society of Canada, Wellman has headed two American Sociological Association sections: Community and Communications/Info Technology and the Sociological Research Association honor society. He has recently published *Networked: The New Social Operating System* with Lee Rainie. The book discusses the implications of the confluence of the Triple Revolution: the turn to social networks, the proliferation of the personalized internet, and constantly accessible mobile connectivity.

Müberra Yüksel is Assistant Professor at Kadir Has University, Turkey. She completed her PhD in the Department of Political Science, Binghamton University, USA, in 1989, and has experience in organizational theory, communication, conflict management, and policy analysis. She has managed a World Bank project and led research on comparative vocational standards within the US, the UK, and Germany. Previous academic positions include Assistant Professor in the Political Science Department, Bilkent University (1991–95), Adjunct Lecturer at Bilgi University (1998–2003), and Chair of the Advertising Department of Kadir Has University (2004–10). Her research interests include strategic management, organizational behavior and conflict management, and corporate and marketing communication.

Matthew Zook is Associate Professor of Economic and Information Geography at the University of Kentucky, USA. His research focuses on processes of technological change and the accompanying shifting geographies of globalization. Currently he studies the geoweb – the integration of location information with online data and activity – and the possibilities and challenges of these rich sources of data on the time and location of the social and economic processes of everyday life. He is a founder of and regular contributor to the FloatingSheep.org blog.

1
Postcards from the Metaverse: An Introduction to the Immersive Internet

Dominic Power and Robin Teigland

Beginnings

The internet is by now a stable foundation underpinning many aspects of daily life in the developed world. It has evolved to become central to the ways in which we experience others and ourselves as well as the way we interact with all manner of cultural, social, economic, and political processes. As we have adapted to, or been born with, the internet, we have become more and more immersed and enmeshed in the information and interactions the technology allows us to create, share, and view. To date the internet has mainly taken the form of a text-based, two-dimensional medium with the odd splattering of images, videos, and sound. It has largely been a curated space – a set of spaces designed for us to be attracted to and sometimes even to contribute a little to. The internet has permeated our lives, at best as an engaging and fascinating resource and at worst as a strangling cage of processed information.

In recent years the internet has begun to develop into a much more immersive and multidimensional space, and it is this emerging 'Immersive Internet' that is the focus of this book of short thought pieces by some of the leading thinkers in the field. Three-dimensional spaces and sites of interaction have not just gripped our attention but have begun to weave or be woven into the fabric of our professional and social lives. This is likely only to go further as platform and interface developments in augmented reality, social networking sites, online games, virtual worlds, and the 3D internet signal a move towards communication technologies and virtual spaces that offer immersive experiences persuasive enough to blur the lines between the virtual and the physical. Partly this immersive potential is based upon a greater variety of ways in which we can interact with others as well as with virtual and augmented spaces and sites, and even with artificial intelligence. Partly it is based on the ever-increasing quality of the aesthetic, visual, auditory, and sensory experiences of computer-generated and internet-mediated environments.

Thus, new waves of internet and information technology are likely to promise ever richer and more immersive ways to connect with technology and with each other. If the internet has so far been founded on the myriad combinations of information and communications technologies, then a possible future is one in which the internet becomes founded on *immersion* and communications technologies. Indeed, as our lives become ever more virtual and the virtual takes on ever more convincing and engaging forms, we must think of these not as purely virtual or abstract phenomena but as lived spaces.

At the center of such lived or intimate spaces is the *one* to be immersed: the individual or group of individuals who will engage with the people and spaces they find in computer-mediated spaces. The avatar is the appearance, incarnation, or manifestation of an individual in virtual or computer-mediated spaces. Avatars can take many forms: from character-like representations for use in games or 3D worlds complementing one's physical world identity to cohesive online presences such as well-developed social network profiles in which one's entire identity is tied to one's avatar. Of course, the Immersive Internet will not just be about the agency of avatars, or their conscious and strategic actions. It will equally be about the spaces, structures, software agents, and systems the avatars will encounter. While many such structures and spaces will be open and accessible, many will be closed and proprietary. In both cases those who control the spaces within which avatars immerse themselves will have crucial roles in defining the 'rules of the game'. The Immersive Internet may not only be about the structuring and strictures of single spaces. As users delve into many different spaces, and as firms, other organizations, and operators work together, it is likely the Immersive Internet will be one where spaces and sites are linked together, as in the internet we know today. While these links might or might not involve interoperability, the spaces will definitely be linked by the experiences and expectations individuals and avatars have built through immersion in multiple spaces and generations of spaces. As these more intimately experienced spaces become linked, spill over, and cross-pollinate each other, we may begin to perceive the foundations of a more or less patchwork landscape of virtual spaces and layers as well as collective shared online spaces: what Neal Stephenson dubbed the 'metaverse' in his novel *Snow Crash*.

The avatar creates the world

The Immersive Internet has, to date, often involved users in the foundation and creation of the very spaces and worlds they experience. In some cases this will, as with Linux, mean that users are involved in the very genesis and coding of online spaces and experiences. In other cases this will involve the creation and building of not just objects but entire landscapes that they and others can then experience. In still other cases, users will define the worlds, spaces, sites, and networks by providing them with content, meaning, and movement. As computer power, broadband, and interfaces improve and as organizations open their domains and code to users, we will see users not just participating but actively innovating and creating the 'stages' on which they will move.

Virtual spaces, no matter how beautiful or complex, are, however, ultimately empty and abandoned code without participants. Participants add their actions, interactions, and performances to generate the layers of meaning and interaction that create the lure with which others become entangled. It is these individual acts that ultimately create the immersive potential. In addition, it is through individuals' footsteps and contact with others that immersive networks become attractive: individual acts of participation both build the network and signal its existence. The agency of avatars and those individuals behind them will shape and determine the spaces and processes that emerge from technological advances.

When the Immersive Internet takes the form of a three-dimensional virtual world, one generally must create an avatar in order to use the space. Just as there are numerous worlds, individuals also have the option to create a myriad of avatars – such as one for playing games, one for corporate activities, one for family interactions, and so on. Yet, as individuals invest more of their time in participating in the Immersive Internet, their online presence represented through one specific avatar can become an important, if not central, part of the person's social identity as well as a tool in the projection of their identity in different arenas. This means that individuals will likely invest considerable effort and resources in the construction of not only their avatars but, through their avatars, the worlds and interactive spaces they encounter and create. As Bourdieu pointed out, the exercise of taste and classification is a central aspect in how individuals and groups carve out and fight for socio-cultural contexts and spaces (Bourdieu, 1984). With so much hinging on identity formation and politics, it is likely that avatars and their contexts will be subject to constant attention, negotiation, and even conflict. This raises many questions about the relations between our physical and virtual selves, and, crucially, our relations with other actors and avatars. As more of our time is spent 'in world', the question thus arises as to what this means for us as social interactive beings. On the one hand, researchers such as Sherry Turkle caution that we are entering a world where we are increasingly 'alone together', while others, such as Wellman, argue for expanding opportunities in this age of increasing 'networked individualism' (Wellman, 2001).

Our lived spaces and practices are constantly being shaped and reshaped by our need and desire for sociality as well as our desire for intimate experiences. Our avatars will bring these needs and desires into the worlds they build or encounter. The Immersive Internet will likely be both an intimate internet and an invasive internet as our selves, identities, feelings, emotions, and memories become entangled online and in our avatars. This means that there is a vast series of crucial questions to be asked and issues to be addressed. For example, if identity formation and maintenance are central to interactive virtual performances, how much of us will we need to invest in order to keep up appearances? How will you fall in love through a technology? If our self-image and constructed body are damaged or depressed, what role can our avatar take and how should we be treated? What and where will our memories be?

Many of the questions above are already salient in populations where, increasingly, people meet and date online, build communities online, and display all manner of memories and emotions online. In the future, as we further project ourselves into our avatars, which will more than likely become more human, leading us through the uncanny valley, and as we interact with the environment and objects through brain–computer interfaces, we may explore new realms for physical and mental activity. Yet how will the memories that we create through our avatars interact with our memories created in the physical world and vice versa? To what degree will our basic human feelings and our very sense of being a human be impacted? The internet and immersive technologies are latecomers to the human scene, but neuroscience has revealed that the human brain is highly adaptive to new technologies; however, it has also revealed that it may be highly vulnerable. While many see the possibilities of the Immersive Internet, some researchers have raised critical voices. For example, Susan Greenfield, one of the world's leading brain researchers, has gone so far as to say that the immediate feedback that individuals can receive in social networks, virtual worlds, and virtual world gaming may be negatively impacting our ability to link the present to both the past and the future, a characteristic that distinguishes us as individuals and humans.

It is not only our individual desires and identities that will structure the emerging Immersive Internet; it will also be our aspirations and creative and entrepreneurial spirit. A central issue of how the internet will evolve does not simply lie at the level of structural and corporate provision – how large or small firms will plan and structure the worlds we encounter and create – but also involves how individuals will try to push forward the commercialization and commodification of immersive spaces to suit their own ambitions and material needs.

Becoming immersed by interacting through one's avatars does offer many functional and commercial possibilities. Applications within the healthcare, education, and entertainment arenas not only seem endless, but also promise to impact and blur the boundaries between these arenas and even others. Regardless of the arena, entrepreneurial spirit will likely continue to drive the development of new Immersive Internet applications. To date, 'avapreneurs' – a concept proposed by Teigland for those solely conducting entrepreneurial activity online through their avatars – have created entire fashion and other industrial ecosystems in various virtual worlds (Teigland, 2010). In fact, this virtual agglomeration of economic activity directly contrasts with the regional agglomeration of an industry in the traditional geographic sense in which individuals, organizations, and firms are in close geographical proximity to each other and attract others to translocate from across the world. In both virtual and geographical contexts, it is the proximity and the level of concentration between related actors that seem to breed synergies, innovation, and economic development. Yet what will proximity and concentration in virtual economic and industrial interactions mean, and on what will they be based? How will virtual proximity intertwine with geographic colocation and economic relations?

Furthermore, as 3D printing becomes integrated with the Immersive Internet as well as commonplace for household and industrial objects, we will not only be able to design and experience objects in these virtual spaces; we will also be able to simultaneously produce these objects in our garage or workplace. Thus, not only will the borders between industries be blurred, but the entire value chain – from the sourcing of inputs and production in the supply chain through to distribution and consumption by end users – will be revolutionized due to the convergence of the Immersive Internet with material, production, and other related technologies. The questions arising here are of deep importance for governments and public sector bodies at all levels. How should taxation and legal systems be designed so as to promote innovation as opposed to hindering it? How should resources be invested in virtual, transnational clusters of economic activity such that this investment benefits local taxpayers and citizens?

Here the Immersive Internet is not only the focus of new products and services, but it also offers an immersive working and networking space. In these environments, entrepreneurs may collaborate on value-creating activities with one another as well as with other individuals from both large and small firms, academia, hobbyists, and the public sector, regardless of physical location. This has already been clearly demonstrated by the OpenSimulator project, an open source virtual world platform project, in which the expression 'meeting face-to-face' has lost its physical meaning to indicate instead a virtual meeting of avatars in a 3D online space. Of further interest is that the number of freelancers in the world is, for various reasons, rapidly increasing. One recent study reported that the number of freelancers in the US had passed one-third of the workforce in 2006 and that this number continues to rise. As anyone sitting at his or her kitchen table (provided they have access to a kitchen table and the internet, that is) will be able to learn just about anything and engage in a world of economic opportunities through the Immersive Internet, the number of freelancers across the globe will only continue to rise. Moreover, individuals who have previously been hindered from entering the workforce due to physical disabilities or peripheral locations will be able to learn and work through the Immersive Internet. One significant question that this raises is how this 'mobility' of labor and the 'mobility' of physical goods due to 3D printing will impact the competitiveness of regions and nations.

Through the Immersive Internet, we are finding indications of 'open entrepreneurship', or the process of entrepreneurs openly engaging in social capital-building activities through the free contribution of intellectual property and other resources to the public, with the purpose of pursuing individual business-related interests while contributing to the pursuit of collective goals. While these entrepreneurs may give away their intellectual property, knowledge, time, and other resources for free, they do so in the pursuit of creating a social structure that enables them to overcome the inherent difficulties in attracting the necessary human, financial, and other resources due to the uncertainties of their new venture and the liabilities of newness and small size (Aldrich and Ruef, 2006; Baker and Nelson, 2005). Through the Immersive Internet, entrepreneurs may more easily overcome these liabilities – factors that traditionally have disadvantaged small firms compared with large organizations and that have generally led to their failure. Furthermore, we are beginning to see signs that the Immersive Internet is leading to, or implicated in, a migration from an economic model characterized by centralized hierarchical firms controlling in-house resources to a model of decentralized social production by communities of globally distributed firms and workers. Such fundamental changes clearly bring into question how and to what degree well-established multinational organizations and their brands will continue to dominate economic activity.

While these technological developments, combined with political and societal changes, continue to change the world as we know it, it is important to view these changes in the 'longue durée'. While we may seem to be moving forward, many also profess that our technological and societal advances have led us to the edge of the cliff of the anthropocene era – the period during which human activity has globally impacted the planet. Dukes writes that we entered this era in 1763, when the available data indicate the beginning of a growth in the atmospheric concentrations of several greenhouse gases (Dukes, 2011). The Immersive Internet, however, offers promise in reducing the pressure of growth on large cities across the globe. A McKinsey study recently reported that this trend of large city growth has been broken in countries such as the US and India as smaller cities and rural areas are gaining in popularity across age groups. Yet how we further develop the Immersive Internet and its potential to secure the future of the planet for generations to come is unclear; building roads tends to increase traffic rather than relieve it. Recent research in entrepreneurship has recognized the basic human paradox of seeking to simultaneously fulfill both individual and collective interests. The question remains as to how the Immersive Internet may impact this dialectical nature of human beings – to encourage us to act more collectively or perhaps more in our own self-interest.

The formative role of avatars in the construction of online flows and spaces may be benign if we use behavior such as escapism, fun, and game mechanics to dominate the tone of our online interactions. But avatars and the individuals behind them will not all be altruistic, and conflict will always be a part of the worlds that avatars populate. Profiteering and swindling will be rife, as will be violence, theft, bullying, and coercion: as, indeed, actors within some virtual worlds have already experienced. Such issues clearly indicate that the Immersive Internet is facilitating changes in our social, economic, and governance models, and it will have an even greater impact as the technologies develop and the next generations who have grown up using these technologies enter society and the workforce. These issues and their questions are endless, and clearly of deep importance to leaders and other individuals throughout society and the globe.

The world creates the avatar

While the Immersive Internet may allow actors to construct worlds and experiences in their own images or in 'make-believe', the worlds and experiences also create the avatar and control and shape the actions of avatars. By entering mediated spaces, avatars are subject to the conventions and rules that govern these spaces, and in many cases they will be subject to the owners or creators of these worlds. It is important, then, that we think carefully about the multiple ways in which such rules, controls, and ownership relations will determine interactions and actions online.

If actors and avatars are engaged in performances, then performativity theorists, such as Judith Butler, point out that even our most personal acts and identities occur on stages that are in many respects subject to scripts laden with social conventions and hegemonic ideologies. The stage is far from always being a tabula rasa open to the whims of those actors who find themselves there. These scripts may be literal scripts, such as those that govern the narrative trajectory of online games, and these narrative scripts define the interface and the options open to actors.

Whether they are literally scripted or not, we find that social conventions and ideologies play a subtle but definite role in defining both actions and the parameters within which avatars may act. Of course, social conventions rooted in the 'real' world have many positive sides and are often reflections of deeply rooted social and ethical standards that make interaction both possible and palatable. It is true to say that the majority of the conventions and ideologies with which we surround ourselves are phenomena that often deeply impact us as we create and maintain them. Nonetheless, there are equally many social, political, and cultural conventions within which individuals may not want to be immersed, and the danger of censorship and restriction in online stages is strong. The intimacy avatars may look for in performance in some ways opens up the very real possibility that it is the *Invasive Internet* within which they find themselves.

There is also the general concern in society that we have less and less choice but to join the masses in creating an avatar or an integrated set of public profiles on social and professional networking spaces. As our immersion in these types of spaces is increasingly expected and even demanded of us, there is the danger that we may experience less a feeling of immersion and more a feeling of drowning or losing control. As many aspects of social life migrate to online interactions – you will never see the party invitation without being on the same social network as your friends – and as business functions also migrate – your Rolodex is a historical artifact but your website and professional network profile are both your address book and your resumé – we are forced to abide by the 'policies' imposed on us by the networks we must use, just as we are forced by terms of use to cede ultimate ownership of our contacts, network information, and even likes and dislikes to platform owners who might have very different ideas of privacy and profit from those we would choose for ourselves.

Moreover, many of the stages upon which performances are conducted are not just scripted but tightly defined and structured in such ways that the avatar seldom has complete freedom of movement or expression. For certain purposes, the fact that the world places a structure upon the avatar is no doubt both useful and necessary. Virtual training and educational spaces must be open to the avatar's own actions, but must also enshrine learning objectives and standards. The growing popularity of the Immersive Internet in education and training is no doubt set to continue, as it not only allows deeper educational experiences than many textual forms may permit but also allows users to access and experience knowledge that could be difficult to find locally. Educational and training spaces will give individuals, through their avatars, new chances and possibilities not only to interact with educators and other students, but also to see, hear, and manipulate knowledge in new and exciting ways.

Communication through sight, sound, and movement are central. When we move through virtual spaces, the space itself is vital to our experience. In other words, we must be careful not only to focus on interaction and others in spatial experiences but also to understand the role of landscapes and passive interfaces. The Immersive Internet is perhaps as much about how it looks and how we observe it as it is a place for interaction between individuals. Just as we may go to a gallery to look at paintings or a park to look at trees, we go online to be immersed in sensory, auditory, and visual experiences. This means that, in order to understand the Immersive Internet, there is a range of questions about the status of all those objects, sights, and sounds with which the avatar is faced.

As Bruno Latour argues, actors constantly come into contact with, and must deal with, non-human agency. Nowhere is this more so, perhaps, than in computer-mediated environments where users must interact with and observe actant-generated objects and environments as well as objects and spaces that are reactive or endowed with artificial intelligence. The human and the non-human elements of such spaces cannot be seen as mutually separate, but need to be seen as mutually interrelated. Future iterations of the Immersive Internet will see the role of the look, sound, and feel of the spaces continue to be central to how avatars experience the virtual spaces they enter. We must, though, remember that much of how we currently see virtual spaces is based on our experience of current interfaces, which are often entirely online, screen-based and computer-generated realms. However, technology seems to be increasingly portable and mobile in real space, raising exciting questions of how virtual interfaces will recreate and represent the physical and material world around us, and how the newly overlaid and interfaced world will recreate and represent us.

Of course, it is not only the avatars' performative abilities that can be structured and conscribed by the spaces and platforms within which they find themselves; it is also the assets and liabilities they collect or encounter within immersive spaces: what they have on their person. In cases such as virtual worlds or online games, the currencies and assets users need are often controlled and regulated by the platform provider. Issues of ownership, jurisdiction, and transferability are in these cases seldom to be decided by individuals' agency.

Clearly, one of the major issues related to entrepreneurial and other commercial activity through the Immersive Internet is the appropriation of returns from one's value-creation efforts as well as its control. The regulatory system developed for the production and trade of physical goods within and across nation states with their own national currencies will have to be reconstructed. Issues of intellectual property and copyrights will need to be revisited as the value of virtual goods and their subsequent 3D printed versions in the global economy increases. This raises a series of important questions: How will virtual currencies and the financialization of virtual spaces affect our agency? How do we deal with the ephemerality of digital goods? As we interact with others, how will we be able to pass on or inherit digital goods? What will happen to indebted or bankrupt virtual presences? With transactions, assets, and liabilities held in one or more virtual spaces, what sorts of rule of law and contract will apply? How will we deal with trust and guarantees in virtual spaces? By whom, how, where, and in what format will tax be paid?

Such questions are crucial to the economic and resource sides of our lives and interactions as more and more economic activity occurs in online and computer-mediated markets. How virtual interactions and actions link to market processes and how they lead to very real financial and business outcomes is a crucial issue. Just as the marketplace on the high street is a forum for the creation of differential outcomes for individuals in the 'real' world, online and virtual market spaces will mean very real material outcomes for different people.

There are many different business and organizational models that can govern the provision of the spaces and technologies we will use, but, if the present day is anything to go by, then it seems likely that for-profit corporate interests will dominate. The running and provision of the largest spaces and interactive platforms on the internet currently seem to favor vertically integrated corporate monopolies rather than garage band dynamics. As the Immersive Internet brings with it more technological and functional complexity, it seems likely that vertically integrated corporate bodies will be needed, and, as Metcalfe's Law suggests in networked environments, near and total monopolies are likely to gain the upper hand. While many corporate bodies will no doubt exercise care to serve their customers' best interests, this is not something that individual avatars will always be able to affect or count on.

As people spend time in Immersive Internet settings, we may wonder what effect this will have on their expectations and dreams for the spaces and environments their fleshy avatars meet in their homes and regions. Will we start to design our real world spaces to be integrated with or reflective of the values and possibilities we may find online? Will our homes and towns be designed with aesthetic memes founded in virtual worlds? As new information and augmented reality technologies lay bare our surrounding infrastructure and environments, will we find new ways of using, imagining, and building the world around us?

The rest of this book

As can be seen from the above, we are deeply uncertain as to what form or forms the Immersive Internet will take and what it will mean for individuals, society, culture, politics, and the economy. As these spaces, practices, and technologies progress, a more intimate and immersive internet and virtuality will emerge. At the same time as the Immersive or Intimate Internet gathers pace, it is likely that its opposite – the *Invasive Internet* – will continue to encroach on our lives, societies, politics, and economies. At present there are simply so many questions and unknowns about what might happen. But what we are sure of is that the evolution of such spaces and technologies will mean much for both the avatar/individual and the world(s) around it/us.

This is the background on which the book in front of you rests. It is a collection of short thought pieces that we think critically engage with the future directions that the Immersive Internet might, should, or even should not take. The book emerged as a way of trying to collect ideas and opinions from a wide variety of people who have been heavily engaged with these sorts of questions and issues. Since the Immersive Internet – including social media, augmented reality, virtual worlds, online games, 3D internet and beyond – is still nascent or emerging and is being explored by a number of different disciplines, we assembled participants from a wide range of academic disciplines and professional backgrounds. What all these thinkers share is a deep engagement with the possibilities, both positive and negative, of a progressively more immersive and intimate set of internet-mediated spaces and interactions. The idea was not to collect a series of empirical pieces on the current state of the art but to collect pieces that provoke and attempt to take in the big picture and the long term: what we think of as, in short, Postcards from the Metaverse.

References

Aldrich, H.E. and Ruef, M. (2006) *Organizations Evolving* (2nd edn). Thousand Oaks: Sage.

Baker, T. and Nelson, R. E. (2005) 'Creating Something from Nothing: Resource Construction Through Entrepreneurial Bricolage', *Administrative Science Quarterly*, 50, 3, pp. 329–66.

Bourdieu, P. (1984) *Distinction: A Social Critique of the Judgement of Taste*. London: Routledge & Kegan Paul.

Dukes, P. (2011) *Minutes to Midnight: History and the Anthropocene Era from 1763*. London: Anthem Press.

Teigland, R. (2010) 'Born Virtuals and Avapreneurship: A Case Study of Achieving Successful Outcomes in Peace Train – A Second Life Organization', *Journal of Virtual Worlds Research*, Special Issue on Virtual Economies, Virtual Goods and Service Delivery in Virtual Worlds, 2, 4.

Wellman, B. (2001) 'Physical Place and Cyber Place: The Rise of Networked Individualism', *International Journal of Urban and Regional Research*, 25, 2, pp. 227–52.

2
Niggling Inequality: A Second Introduction to the Immersive Internet

Edward Castronova

The people in the background

Over the next few hundred pages, you will read a series of postcards from the metaverse. Some are pictures of sites the authors are fond of, or that made them ponder the wonderful. Some are pictures of the authors themselves, standing in front of monuments they made. In this essay I hope to set some context for the images and at the same time point out some common details in them. It often happens that authors will share a context but miss interesting patterns across their contributions. A photograph of nature thrills us with color and tenderness, as the photographer intends, but among any 1000 or 1 million photographs of nature there is a fearful trend: each was taken by a person; nature was not alone there, in that moment. As nature imagery documents our domination of the earth, so the little details common across these metaverse postcards reveal something of our own treatment of that place.

That place, the metaverse – what is it? The chapters here answer the question in many different ways. Collectively they give as good an answer as any. The metaverse is art in which we live. It is a drama in which we are all actors. It is a book, about us, that we are writing as we go along. We imagine something; we wave our hands and that thing acquires (digital) representation along with a supporting world; we step into the representation and manipulate it; while doing so, we imagine something; and the cycle continues. Indeed, it can go on without us: if we merely once imagine and build a thing that can itself imagine and build – and we have already, many times; they are called 'artificial intelligence' – then we need no longer be a part of the cycle. The metaverse runs by itself. Our histories and aspirations are all the raw material it needs. Nor is the metaverse limited to digital existence: plastics printers turn thoughts into toys. The authors here universally judge the metaverse soon to be an everywhere all-the-time phenomenon, and we the fish in an aquarium that builds itself.

We fish can look forward to joys as well as perils. Technology does nothing good or bad, but people make it so. In these pages you will read of wonderful educational experiences, of comforting online volunteer communities, of vast profits and glorious aesthetics. You will also read of addiction, capitalist shenanigans, and state control of the mind. Big change is coming, that much we know.

'We' – who are 'we' in these postcards? We are professors and artists and designers. We are expert cultural critics, masters of managerial informatics, high priests and priestesses of semiotics, sensei of technology. An active lot, this. Active folk get up off the couch and go places, places from whence a postcard merits dispatching, or a photograph of yourself. Active folk are touched by what they see. They consider and reflect. They process and judge. They remember. They return formulating schemes of change. They get busy.

Not everyone is like this. Collect 1000 or 1 million photographs of active people on trips. Now look at the people in the background. Not the subject people, but the context people: the ones who are not on a trip. What are they up to? Not much. Almost nothing, really. Going about their daily business. And what is daily business? Talking with and touching family and friends; doing jobs; eating, voiding waste, sleeping.

How does the metaverse touch them? It is an important question, because for every sensei of technology there are 1 million people merely going about their daily lives. They are different folk. The differences in aspiration and motivation and energy can only lead to unequal outcomes as the metaverse washes over them, and us. What if all the grand and wonderful or frightening and awful things that the metaverse may bring, happen only to a few? What, then, for everyone else?

Niggling

I predict a great deal of niggling. I am drawn to the term by J.R.R. Tolkien's short story 'Leaf by Niggle'. Niggle is a painter who works on one painting all his life. He shows it to no one but spends countless hours improving it here and there. Tragically, he never finishes. He devotes so much attention to detail that major parts of the overall picture are left untouched, right to the end. The word *niggle* means 'to do something in a painstaking, finicky, fussy, or ineffective manner; to trifle, fiddle; to waste effort or time on petty details'. It is not a happy term. It acquires its negative connotation through the concept of waste: the person niggling really should be doing something else, something more. They should focus on getting things accomplished rather than simply work and work on petty things. This seems to go against the teaching that the journey is more important than the destination; Niggle's act of painting is the point, not the finished artwork. But note that the definition of *niggle* emphasizes the petty nature of the distractions. We are not stopping to smell the roses, we are stopping to look yet once again at our sandals and make sure the strap around the ankle is right where it is supposed to be, no more and no less than 3/8" above the ankle bone when the foot is at full rest.

Niggling is failing to see forests for the trees; it is failing to get the big picture. Some people niggle because they simply can't see the big picture, much as they try. Or they do indeed see the big picture, but a mental compulsion convinces them again and again that no effort can be made to address the big picture until every preparatory detail has been arranged. Or, and I suspect that this is by far the most common grounds for niggling, people niggle because they don't care about the big picture.

Niggling because you don't care is a vice. It even has a name, *acedia*, which, as Reinhard Hütter notes in a recent essay, is normally translated as 'sloth' but comes closer in meaning to 'spiritual apathy.'[1] Hütter advances acedia as a vice that belongs uniquely to our time. If you just don't care, this is a wonderful time to be alive! The real world is indeed held to be largely empty of meaning, confirming your foundational stance. And, while that might make existence frightfully boring, at just the right moment technology has come to the rescue in the form of these amazing worlds built just for your dawdling. There may be nothing to live for, nothing really to do, but at least there's entertainment while the time ticks away between womb and tomb. Hütter objects to the stance, as I am sure most readers do. The authors and experts who constitute the community from which these postcards are drawn are a special case. The digerati agree, sighing, with the age's secularism and the resulting meaninglessness of human action, yet heroically they find energy to explore, seek, analyze, and build. No spirit, but no spiritual apathy either. This, however, is not the case with the people in the background. They live contented, acedic lives. They are happy to niggle away their time.

What does an acedic niggler do with the amazing new technologies of net, web, 3D, and interaction? Sit there, mostly. They watch a lot of TV, a lot of TV. The average in the US is more than four hours per day.[2] They watch TV on their TV, as of old, but now they also watch TV on their smartphones, their work computers, their tablets. They watch TV in the living room, the kitchen, the bedroom, the bathroom. They watch TV on the bus and in the tube, at work and at play, at home and on the road, inside and outside and everywhere. The amount of watching is rising.

The word 'TV' doesn't capture all of the watching behavior. The watching that people do involves film and video but also streams of information, pictures, and short sentences. People watch plenty of moving pictures but also stills and comics. They watch captured scenes of people and things intentionally or unintentionally being interesting, but also short blurbs about someone seen in a bar last night and crazy forum posts about crazy topics. The niggler's experience is to sit, surf, select, and scan. If this is 'interaction', it is interaction of a very limited sort.

Of course, some things in the emerging metaverse require a great deal more interaction, spark, and energy. Big games certainly do. It seems that lots of people play the big immersive games. These are all 3D, with talking non-player characters, thousands of quests and missions, and a huge map to explore. Yet, as I write, there is a disturbing trend. The games that make the most money are quite frankly 'button-mashers', games that really do not require much acumen or forethought or even energy. You sit on the couch, go into the map, kill what's there (or solve a simple puzzle), and then go to the next map. Anything challenging? Look up the solution on the net. Even the hard games are being streamlined towards passivity. The player is enabled to do exactly what feels good to do at that one moment, and the system handles everything else. Too hard to make up a character background or do some roleplaying? No worries, the game gives you a couple of stock characters and walks them through cut-scenes for you to – yes – watch. Too hard to explore a map or a community? No worries, the game puts arrows on the ground and exclamation points over peoples' heads, showing you where to go. The successful handheld and social network games are, of course, a complete time sink, productive of nothing.

It is true that there are extremely active gamers who fiercely pursue every avenue to excellence, physical, and strategic, and social. Increasingly, I view them as an elite. There are also lots of people who pursue athletic excellence, and then there are sedentary people like me.

My kind of sport – my antisport – vastly outnumbers theirs, so much so that in America we have an 'obesity epidemic'. Is it a good thing? Certainly not. But that's how it is. Elite gaming is limited to a rather small demographic, typically young, typically male (though, of course, not exclusively so); everyone else mindlessly presses buttons or just watches stuff.

In the end, has there been an experience worth postcarding here? Have these users smelled roses? Or have they rather just walked away the hours chatting to the air about nothing at all?

The vast acedic niggling landscape that will dominate the metaverse is not a result of the technology at all; it is a core aspect of the human condition that merely manifests itself powerfully now that we have achieved a state of wealth such that most of the things humans feel compelled to do are not that hard to get done. Maslow's hierarchy is true, but it neglects something quite important: while everyone is always desperate to get the bottom few stages taken care of, fewer and fewer even care about the top tiers. Let us take a mental trip together into the lands of your fathers and mothers and all the people you have seen on the streets in your many journeys, all the people in the background of your postcards. There we will see together the thousands and thousands and thousands of people who are have everything taken care of in terms of the fundament of Maslow's pyramid: they eat and mate and sleep in peace. And, so far as any of us can tell, they are utterly unconcerned about the top of the pyramid, the 'self-actualization' that so dominates our stressed-out little lives. Thoreau was wrong – most people do not lead lives of quiet desperation, even if most people *like him* may do so. Most people are not like him, or like us. They don't really care.

A metaverse that consists of 1 million acedic nigglers for every one digeratus will have specific features worthy of note. One of them is inequality.

Inequality

Imagine a wonderful metaverse, the vast majority of whose users do nothing, just goof around. As part of goofing around, the users forage – they sit, surf, select, and scan. But nothing more. At the same time, there are a few very active people, who go out to explore, create, invert, and repurpose. Who will be paying whom in this scenario? Who will have the scarce and valuable skills, and who will be on the short end of the market stick? For the invisible hand caresses and it ignores.

It seems beyond question that a good recipe for poverty in coming decades would be to while away one's hours consuming the offerings of glorious technology without making any effort to understand them, much less refashion or invert them. How many even have the cognitive capacity to understand code, or to work with a website? True, new tools are being built every day, to help those without technical skills to make things. Let's grant this, for the sake of argument, and assume that at some future date every creative opportunity available in contemporary technology will be fashionable by anyone through a simple point-and-click middleware. It is an easy assumption to grant because we are already there in terms of writing and art and sculpture. Anyone can pick up a hammer and start hitting a rock. Anyone can write sentences on a piece of paper. Anyone can scrawl on a canvas. Therefore, suppose that in the future anyone can make a glorious immersive 3D experience – *if they want to.* How many people today desire to make paintings? Plenty, I suppose. One, two, or three million. Perhaps 30 million? It is not much in a population nearing 7 billion people. Even so, how many of these desire to make paintings so much that they hone their mastery of that technology to the point of excellence? Not as many. Among them, how many strive to grasp the human condition to such a depth that their paintings move us? Not many at all. How many succeed in this striving? A couple. Out of billions who have access to creative tools, only a handful ever create something that others see. YouTube changes nothing. One billion videos are made, 100,000 are seen by a few people, 10,000 are seen by more than 100, ten are seen by a million or more. The inequality that's coming really has nothing to do with access and affordances, and everything to do with the power-law distribution of desire combining with luck and talent.

The actions we hope to see in the metaverse will only happen for people who actually can and do pursue them. The people who have the desire and skills will be in a position to make, shape, and create the metaversal experiences that others, the vast majority, will receive. Those others, not caring about much at all, will do little. Doing little, they will be unskilled. Being unskilled, they will receive the metaverse, not make it. Naturally they will be asked to pay for the service, and they will, to the extent of their ability. Packages will be designed that balance the ability to pay against the cost of production. A few will be creating, designing, producing. Most others will be watching: sitting, surfing, selecting, scanning.

Will these acedics be happy, niggling away time with their pictures, their likes, and their gold coins? This raises big questions. What is happiness? What is the good life? Can a person be content without living a Good Life as defined by some philosopher or priest? This isn't the place to suggest an answer, but there is actually a science of happiness and it says this: what makes people happy are things like families and communities and vocations: a place, a home, a calling. Meaning.[3] Our measures of happiness often do not accord all that well with a person's characterization of their life. A Californian will exclaim about how wonderful the weather is there, while the data show that satisfaction with the weather is actually no different in sunny California than in snowy Buffalo. We adapt to circumstances. Winning the lottery has no long-run effect on happiness. Neither does losing a leg. Thus, if we check to see whether people are content with their reception of media, today, tomorrow, or in ten years, we will find that they generally are. Even if the quality and richness of the media change, for better or for worse, sadness and happiness will not change much. An acedic niggler is content to just mosey along, and will be happy or not depending on the little things, like family, village, and day-to-day work. It's not clear that the metaverse will impact these things in any significantly different way from the impact TV has had already. Hang out with family and friends; go to work; then sit, surf, select, scan; sit, surf, select, scan; sit, surf, select, scan. Asked if he is happy, the niggling acedic says, 'Sure. Happy enough.'

Rather than ask about subjective well-being, we might assess contentment through behavior: what do people do? A person may express deep dissatisfaction that she never became an executive chef. We may examine her life and ask – what steps did she take to *become* an executive chef? If she never actually did anything about the dream, we cannot locate the source of her dissatisfaction in the system that selects, trains, and employs executive chefs. It may be there – there may have been barriers. But the fact is, the putative barriers were never tested. This does not invalidate the woman's dissatisfaction, but it does put it in context. When an overweight man like myself expresses sadness at his weight, we might respond, 'As sad as you say you are, you're apparently not sad enough to do anything about it!' We would thus judge our acedics as content simply because of their acedia – they're not doing anything about the metaverse, they don't really care. Even if they might complain that stealth is overpowered in Guild Wars 2, they're not actually doing anything about it. Even if people say they wish something would change, or that something is wrong, or that they are devoted to this or that cause, not many actually do anything. How many have exited a first marriage declaring that they would change their lives completely so that they could have true love? And how many then become divorced two, three, four times, or more? How many give up completely on the idea of a long-run, stable, intimate relationship with another human being? How many diets are begun in earnest, with proclamations and purchases and club-joining and power-walking, only to be silently abandoned after a few weeks? This is not an exception, it is how people live today. Whatever we may say about our desire to do something, to change, to be active in one way or another, for the most part we don't do anything at all. Our passivity implies that, actually, we don't want to do much about change; certainly not if it gets in the way of [*insert TV show here*]. Similarly, the passivity of most folks with respect to the media implies that they are essentially fine with things as they are.

A third way to ask about happiness is to take an external view, building a notion of a 'good life' and then asking, is acedia part of a good life? Well, of course not – the word refers to a vice, after all. Niggling is not good. You're supposed to stop *and smell the roses*, not prattle on about yesterday's news. I once thought that the interactive age would be special because software, unlike movies, gets people to *do* things, to overcome their innate tendency to sit back and relax once fed and sexed and sheltered. This was before I realized that one can fill up a life with empty doings and that the metaverse may be inclined for commercial reasons to aim at precisely that. What is the opposite of an empty doing? A meaningful doing might build a connection to other people, such as, but not exclusively, raising a child. Or it might be part of the pursuit of a valid vocation. These are the founding stones of a good life. Niggling on the internet can prevent a person from building those foundations. Is that the fault of the internet? Perhaps it is. There has always been a temptation to diverge from a good life. Maybe the metaverse increases the temptation. If so, then, no, the acedics will not be happy at all. They'll have reason upon reason upon reason, once they've got food, shelter, and the other basics, to sit back and do nothing.

Thus there's some tension in the media passivity that looks to extend into the metaverse. Most people will be content and will not actually do one in a million of the things made possible by the metaverse. But, by objective standards, we may not judge their lives to be good. On the other hand, the world is not particularly enamored, comfortable, or even learned in the handling of objective standards, so it may not matter whether the nigglers are happy or not, in any of the three senses just discussed.

Whether or not there will be inequality of happiness, there will certainly be inequality of income. The nigglers may or may not be poorer in spirit, but they will certainly be poorer in wallet. They will also be scorned. Some will rail at their apathy. Others will scold them, with Hütter, for devoting their precious lives to spiritual nothingness. Many criticize those who eat McDonald's; others are angry at the entire culture that makes such things possible. It is indeed a sad affair; Burger King is much better. Yet the profits of McDonald's only underscore how vastly outnumbered are those who think they know a thing or two about good food. Not much money is made serving black-truffle-studded foie gras. Those who understand such things must also try to understand the mentality of their brothers and sisters on the earth, who don't really care about taste. Or anything else.

As a step towards understanding acedia, let us ask, can we really blame a person for not caring? In our time, the world has been drained of meanings and the iconic creative person these days makes irony his primary tool rather than the healthy correction it ought to be. The metaverse is coming upon us in an age not of cultural decay but of active cultural demolition. This leads to niggling, goofing around on the internet, because the myths and fantasies destroyed or corrupted in the real world are merely being rebuilt in the metaverse, in sugary forms, to be enjoyed by all – for a small fee. So how can we expect anyone to care about global warming, or the fate of the starving, or their own education – all these things that the metaverse might get them involved in, but probably won't – when the constant message of our culture is that this world consists of proteins swimming around in a self-building fishtank – and nothing more? From the standpoint of an average person born in 1990, there doesn't seem to be anything truly of import outside the tank. And, while there's nothing of import inside the tank either, at least there are cool crafted plastic gizmos in there that pass the time. And if this situation results in the few having richer, fuller lives while the many wallow in a state that they accept peacefully enough, bad though it may be – what of it? On what grounds can this situation be criticized? For the acedic niggler, there aren't any.

A breathtaking inequality is in the works, and we need to develop an answer to the challenge it will present. Some people will step into the metaverse with energy and zeal; they may be born with that energy, or born with enough money that good teachers and mentors will be brought to bear, to bring about a conversion into activity and creativity and growth. These folks will have a special time, for good or ill, with the metaverse, and all the things said about it in these pages will ring true for them. As you read, though, consider the nigglers, those who don't care at all, who won't try, and for whom the metaverse will primarily serve to pass the time. They stand in the background of these postcards, but their fate is no less important for that.

Notes

1. Reinhard Hütter, 'Pornography and Acedia', *First Things*, April 2012.
2. Brian Stelter, 'Youths are watching, but less often on TV', *New York Times*, 8 February 2012.
3. Jonathan Haidt (2006) *The Happiness Hypothesis*. New York: Basic Books.

3
The Distributed Self: Virtual Worlds and the Future of Human Identity

Richard Gilbert and Andrew Forney

This theoretical work develops two central premises. The first is that human identity, defined as a person's conception and expression of his or her individuality, is not fixed and immutable but changes in response to revolutionary developments in culture and technology. The second is that we are currently in the early phases of one of these profound techno-cultural transitions: the rise of 3D virtual worlds and the formation of a ubiquitous, photorealistic, seamlessly integrated, and massively scaled metaverse (Dionisio et al., in press) that will dramatically reshape our conception and experience of the self.

Conceptions of human identity: a brief history

Psychologists, historians, and philosophers of mind generally divide the history of human identity into three stages: (1) the Pre-modern Stage, (2) the Modern Stage, and (3) the Post-modern Stage (Table 3.1). During the Pre-modern Stage, a person's identity (The Social Self) was based upon his or her roles and standing in the social order rather than on a unique organization of behavior and internal experience. In this era, a person was a peasant, merchant, landed gentry, or lord; he or she was a farmer, blacksmith, soldier, or knight – not merely someone who happened to occupy one of these positions and social statuses. Thus, the socially embedded self is not described by a unique and distinctive pattern of feelings and thoughts but by a set of status identifiers that reflect the person's fixed roles within the social order .

The Pre-modern conception of identity as external (outside the individual) and contextual (rooted in the individual's place in the social order) gave way to a 'modernist' view of identity as personal, unique, and internal (The Psychological Self) following major historical

Table 3.1 Stages of human identity

Stage	The social self	The psychological self	The multiple self	The distributed self			
				Expressive distribution	Intelligent distribution	Intelligent distribution with dynamic attributes	Dynamic intelligence with server capabilities
Features	Contextual, embedded in fixed social order	Internal, embodied, stable, individual	Fragmented, embodied, unstable. Changes with context and personal desire	Embodied consciousness distributed to multiple digital platforms and selves	Distributions to entities capable of action without direct input from embodied consciousness	Distributions to entities capable of learning and being changed by experience	Distributions to entities with the ability to distribute their own informational patterns
Societal context	Feudalism	Enlightenment; industrial capitalism	Globalization; post-industrialism/age of information	Post-industrialism/age of information			
Technological context	Agriculture	Geology; archeology	Windowed operating systems	Cloud computing; immersive virtual worlds	Artificial intelligence	Advanced artificial intelligence; human–machine singularity	

developments that occurred in the 17th through 19th centuries. These included the Enlightenment, with its emphasis on internal processes of reason and cognition, and the rise of industrial capitalism, with its emphasis on private property, individual rights, and a fluid social system that enabled greater personal change relative to the old feudal order. In the modernist conception, identity is viewed as being internal, unique, divided between conscious and unconscious awareness, largely continuous but subject to change, consistent with developmental experience, unitary or singular in its organization, and physically embodied – all assumptions that are reflected in the classic theories of personality from Freud to the cognitive behaviorists. Each theory assumes that developmental experiences interact with inborn tendencies to create a relatively stable internal organization that is unique to the individual and subject to accurate description.

In the latter half of the 20th century dramatic advances in transportation and telecommunications turned the world into a global village where individuals were constantly exposed to new perspectives, narratives, and styles. The sheer volume and diversity of these voices and perspectives challenged the very notion of objective truth. How could one believe in the truth of any position, including propositions regarding human identity, when a range of counter-positions was constantly available? In this broad context of intellectual uncertainty, modernist conceptions of a singular, objectively describable, self came under attack by post-modern theorists who argued that there is no stable, consistent, coherent individual identity (Gergen, 1991). Instead they maintained that human identity is fragmented, multiple, and constantly shifting (The Multiple Self). In essence, the multiple self represents a qualitative shift in how human identity is viewed, because it does not assume the existence of any structure that constrains the range of self-expression – either an external structure like the fixed social order of pre-modernity, or the internal, psychological structure at the heart of modern conceptions of personality.

The post-modern, multiple self can be understood with reference to developments in the area of computer science (Turkle, 1995). Like a windowed computer operating system that serves as the executive controller for many functionally different applications (only one of which is active and displayed on the screen at any time, while many others are available but in an inactive or latent position), the self is conceived as an entity capable of 'maximizing' or 'minimizing' multiple aspects of identity according to personal desires and the demands of a particular context without regard to whether they form a consistent, coherent structure. Thus, the Multiple Self is analogous to an operating system that manages a shifting collection of active and waiting processes.

Virtual worlds and the future of human identity

The distributed self: an overview

The rise of 3D virtual worlds and the introduction of avatar-mediated forms of expression have the potential to once again reshape humanity's conception and experience of the self and usher in a fourth stage of identity, one which can be termed 'The Distributed Self' (Gilbert et al., 2011). In this conception, consciousness and aspects of the self will be increasingly externalized and distributed into three-dimensional digital forms (i.e., avatars) reflecting any number of combinations of age, gender, body type, race, ethnicity, style, personality, and physical health. Several studies have shown, for instance, that participants in 3D virtual environments such as Second Life often create avatars that, relative to their physical self, are younger, have a better body or physical appearance, and are ascribed a more positive or idealized personality (Au, 2007; Bessiere et al., 2007; Gilbert et al., 2011). Moreover, Gilbert et al. estimate that, among the overall user base of Second Life, 18 per cent have a single 'alt' (i.e., a secondary or alternative avatar) in addition to their primary avatar while 32 per cent operate two or more alts (Gilbert, 2011). In approximately 70 per cent of these cases, one function of the alt or alts is to experiment with different aspects of identity or personality.

Taken as a whole, these data indicate that about half of active users of Second Life are coordinating a multiple personality system consisting of a physical self plus two virtual identities (a primary avatar and one alt) and about a third are coordinating an identity system involving four or more components (a physical self and three or more virtual identities). As depicted in Figure 3.1, when the allocation of consciousness to non-immersive digital forms such as email, Facebook, Twitter, or LinkedIn is added to the physical and 3D virtual components of the overall identity system, the structure of the self becomes more like an organizational flowchart rather than the singular entity in modernist conceptions, or the diverse, but device-constrained, model of post-modernism.

Whereas the windowed operating system serves as the technological analog to the post-modern conception of The Multiple Self, the rise of 'cloud computing' (i.e., the virtualization of computational resources on the internet so that they can be allocated, replicated, or distributed on demand across multiple platforms and devices) forms the technical basis for the new, distributed conception of identity and self. Within this

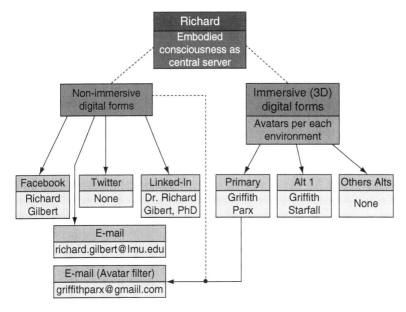

Figure 3.1   The distributed self

new model, the source of consciousness remains internal and embodied (in the 'cloud' of consciousness), but the expression or enactment of this consciousness becomes increasingly external, disembodied, and distributed on demand to multiple digital forms. Reflecting on this trend and growth projections for 3D virtual worlds, Gilbert et al. note the following:

> As 3D virtual worlds and the global population of avatars continue to grow, creating and coordinating a system composed of a physical self and a diverse set of online identities will increasingly become a normative process in human development. Individuals will manage their multiple personality orders in a manner akin to a choreographer managing a company of dancers or a conductor leading an orchestra and the operation of personality will take on a quality of performance art.
>
> (Gilbert et al., 2011, p. 232)

'Expressive' distribution

Thus far in discussing the distributed self, all of the digital forms that make up the disparate identity system are merely *expressions* or *reflections* of the embodied consciousness. That is, every act, comment, or gesture that emanates from any of the constituent identities must originate and be under the direct control of the authoring consciousness in real time. Without the initiative and guidance of the central consciousness, the component identities are devitalized and, like actors stripped of a script, are unable to engage in action or communication. Thus, the function of the divergent digital forms as currently presented is solely to express aspects of the authoring consciousness across a variety of domains or realms and is therefore referred to as 'Expressive Distribution'.

From expressive distribution to distributed intelligence: integrating artificial intelligence into the poly-form identity system

A qualitative advance from a purely expressive distribution of consciousness would require aspects of consciousness to be transferred to one or more avatars that make up the immersive portion of the online identity system in a way that enables them to act in the absence of direct and immediate control by the embodied mind. That is, avatars would need to be equipped with at least a basic level of artificial intelligence (AI) that allows them to independently carry out functions prescribed by the authoring consciousness. Norbert Wiener and the Cybernetics group at MIT (Wiener, 1948) provided the theoretical underpinnings for this possibility by advancing the position that human consciousness and identity is best viewed as a pattern of information unrelated to a biological or any particular material substrate. In Wiener's famous phrase that captured the Cybernetic viewpoint, 'Information is information, not matter or energy' (1948, p. 132). Thus, from a cybernetic perspective, patterns of information could theoretically move between different substrates without a loss of meaning.

Decades after Wiener's foundational work, Hans Moravec, in a 1988 volume on the future of robot and human intelligence, became the first scientist to specifically suggest that, because human mentality is essentially an informational pattern, it could be moved from carbon-based organic components and instantiated in silicon-based electronic components without a loss of functionality (Moravec, 1988). Later, in a comprehensive treatise on 'post-humanism', Hayles (1999) reasserted the cybernetic conception of identity as informational patterns independent of the material substrate in which they are housed. According to post-humanists, the embodiment of human thought in a biological substrate is a vestige of history rather than an inevitability of life, and the body is viewed as the original prosthesis of the mind that can be extended or replaced with other prostheses. They believe that human consciousness can be seamlessly integrated with intelligent machines and that there is no essential or absolute demarcation between bodily-housed consciousness and intelligent computer simulation. From the post-human perspective, the insistence that consciousness must be permanently and solely housed in a fixed physical body that is highly limited, requires continuous feeding and cleaning, experiences pain, and eventually withers and dies, represents fear of change, imaginative limitations, or a form of prejudice that could be labeled 'bioism' or 'carbonism'. Finally, the legendary futurist, Raymond Kurzweil, characteristically pursued the possibility of distributed intelligence to its logical extreme by asserting that the *entire* human brain could be transferred or simulated in a computational substrate. As the brain is a massive computational system, he specifically proposed that 10^{16} cps or Hertz of computation and 10^{13} bits of memory would be required to emulate human levels of intelligence, while 10^{19} cps and 10^{18} bits would be needed to capture the salient details of each of our approximately 10^{11} neurons and 10^{14} interneuronal connections (Kurzweil, 2005).

The distribution of information and action patterns from a human driver to an avatar is not just a conceptual possibility. It is currently taking place, albeit in a highly simplified form far removed from the ambitious scenarios just discussed. In virtual worlds such as Second Life, 'bots', intelligent agents that are visually indistinguishable from avatars directly controlled by a human driver, are being programmed to perform simple functions that previously had to be performed by an avatar operated by a human intelligence in real time, for example, greeting customers at a virtual store or club, answering basic questions about the location or use of inventory, taking messages, contacting the owner of the virtual environment. However, as discussed by Burden and the Daden Limited report on the Future of Virtual Worlds, it is widely speculated that next-generation bots with human-equivalent AI components may be able to pass a virtual Turing Test whereby they cannot be recognized as an intelligent agent by a majority of human-controlled avatars after five to ten minutes of interaction within the virtual world (Burden, 2009; Daden Limited, 2010).

Looking further over the horizon, it is anticipated that intelligent agents with ever more sophisticated AI components will be able to serve as effective virtual assistants for their affiliated human intellects by meeting other avatars and attending events when the human driver is unavailable and reporting back on these activities to the human intelligence. Eventually, it is assumed that the level and sophistication of the transferred intellect, that is, its information and behavioral patterning, will reach such a point that, in conjunction with photo-realistic graphics, it will be difficult to distinguish the bot from the person it is representing even by associates and friends in the physical world. It is important to note, however, that this achievement would represent a significant advance over current AI-equipped avatars, and thus it is more likely to be a medium-term rather than a near-term development.

Implications of distributed intelligence

The current and anticipated developments in distributed intelligence that have been discussed thus far have profound implications for human psychology and culture, which are discussed below.

The multiplication of the self

When the information patterns of human mentality are successfully instantiated in a digital form, the potential arises to make a large (theoretically unlimited) number of copies of the autonomous agent. Each replica or simulated self will then be able to perform functions that previously required the direct control of the embodied consciousness, thus creating a group or army of selves to multiply the impact and functionality of the authoring consciousness. In contemporary culture, the benefits and drawbacks of multitasking, that is, dividing consciousness into more than one activity at the same time, are often discussed and debated. In an immersive world filled with AI-equipped avatars, the self will have the unprecedented ability to simultaneously execute multiple tasks with each of its intelligent agents being able to fully focus on its assigned activity. Thus, the development of autonomous agents will help achieve the coexistence of multitasking and undivided attention.

The virtualization of time

One of the great achievements of the 20th century was the virtualization of space. The development of the radio, telephone, and digital communication technologies enabled individuals to instantaneously project their consciousness across vast distances. However, the embodied consciousness and its spatially distributed form (text, audio, video) both needed to operate at the same time. In contrast, when intelligent agents are capable of action outside the direct and immediate control of their physically housed consciousness, these digital 'stand-ins' or 'representatives' can simultaneously operate in multiple time zones. For example, while the embodied consciousness is sleeping, the distributed consciousness is rising; while the embodied consciousness is working, its intelligent agent is socializing, leading to the even more radical achievement of the virtualization of time. In a world teeming with intelligent agents, the self is not only capable of being in two (or many more) places at once; it can also be simultaneously projected into multiple time zones from a single position in space.

A new conception of immortality

For most of history, the only way that human beings could respond to their fear of death and desire for life extension was to invoke metaphysical notions such as an afterlife or reincarnation. More recently, advances in genetics and microbiology have introduced possibilities such as organ regeneration, cloning, and modifying cellular processes involved in aging and death as mechanisms for life extension. Now, with the rise of avatar-based distributed intelligence, another possibility has emerged other than invoking concepts of an eternal soul or extending the life of the physical body. This involves the immortal preservation of an individual's consciousness (Geddes, 2010), or at least his or her appearance and a large set of behaviors, attitudes, personality traits, and patterns of thought in a three-dimensional digital form, an outcome that Blascovich and Bailenson have termed 'virtual immortality' (Blascovich and Bailenson, 2011).

Experience with historical figures

The preceding discussion of immortality pertained to the timeless preservation of the self. However, the self is not the only person whose identity could be endlessly maintained. The physical and psychological features of parents and grandparents could also be distributed to highly realistic avatars so that subsequent generations within a family would be able to interact with a persuasive 3D simulation of their ancestors in a manner that was far more powerful than non-immersive experiences such as viewing photographs or videos of their deceased relatives. In addition, the same mechanism could be applied to provide individuals with immersive experiences with simulated historical figures, such as past presidents, for educational purposes. For example, Project LifeLike, a collaboration between Avelino Gonzalez at the Intelligent Systems Laboratory (ISL) at the University of Central Florida and Jason

Leigh at the Electronic Visualization Laboratory (EVL) at the University of Illinois at Chicago, has developed an avatar that has captured the appearance, gestures, speech idiosyncrasies, and personality characteristics of retired NSF program director, Dr Alex Schwarzkopf, for historical preservation.

Reconsideration of a mind–body dualism

For much of its history, the field of psychology has embraced monism, that is, the belief that the mind is housed in the physical body and is part of a unified entity. Dualistic assertions that the mind is separate from the body have been disputed on a variety of grounds, including the following.

Problem of causal interaction: having something totally non-physical causing physical events such as neuronal firing violates the physical laws of the deterministic universe.

The argument from brain injury: if the mind were completely separate from the brain, how could it be possible that every time the brain is significantly injured, the mind is also affected?

The argument from biological development: human beings begin their existence as entirely physical or material entities and, since nothing outside the domain of the physical is added later on in the course of development, then we must necessarily end up being fully developed material beings.

The argument based on simplicity: why is it necessary to believe in the existence of two, ontologically distinct, entities of mind and brain when the same events and properties can be explained in terms of one?

If, however, patterns of thought are successfully distributed from an embodied consciousness to a three-dimensional digital form, long-held assumptions about the unity of mind and body will need to be revisited.

From distributed intelligence to synthetic evolution

The future scenarios that have been outlined thus far, as radical and consequential as they may be, are all limited in the sense that they involve transferring fixed elements of the embodied consciousness to a digital form. That is, after the process of transfer takes place, the avatar independently executes the distributed pattern of information in a manner that never changes, in a uniform or 'static' manner over time. However, there are two extensions, which add an element of change or variability to the process, that would be truly revolutionary.

The first extension involves the *addition of dynamic attributes*. It occurs when agents equipped with distributed intelligence are able to learn from, and be changed by, their experiences in executing elements of the authoring consciousness. This capacity for experiential learning or adaptation would mean that, over time, there would be a growing discontinuity between the embodied consciousness and its digital representative, because the two entities would increasingly be shaped by tangibly different histories. While the digital actor's interactions with the environment could be predicted from their attributes at the time of construction, the uniqueness afforded by the actor's divergent experiences would produce qualities and attributes that could never have been foreseen by the human architect/server. Under these conditions, the only way to maintain the intelligent actor's fidelity to the human user's consciousness would be to undertake the process of frequent, if not continuous, updates. Because this process of ongoing synchronization would almost certainly prove to be unwieldy, if not impossible, the more likely outcome would be that the intelligent agent begins to evolve in ways that are not direct or obvious reflections of the original, authoring consciousness. When this occurs, avatars equipped with distributed intelligence will become more like digital offspring of the initial, embodied consciousness rather than a direct expression of it. Moreover, because these entities exist in digital space mediated by contemporary processing power that far exceeds the human capacity, it is not difficult to imagine such electronic progeny being capable of development at a blinding pace, one that shatters the comparably snail-like pace of the biological human. On a philosophical level, at a certain level of discontinuity between the embodied and disembodied mentalities, fundamental questions can be raised about whether the evolving avatar intelligence has any connection to humanity as a whole (Is it human?) or the particular identity of the human who served as its architect (Is it me?). At advanced levels of discontinuity, one could reasonably argue that the evolving avatar is no longer a component of the distributed identity of the authoring consciousness and has acquired a unique identity of its own.

The second extension involves the *addition of server capacity*. This means that avatars loaded with information patterns from the embodied consciousness acquire the capability to act as servers or computational sources in their own right and transfer information patterns to a next level of avatars, that is, avatars twice removed from the original, embodied mind. In this way, the distributed self gains potentially infinite depth, with each created agent harboring the potential to project their own actors, who in turn may create their own offspring, ad infinitum. In this conception, avatars that have acquired server capacity and exercise their ability to transfer information patterns are termed 'proliferating avatars' while those that do not are designated as 'non-proliferating avatars'.

The implications of a dynamic, autonomously proliferating collection of digital selves tracing back to an initial, embodied consciousness (the virtual equivalent of a line of descent or genealogy) are difficult to grasp. However, when considered in concert with the laws of accelerated returns that accompany digital as opposed to biological development (Kurzweil, 2005), it is conceivable that a single, embodied consciousness could spawn an enormous community of actors whose development might proceed in a vast number of directions. It is also possible that human beings would try to close Pandora's box and seek to limit the transfer of information patterns across generations of avatars. This might be accomplished by requiring every avatar operating in the virtual world to be sponsored by a human being and tied to physical world data such as a bank or credit card account. This would ensure that the human consciousness was the ultimate determinant of the number of avatar levels in the distributed identity system, and reassert human authority.

Another possibility, raised by evolutionary biologists, is that there are inherent barriers that will block the capacity for avatars to independently transfer information patterns to other avatars and create unlimited levels of distributed identity. From an evolutionary perspective, the ability for an avatar to undertake a process of transferring its mentality or information patterns to another avatar implies a level of consciousness or awareness on the part of the transferring agent that currently does not exist and may never be possible to develop. This is due to the assumption that consciousness and cognitive prowess is a latecomer to evolution that arose only after deeper layers of perception had been built over millions of years of biological progression. They argue that efforts to short-circuit this process by attempting to program advanced intelligence into a disembodied form are destined to fail, no less than one could hope to construct a roof without first building the house.

A logical answer to the objections of evolutionary biologists might be to note that the problem itself (transferring something closely tied to biology into a non-biological substrate) also suggests a solution.

Assuming that the evolution of consciousness is the product of a long line of development, this time frame could be dramatically compressed due to exponential increases in the speed and power of computer processors. Cognitive evolution that may have taken millennia to produce in conventional, biological terms may occur in a micro-fraction of time due to this accelerated state. At the same time, it should be noted that exponential advances in computational power and speed alone might not be sufficient to simulate higher-order human mentality. Regardless of the capacity of the hardware (even assuming near-infinite capacity), new computational methods or techniques (e.g., algorithms, paradigms, theories) will be required for synthetic agents to, for example, understand natural language in the way a human being can. It is even possible that these complex cognitive capacities will prove to be 'non-computable' for any device, regardless of capacity or speed, into the distant future.

It is impossible to know where on this continuum of possibilities the distribution of the self and human identity will ultimately fall. Due to challenges in AI and computational methods, will we merely see slow and incremental increases in the capacity to instill patterns of human mentality into non-biological entities that have a limited ability to perform simplified tasks in defined contexts within the virtual world? Or will distributed intelligence allow us to create more skilled and flexible agents that can serve as our personal representatives in more complex and varied immersive settings? In the extreme, will these digital representatives eventually develop the dynamic ability to learn from experience or execute transfers of their informational patterns to other avatars and usher in a process of synthetic evolution? The future will answer these questions. However, given the exponential pace of technological development expressed in the laws of accelerated returns, including advances in miniaturization and nano-technology (the likes of which Kurzweil and others posit will be critical to the digitization of human mentality), it is likely that patterns of information that make up the self and human identity will be increasingly distributed beyond their embodied roots, and current assumptions of a unity of mind and body will be replaced by a resurgent dualism.

Acknowledgments

The authors would like to thank Dr John Dionisio, Associate Professor of Computer Science, Loyola Marymount University, for his thoughtful comments on an earlier draft of this manuscript.

References

Au, W. J. (2007) Surveying Second Life (Web log message, 30 April 2007) http://nwn.blogs.com/nwn/2007/04/second_life_dem.html

Bessiere, K., Seay, A. F., and Kiesler, S. (2007) 'The Ideal Self: Identity Exploration in World of Warcraft', *Cyberpsychology and Behavior*, 10, pp. 530–5.

Blascovich, J. and Bailenson, J. (2011) *Infinite Reality: Avatars, Eternal Life, New Worlds, and the Dawn of the Virtual Revolution*. New York: William Morrow.

Burden, D. (2009) 'Deploying Embodied AI into Virtual Worlds', *Knowledge-Based Systems*, 22, 7, pp. 540–4.

Daden Limited (2010) *The Future of Virtual Worlds*. Unpublished whitepaper.

Dionisio, J., Burns, W., and Gilbert, R. (in press) '3D Virtual Worlds and the Metaverse: Current Status and Future Possibilities', *ACM Computing Surveys*, in press.

Geddes, L. (2010) 'Immortal Avatars: Back up Your Brain, Never Die', *New Scientist*, 2763.

Gergen, K. (1991) *The Saturated Self: Dilemmas of Identity in Contemporary Life*. New York: Basic Books.

Gilbert, R., Foss, J., and Murphy, N. (2011) 'Multiple Personality Order: Physical and Personality Characteristics of the Self, Primary Avatar, and Alt', in Peachey, A. and Childs, M. (eds) *Reinventing Ourselves: Contemporary Concepts of Identity in Online Virtual Worlds*, Springer Series in Immersive Environments. London: Springer, pp. 213–34.

Hayles, K. (1999) *How We Became Posthuman: Virtual Bodies in Cybernetics, Literature, and Informatics*. Chicago: University of Chicago Press.

Kurzweil, R. (2005) *The Singularity Is Near: When Humans Transcend Biology*. New York: Viking Press.

Moravec, H. (1988) *Mind Child: The Future of Robot and Human Intelligence*. Cambridge: Harvard University Press.

Turkle, S. (1995) *Life on the Screen: Identity in the Age of the Internet*. New York: Touchstone Press.

Wiener, N. (1948) *Cybernetics or Control and Communications in the Animal and the Machine*. Cambridge: MIT Press.

4
Meta-Dreaming: Entangling the Virtual and the Physical

Denise Doyle

> Far from the immensities of sea and land [...] isn't imagination alone able to enlarge indefinitely the images of immensity?
>
> (Bachelard, 1994, p. 183)

Introduction

> Each decade (piece of time) has its own curiosity. We move in waves. There are few curiosities here. There has not been the time to build those objects that exist and embody something of their own 'time'.
>
> (Wanderingfictions Story in Doyle and Kim, 2007, p. 217)

This chapter explores virtual worlds, or the metaverse, as spaces of and for the artistic imagination, in which the entanglement of the physical with the virtual is being exploited for its creative and imaginative potential. In particular, there are opportunities to investigate, subvert, invert, and even question our current understanding of virtual space (and the concept of the metaverse itself) through an exploration and manipulation of time, space, and identity. Creative opportunities not ordinarily available in physical world spaces are enabling artists to create new spaces of the imagination that are almost tangible, almost physical, and most certainly a 'real' experience for the audience. For Patrick Lichty, it is the particular characteristics of virtual worlds that closely echo the logic of the physical world that are providing 'an existential overlay' to the experience of virtual world spaces, and he considers how the 'invocation of this metaphor [raises] questions about the intent of the creation of such worlds and how (or if) artists will choose to engage with virtual environments in this manner' (Lichty, 2009, pp. 2–3). However, it is this 'play' of the imagination between the virtual and physical that underpins many of the themes explored by artists in projects developed on one virtual world platform, Second Life, during its lifetime (Doyle, 2010).

Second Life has been the space inhabited by Wanderingfictions Story, my avatar or virtual counterpart, for what is now a significant (if not quite substantial) period of time. The island associated with Wanderingfictions activities is Kriti Island, sitting somewhere within the wider reaches of the metaverse between the island of Symobia and the Conch Republic. Her 'voice' is heard in this chapter through her initial writings in 2007, which are included here as a prelude to each chapter section. She is also the subject of the Meta-Dreamer project discussed further below. As such, the chapter implements a playful exploration of narrative discourse through a series of snapshots of Wanderingfictions Story and reflects on the artist's persona and creative responses to a space that deliberately entangles the virtual with the physical.

Body

> I have the experience of embodiment although I know my body is virtual. Of course I do. There is little true form here, only a series of associations. I took a friend of mine to a volcano last night. He was in awe of it. In his mind's eye, in his imagination he saw before him a 'real' volcano. Well, real enough to evoke his awe. Is that not 'real' enough for it to contain a form of reality? A form of presence?
>
> (Wanderingfictions Story in Doyle and Kim, 2007, p. 216)

Working within the realm of art and technology (and as an artist who is interested in narrative), my exploration of virtual space over the last decade has often been based on the retelling of narratives in a new context. An early practice-based project was to reinterpret Italo Calvino's *Invisible Cities* (Calvino, 1997) through an interactive artifact. The story was of Marco Polo's adventures to imagined cities, with Calvino providing the descriptions of the fantastic, symbolic, and often conceptually based places. In the introduction to the project, I considered the following:

How do we understand time in virtual space? Real and imaginary, real and virtual. Is this a suitable dialectic offered by the introduction of 'net space'? Is it truly a dialectic, or a 'parallel' world we can draw upon to explore issues of time, our experiences of the world as, in fact, a type of non-linear time, a time mixed up with past, present and future?

(Doyle, 2000, p. 4)

Of equal note were my closing remarks for the project, where I suggested that the creation of a figure in the virtual space, that of Eleni, was worthy of further study.

To produce Wandering Fictions for the web remained essential for the concept. The impact on the process, above technical constraints, of constructing a character to exist within this space was continually evident. The net space, if it has borders and boundaries, is not yet visible. A very different potential space could still emerge.

(Doyle, 2000, p. 24)

In Figure 4.1, two stills can be seen of Eleni, the protagonist in the interactive arts project. Here a vectorized film of movements of a figure was created in an attempt to create a figure that could explore the virtual spaces of Calvino's imagined cities. What was of interest was this exploration of online, or cyberspaces, in a human form.

Figure 4.1   Studies of Eleni
Source: © Denise Doyle (2000).

Following my introduction to Second Life a few years later in 2006, it was a relatively short time before I created Wanderingfictions Story.[1] The origin of her first name was based on Siegfried Zielinski's early writings on the internet, in which he notes the following:

> In the motion of crossing a border, heterology encircles the impossible place, that is unlocatable, that is actually empty, that in practice is created in the motion of crossing the border [...] this is what taking action at the border, that which I call subjective, targets in relation to the Net: strong, dynamic, nervous, definitely process-orientated aesthetic constructions, that are introduced into the Net as *Wandering Fictions* [my emphasis].
>
> (Zielinski, 1996, p. 285)

This name, Wandering Fictions, became emblematic of my interest in virtual space and instantly made sense in the context of the Second Life space. If translated back into physical space Wanderingfictions Story would be over seven feet tall, brown-skinned, with a wardrobe full of saris. This form of representation was the result of a piece of performative writing practice undertaken in collaboration with artist Taey Kim (Iohe).

The outcome was a written dialogue of exchange through a series of virtual postcards and subsequently the publication of *Embodied Narrative: the Virtual Nomad and the Meta Dreamer* (Doyle and Kim, 2007). In conversation with Dongdong, whose presence was in Web 2.0 space, Wanderingfictions Story attempts to describe her experience of being in the Second Life space. Seen through new eyes, comparisons were made between the early travelers exploring and discovering new lands. Through this performative writing experiment, there was the attempt to explore the implications of living multiple (and concurrent) realities in relation to Second Life. If there is a cultural dream pool, it now includes the very real, or lived, experience of embodiment in avatar-mediated virtual worlds and spaces, and this is enabling new narratives to emerge. Katherine Hayles considers narrative to be 'a more embodied form of discourse' (Hayles, 1999, p. 22), and describes the dynamic between narrative and what she terms 'possibility space' where narrative 'capitalizes on and reinforces human presuppositions that make the world make sense, possibility space carries the scent of the non-human, the algorithmic, the procedural, the machinic' (Hayles, 2005, p. 179). Hayles (2005, p. 180) further states, 'An optimistic interpretation of the infiltration of narrative by possibility space, then, is that humans are now able to go beyond their evolutionary inheritance into realms that cannot be easily imagined or represented by the human mind alone.'

For Hayles, possibility space can also be understood as 'opening the human to the unthought and unrecognized otherness of a universe much bigger than human conception can hold' (Hayles, 2005, p. 180). This notion of possibility space and the narrative infiltration indicated by Hayles have implications here in the sense that virtual world spaces such as Second Life offer the chance to reconsider relationships that have come to be embedded culturally and socially (and personally) as the logic of our physical world rather than the unthought otherness of an as yet unrecognized universe.

Actual virtual body

> Of course I can fly here. But it's like having invisible wings that you cannot really spread widely or fully or freely enough. Some-times I fly upwards as fast as I can, so I can feel that sensation of freedom, and I can dream of flying a great distance along the horizon. Eventually I get to a point where gravity pulls me back down, but I do seem to be able to have the fantasy of escaping gravity, at least for a moment.
>
> (Wanderingfictions Story in Doyle and Kim, 2007, p. 214)

Having already developed a number of artist projects utilizing and investigating the Second Life platform as a space for artistic experimen-tation, in 2009 my interest in the notion of Wanderingfictions Story as a manifestation of, and from, virtual space became the basis of a new project, *Meta-Dreamer*. After reflecting on the work of the perfor-mance artist Joseph DeLappe's *MGandhi* series,[2] I began working with digital materialization expert Turlif Vilbrandt[3] to create a series of digi-tally materialized objects of Wanderingfictions Story. By experimenting with digital processes that extracted data from Second Life and inves-tigating different types of physical materials, attempts were made to represent jade and clouded glass, among other textures. The end result can be seen in Figure 4.2. The qualities of the figure are cloud-like and ethereal, as though Wanderingfictions Story, the meta-dreamer, were 'almost there'. The digital object was presented in the Golden Thread Gallery space (as part of the ISEA2009[4] exhibition) alongside DeLappe's figure of *MGandhi 1* (2008). The visitor could also experience the virtual installation on Kriti Island in Second Life that included the presentation

Figure 4.2   Wanderingfictions Story as part of the *Meta-Dreamer* project at the Golden Thread Gallery, Belfast (2009) Digital Object
Source: © Denise Doyle (2000).

of Wanderingfictions Story, the meta-dreamer, through captured images and her meta-dream writing.

This process of extracting data from virtual space to be manifested in some way in physical space forms an aspect of what Lichty terms an Evergent modality of art in virtual worlds. In his article 'The Translation of Art in Virtual Worlds', Lichty outlines a number of interesting questions with respect to artists working between the virtual and what he terms the *tangible* (Lichty, 2009). Further, he presents four modalities of art presented below in which each modality 'refers to the location and vector direction of the work's relation between worlds' (Lichty, 2009, p. 2). He notes that, in terms of artistic praxis (beyond the associated problems of audience and questions of form), it is 'the representational modality and the permeability of the boundary between worlds' that is of particular interest in the creation of meaning in artworks produced in virtual world spaces (Lichty, 2009, p. 1). He explains, 'The nature of communication of the work is dependent upon its location and vector. What I mean by vector is a gesture of direction, simultaneity, concurrence, or stasis in regards to its movements between worlds' (Lichty, 2009, p. 2).

As noted, Lichty suggests that there are four modalities of art being produced in virtual worlds: the Transmediated, the Evergent, the Cybrid, and the Client/Browser work. He explains, 'This epistemological "movement" within and between worlds has four basic structures; work that is essentially traditional physical art translated to the virtual, "evergent" work that is physically realized from virtual origins, the virtual itself, designed entirely for the client/browser experience, and "cybrids" that exist concurrently between various modalities' (Lichty, 2009, p. 2).

According to Lichty, the semiotics of two of the four modalities, the Transmediated and the Client/Browser, are 'a straightforward affair' (Lichty, 2009, p. 2). However, the Cybrids 'are less concerned with continuity but are interested in the differences and distinctions between worlds and scales' (Lichty, 2009, p. 5). Both the Cybrid and the Evergent works demonstrate a 'movement from virtual to tangible, which includes the consideration of works existing in simultaneous physical and virtual components, [and] present more complex models' (Lichty, 2009, p. 2). Manifesting from the virtual to the physical (or tangible) certainly has its parallels with manifesting from fictional worlds. Whatever the movement, this is a complex play and suggests in particular that it is those 'enigmatic liminal works that live between worlds' (Lichty, 2009, p. 11) that create spaces that are the most potent for the imagination, demonstrating an array of creative potential for artists engaging in virtual spaces.

Space (and place)

> In my world, changing destination is easy [...] All I have to do is to find somewhere I want to go and then within a moment I can 'teleport' there. Some would say that that makes it easy to know every place because you don't need to spend your time travelling. You don't need to plan your slower journey, work out what transport you need or where you would need to stay if the journey would take more than a day. But here's the thing: I miss being able to physically move through the space of this world; to travel from region to region [...] That's where we make the connections, crossing the borders, the boundaries.
>
> (Wanderingfictions Story in Doyle and Kim, 2007, pp. 213–14)

It is now official. Recently scientists captured anti-matter for just over 16 minutes, or for enough time to try and study a little of what this inversion of matter might mean – this 'elusive "mirror image" of everything we see around us' (Chivers, 2011) – the presence of which has been known for some time. However, it has been the containment of the anti-matter that has been the tricky bit. I sometimes wonder if Second Life is made up of some form of anti-matter – a mirror world – replicated –

overlaid. Certainly it is a form of mirrored space, yet perhaps this is too simplistic a notion, a literal mirror world – more an overlay, as Lichty suggests. Moving through space (and time) is our basic level of experiential knowledge as we exist in the physical world. Doreen Massey, in an essay responding to the work of artist Olafur Eliasson, attempts to illustrate a set of relationships between time and space by using a narrative account of a journey between Manchester and Liverpool. In the process of traveling, she suggests, 'If movement is reality itself, then what we think of as space is a cut through all those trajectories; a simultaneity of unfinished stories' (Massey, 2003, p. 111). Further, she writes,

> Space has its times. To open up space to this kind of imagination means thinking about time and space together. You can't hold places and things still. What you *can* do is meet up with them [...] 'Here', in that sense is not a place on a map. It is that intersection of trajectories [original emphasis].
>
> (Massey, 2003, p. 111)

If each space has a particular time, as Massey implies, then it may be that virtual world spaces may also have a particular time (or times) attached to them. Not only, then, could there be different sets of time-spaces that may be located in the Second Life experience; the space could also enable a particular reflection upon different time-spaces as phenomenal experience. These new time-spaces may also share their qualities with mythic time. Of mythic stories, Griffiths writes, '[They] talk time out of mind, charm time and trick time, clogging it or stretching it: fables make time fabulously paradoxical, a stubborn blot on the face of clock-time but true to the time of the psyche, where past present and future are kaleidoscope' (Griffiths, 2004, p. 66).

Remote islands

> Ah, so you are a mapmaker! I wonder what remarks you make of the landscapes that you travel through? Do you have a system of classification at all? Of patterning? Is it to 'capture' what it is to be here or to be there?
>
> I'm uncertain of my own geography. I don't even know where I live. Conceptually, that is. If we looked on the map I would not be able to point to it and say 'there, that is where I live,

that is my home'. Perhaps this is something that happens with a virtual geography.

(Wanderingfictions Story in Doyle and
Kim, 2007, pp. 214–15)

In her *Atlas of Remote Islands: Fifty Islands I Have Not Visited and Never Will*, writer Judith Schalansky (2009, p. 10) suggests that 'the lines on a map prove themselves to be artists of transformation: they crisscross in cool mathematical patterns [...] they ensure the earth retains its physicality'. Having never traveled to these real islands (and never intending to), Schalansky pieces together information and descriptions of these imagined, yet real places.[5] Comparing the earth represented as a globe and through the atlas, she writes, '[...] this Earth has no borders, no up or down, no beginning and no end [whereas] in an atlas, the Earth is as flat as it was before explorers pinned down the white spaces of enticingly undiscovered regions with contours and names, freeing the edges of the world from the sea monsters and other creatures that had long held sway there' (Schalansky, 2009, p. 11).

Rapa Iti, Pingelap, and Clipperton Atoll are but three of the 50 islands that are described by Schalansky (it is hard not to imagine Kriti Island to be the 51st of Schalansky's islands, full of stories yet to be told). Rapa Iti has an area of 40 square kilometres with 482 inhabitants and lies in the Pacific Ocean as part of French Polynesia. Marc Liblin, who lived near the foothills of the Vosges in France, dreamt that he speaks an unknown language. Eventually he meets an old woman who speaks the old Rapa of her homeland. Liblin, 'who has never been outside Europe, marries the only woman who understands him, and in 1983 he leaves with her for the island where his language is spoken' (Schalansky, 2009, p. 72). Of the 250 inhabitants of Pingelap in the Caroline Islands, 75 see no color, 'not the fiery crimson of the sunset, not the azure of the ocean [...] silly talk about the gloriousness of colour makes them indignant' (Schalansky, 2009, p. 98). Clipperton Atoll, with barely two kilometres of land, is uninhabited. Schalansky suggests that the very construction of an island lends itself to narrative, or to stories in literature (everything becomes a stage): 'The absurdity of reality is lost on the large land masses, but here on the islands, it is writ large. An island offers a stage: everything that happens on it is practically forced to turn into a story, into a chamber piece in the middle of nowhere, into the stuff of literature' (Schalansky, 2009, pp. 19–20).

If Kriti Island were to be described in similar ways (if her stories could be told), the space (or place) would not be unlike the islands described by Schalansky. When Kriti Island was specifically placed almost adjacent to Symobia in 2007 there was barely another island nearby. Now, in 2012, it is as though Kriti had become part of an archipelago of islands. Beyond its locality, it is hard to determine the situation of Kriti with any geographical certainty – even now, four years on. But, when I try and 'imagine' the differences and similarities between the real islands in Schalansky's atlas and Kriti, their differences seem to fade and their similarities strengthen – the island offering up a stage writ large.

Conclusion

> The poet confronts us with the simplest motives of a reverie; with him, we enter the chamber of a dream.
>
> (Bachelard, 2005, p. 92)

Whether traveled to physically or in the imagination, the experience of a place can be as a mathematical pattern on a map, or as a virtual island on a virtual grid, or even as a real place imagined. Yet, the heterogeneity of these experiences points towards a complex interweaving and entangling of the virtual and the physical, and that of the imagination with the body, and with space. The question of what is real and what is fiction has always been a tenuous one, and this premise is demonstrated in the stories and descriptions of the islands on Schalansky's map. The narratives are written based on fact, and yet these embellished stories allow us to see the world slightly differently, revealing stories that allow us to make another sense of the world (even to dream slightly differently).

As the real and imagined are no longer strangers (or opposites), it is also true that the physical and the virtual have become more firmly entangled. Ironically, it more accurately reflects the world in which we have always lived – a world that is not Cartesian, but many-layered, with 'times of space' rather than just space itself (Massey, 2003). We do also need time; time to consider and to make sense of the focus of our own curiosities, as we have already seen over the last decade. We need to lay the ground for what will inevitably become a new focus for our curiosities in future times of space. The artist's imagination in virtual worlds reflects the dreams of the poet or the writer, and as we entangle the virtual and the physical new hybrid forms of art emerge. Just as the poet writes in reverie, the very existence of virtual worlds has freed us to dream slightly differently (by entangling the real with the imagined, the physical with the virtual) and to enter the chamber of a dream more freely.

Notes

1. What's in a name? When I joined Second Life, after the briefest of introductions, I was searching through the surnames that were available at that time. The names that can be created in Second Life depend upon when you create an avatar and name it, as there are a certain number of 'family' surnames available at any one time. The day I joined, the family name of 'Story' was available, and as soon as I saw it, it reminded me of Wandering Fictions; Wanderingfictions Story was born.
2. During an artist residency at the Eyebeam Gallery, New York, in 2008 Joseph DeLappe experimented with a range of data materialization processes to produce *MGandhi 1* (8″ rapid prototyped 3D print), *MGandhi 2* (15″ rapid prototyped 3D print finished in genuine gold leaf, and *MGandhi 3* (17′ tall monumental sculpture constructed from cardboard and hot glue).
3. Turlif Vilbrandt is an expert in the field of Digital Materialization. He is currently completing his PhD research at the SMARTlab Digital Media Research Institute, University College Dublin.
4. The Inter Society for Electronic Arts organizes an annual symposium and related exhibitions. In 2009 it was held in Belfast on the island of Ireland.
5. A friend emailed me today from a small archipelago of islands just outside Stockholm, Sweden, from a writing retreat. She told me she has internet but no running water. This is our world: it is 'almost true' that our existence now depends on the internet almost as much as we need water itself.

References

Bachelard, G. (1994) *The Poetics of Space*. Boston: Beacon Press. Originally published in 1958, translated by M. Jolas.

Bachelard, G. (2005) *On Poetic Imagination and Reverie*. Putnam, CT: Spring Publications, Inc. Originally published in 1971.

Calvino, I. (1997) *Invisible Cities*. London: Vintage.

Chivers, T. (2011) 'Cern, Alpha and Antimatter Storage: Why Antimatter Should Matter to Us', *The Telegraph*, 13 June 2011, http://www.telegraph.co.uk/science/8560935/Cern-Alpha-and-antimatter-storage-why-antimatter-should-matter-to-us.html

Doyle, D. (2000) *Wanderingfictions 2.0: Eleni's Journey*, MA Project (Digital Media), Coventry: Coventry University.

Doyle, D. (2010) *Art and the Emergent Imagination in Avatar-Mediated Online Space*. PhD Thesis. SMARTlab Digital Media Institute, University of East London.

Doyle, D. and Kim, T. (2007) 'Embodied Narrative: The Virtual Nomad and the Meta Dreamer', *The International Journal of Performance Arts and Digital Media*, 3, 2–3, pp. 209–22.

Griffiths, J. (2004) *A Sideways Look at Time*. New York: Penguin.

Hayles, N. K. (1999) *How We Became Post-Human*. Chicago: The University of Chicago Press.

Hayles, K. N. (2005) 'Narrating Bits: Encounters between Humans and Intelligent Machines', *Comparative Critical Studies*, 2, pp. 165–90.

Lichty, P. (2009) 'The Translation of Art in Virtual Worlds', *Leonardo Electronic Almanac*, 18, 12. Accessed 5 January 2010, http://www.leonardo.info/LEA/DispersiveAnatomies/DA_lichty.pdf

Massey, D. (2003) 'Some Times of Space', in May, S. (ed.) *Olafur Eliasson: The Weather Report*. London: Tate Publishing, pp. 107–18.

Schalansky, J. (2009) *Atlas of Remote Islands: Fifty Islands I Have Never Visited and Never Will*. London: Particular Books, Penguin Group.

Zielinski, S. (1996) 'Thinking the Border and the Boundary', in Druckrey, T. (ed.) *Electronic Culture: Technology and Visual Representation*. Canada: Aperture Foundation, pp. 279–89.

5
Individually Social: Approaching the Merging of Virtual Worlds, the Semantic Web, and Social Networks

Francisco Gerardo Toledo Ramírez

My body can walk barefoot, but my avatar needs shoes.

Gazira Babeli[1]

Avatars, virtual art, and the metaverse

In my research, I approach the study of virtual world-based art and the avatars that formulate it by focusing on the experiences and performances of avatars involved in aesthetic exchange, encompassed by the term *Second Life-based artwork* (Toledo Ramírez, 2011). The features, behavior, and ethos of avatars creating art in virtual worlds and assuming identities as 'artists' are key to my work and contribute – to some extent – to the discussion of a future Web inhabited by 3D avatars. In my research, these subjects are approached from mixed methods centered on qualitative inquiry, case studies, and a mix of analytical perspectives from distributed aesthetics and media studies. I am persuaded that analyses of the future of the internet, avatar interfacing, and semantic and social media could obtain greater value if they come from multidisciplinary perspectives that merge the social sciences, aesthetic, and media studies disciplines in one single influential point of view. Some research in this field today is enlightening and effective – methodologically speaking – as an analytical framework that contributes to the study of merging social media technologies, virtual worlds, and semantic networks, all pivoting around the crucial future of the web.

A well-rounded thesis about the future of the internet predicts the emergence of the metaverse as a significant transformation of paradigms at the level of the global attention-economy, including 'resources, products and services through 2D and 3D virtual and augmented reality environments' (Metaverse Roadmap, 2007). Worldwide networks become more numerous, complex, hyper-connected, and faster, 'compressing' (literally and metaphorically) physical space/time and creating the impression of collective 'hyper-vicinity' in which everyone must update their social, professional, and personal network cues. More versatile mobile communication devices, more transparent, accelerated, and automated networks, and the massive presence of *intelligent* objects interpenetrated by patterns of information will transform the task of interfacing the world through digital networks as the most common, influential, and strategic activity in human material and cultural productivity.

We are at the first stages of an unprecedented, hyper-accelerated transformation in our relationship to information technology on a planetary scale. The hypothesis of a future web would include a 'browsable' metaverse operating from within a 3D virtual persistent space through avatar interaction in combination with newer and more pervasive social media and semantic networks. This will be a special 'place' in which the boundaries between the real and the virtual have been erased: a 3D environment inhabited by avatars, augmented reality applications, geospatial and GPS data in the palm of 'your' hand, and 'possibly' voice-computer control and talking-avatar interaction technologies. These will become fused into a vast *3D online virtual environment*; controlled and coordinated by an open source *metaverse operative system for the masses*. These not-long-ago separated realms will fully merge, accelerated and enhanced 'as visually and data rich as the physical world' (Metaverse Roadmap, 2007), or maybe richer.

Learning origami with Godzilla

Metaverse economies will also, besides the abovementioned, include games, wireless smart mobile broadcasting, and virtual worlds. This will be the paradigm of an accelerated structural growth as well as incessant change, releasing the transformative power to redesign traditional chains of production – resources–products–services – to more modular and flexible ones. In my research, the analysis of these topics comes from a specific viewpoint: media studies and (distributed, immersive, and diffuse) aesthetics. Quite simply, these are aesthetic 'modes' manifested in the digital that invoke similar media use, modes of reception–perception and convergent creativity process (with or through them). From this standpoint the relevant fact is that, simultaneously, *immersive, diffuse,* and *distributed* aesthetics refer to the common realm of experiencing, reacting to, and working creatively with the 'spatial and temporal flows of information networks: ... immersive and distributed aesthetics also share similar interests in transforming and extending notions of the body and perception through techno-logical mediation' (Bartlem, 2005). This implies the acknowledgment that potential digital culture, virtual worlds technologies, and user phe-nomenology must reconfigure our own epistemologies on the digital, cyberspace, and online interactive collaborative work. This is, in fact, a keystone in contemporary research on the subject. Hence, it is my claim that aesthetically examining these topics contributes greatly to the general theory of digital and virtual worlds, strengthening, in the process, the incorporation of ethnographic, phenomenological, and *multimodal* research methods on digital technology, social and seman-tic media networking, and the future 3D metaverse.[2] The question is indeed intricate and requires innovative collective knowledge con-struction, the operability of which is analogous to the humoristic metaphor I have chosen for the heading of this section: learning the delicate discipline of origami from an instructor with the tempera-ment, size, and *habitus* of that well-known prehistoric mega-monster, *Godzilla.*

As you have probably already imagined, the issues of body and pres-ence (or telepresence) are central to the entire idea of being 'present' in a remote, digital, mediated screen-based environment. The 3D environ-ment with which one could interact becomes transformed, mediated, and symbolized as a representation in the ambiguous figure of the avatar: a device we use today to extend our body and subjectivity, nego-tiating access and presence through mutable and ephemeral states of *absence/presence.* We know that this is based largely on technologies for *immersion* and *illusion*, yet our response to them is real and powerful enough to collapse and transform our relation to space, distance, and presence and, through these dynamics, transform *immersion* and *illu-sion* in the way we perceive bodies, 'consciousness, communities and relationships with digital technologies' (Bartlem, 2005). By examining virtual, interactive, and immersive aesthetics through art and artists cre-ating in the metaverse, we may attest to the synthesizing potential of convergent technologies from subjectivity to social operability, and this definitively matters in the mid to long term. Additionally, in some tech-nology and business models, the transition from a collaborative web to one that is virtually interactive and semantically enhanced – an empow-ered one – is seen as a transformative shift from the model of sequential *engineering–distribution* (for example, from planning to products to services) to a new ethos based on informational and semantic detection, collaborative diagnostics to *imagineer* new 3D interfaces, new devices, and enhanced perceptual ways for mediating reality; in other words, acknowledging that distributive resources, services, and products can revolve around a decentered arrangement of networks, and social and semantic media technologies that are not delayed by outdated and rigid vertical hierarchies.

Semantic coding and the 'sticky' case of media friendship

Imagining a future web in this context may lead to a deep shift in paradigms. For instance, as flexibility and opportunistic–holistic analysis derived from ubiquitous and instant feedback become naturalized and its applicability gains traction and influence in business and marketing cultures, let's think of a 'scenario' where planning too much in advance is no longer (or necessarily) rewarded, nor represents an advantage. In other words, this will be a web comprised of highly immersive and interactive visual components, rich social media interactions, and 3D interactive spaces where one's avatar finds his/her way at ease 'in a real life setting by building machines and buildings, exchanging ideas and socializing with others and doing business' (Mukerjee, 2009).

Although no one can predict with exactitude what the web of the future will be, certain trends and paths are clear indications of the dominant course. Cameron Chapman, a professional web designer and blogger, sees social media and the applications related to it at the forefront of the (future) web for a long time. Nine out of the 15 predictions, or 60 per cent, related to the future of the web – a collaborative blog-project led by Chapman – somehow involve the merging of virtual worlds, social media, and semantic networks packed in a more efficient, secure, and ubiquitous web: 'more semantic: ... from creating artificial-intelligence apps that interpret data much like humans do, to more semantic tagging conventions that make it possible for current online apps and services to make sense of what code means to humans' (Chapman, 2009).

We know that the question of semantic networks and semantic media apps revolves around the way humans, computers, machines, and intelligent 'objects' can 'dialogue' and exchange meaningful categorized information instantly among themselves. New paths in semantic tagging (for example, in coding) may get definitive traction in the next few years, as information architecture, web and data base design, and social network apps converge to share 'semantic labels in their code'

(Chapman, 2009). In predictions #6 and #9, *Augmented Reality In Mobile Web* and *Even More Social Apps* respectively, Chapman and collaborators make remarks concerning the pros and cons of future 'intelligent' mobile devices capable of running augmented reality applications by handling more and more sophisticated active layers of identity, face recognition, and semantic informational environment detection (on service, business, social, and personal levels). These augmented reality applications may carry a number of important 'benefits', from the personal to the social, providing even the possibility of identifying the person sitting across from you at a party without 'real' contact (Chapman, 2009) or helping you find your way around an unknown city.

As you point your mobile's camera at a place or a person, a sophisticated network of cross-reference databases will be put to work for you. This might be quite a concern for security and privacy specialists, as a simple picture of anyone through your mobile device's face recognition app may lead to a match of information via augmented reality applications and the cross-reference to social networking profile databases. So you might get instant access to whatever information that person has decided to make public about himself or herself. If you think of the exposure of your personal content (and that of others) open to accelerated tracking identity devices and your personal info and social media content open to smart mobile technology, then security and privacy issues are a big concern. In prediction #9 (*Even More Social Apps*), despite the convention that social media are still in their infancy with plenty of room for new apps, platform development and 'seamless' convergent design with virtual worlds will break the current 'walled-gardens' principle.[3] Chapman notes, 'Today's kids have been using virtual worlds since they were toddlers (think Webkinz and Club Penguin), so they'll likely want to continue using them as teenagers and adults. Plus, with advances in virtual reality on the verge of major breakthroughs, virtual worlds could come to the forefront of social media' (Chapman, 2009).

Consequently, avatar issues are of primary importance to research, and I think, in any case, the future web will see different kinds of avatars from the ones we know and use today in virtual worlds like Second Life. The reasons are many, but to mention a few centered on embodiment, subjectivity, and auto-empathy of avatars (D'Aloia, 2009) operating in the *liminal* (Lichty, 2009), we must consider the transference or back and forth communication between the virtual and the real. This is an important matter, because the avatars through which people 'live' and interact today in virtual worlds such as Second Life – far from being optimal in design, interaction, or 3D qualitative representation – are, surprisingly, more 'mature' virtual agents who have undergone intensive personal transformations, embodying subjectivity and unintentional personal narratives to the extent that they truly embrace a functional (virtual) 'personality'. This refreshing and rewarding experimentation with the limits and extensions of our bodies and personalities might get lost in radical avatar-standardization, complex software and managing requirements for a 'seamless', 'one-language' platform interoperability defined only by profit, thereby misdirecting the lessons that humanities and aesthetics in (and from) the virtual may teach.

The paradoxical extension of the virtual body from absence

I have referred previously to *multimodality*, and for me this is the essential method and epistemic procedure to approach the dense and dynamic flow of contemporary digital and media networked cultures. Its value resides in its qualitative inquiry features, and hence I advocate the essential recognition that the web, new media technologies, markup languages, semantic search engines, data mining, and multilevel structuring meaning-technologies on the one hand, and computer games, social networks, and interactive virtual worlds on the other, are leading a planetary-level movement towards the 'progressive aestheticization of reality and its main cultural expressions' (Campanelli, 2010, p. 13). This ontology helps to grasp, panoramically, the merging of technologies, media communications, and modes of perception synthesized in the discourse of the metaverse in online collaborative networks of users around the planet. Reflecting specifically from the perspective of studying avatars, the prediction of a future web mutating into the metaverse to form a 3D geospatial world or virtual space in which new and expanded resources for web users and the use of 3D avatars are developed might not necessarily be the norm.

Aesthetics and media studies research perspectives applied to virtual worlds are a valid standpoint nurturing this conjecture. The 'merging' into a possible future web phenomenon studied through phenomenological and ethnographic methods is constantly challenging, interrogating, discussing, refuting, and confirming its object of study, critically engaging and – sometimes – superficially mystifying interpretations and concepts around the aesthetics of digital media. Nevertheless, this is the best proof of their vitality and robustness as methods contributing to cross-disciplinary 'dialogue' and cross-fertilized interpretations.

In conjunction, the analysis may instigate a much-needed dialogue on the emergence of a collective consciousness through a *multimodal* focus on all the fields involved. This is illustrated in the work of virtual aesthetics, digital, and virtual culture researchers such as Florian Cramer, Vito Campanelli, Katherine Hayles, Tom Boellstorff, Edward Castronova, Angela Ndalianis, Sherry Turkle, Boris Groys, Oliver Grau, and Anna Munster, to mention a few.

The aesthetic and media studies factor

A *multimodal* view also contributes to acknowledging the profound capability of new digital media technologies to reformulate our own epistemologies about media and the multiplied, dialoguing, and intermittent positions in which users can reinvent their identities and assumptions, repositioning them culturally towards the web, the digital, and the virtual. Contemporary media do not substitute for 'old' media (overcoming them); rather, they reconfigure and assign them 'new' locations, semantic value, and syntactic functions within 'new media'. This is an idea strongly stated early on by Grau, quoting Friedrich Kittler,[4] when reflecting on how phenomenological and ethnographic approaches to electronic virtual art and new media favor the allocation of newer definitions, categories, and interpretations of 'older' media: 'understood in this way, new media do not render old ones obsolete, but rather assign them places within the system' (Grau, 2003, p. 8).

On the other hand, Munster affirms that, in the context of distributed and shared aesthetics experiences, the body is 'insoluble' (Munster, 2006, pp. 178–86), implying that *embodiment* and *presence* (or telepresence) are not fixed (keystone) processes but, rather, mutating and flickering-meaning ones. It is better inscribed, I think, in Deleuze's notion of *the fold* (as simultaneously *form* and *process*) and the idea of *blocs* of sensations. From this, I envision an articulation between embodiment, techniques for self-representing, and technologies responsible for producing *blocs* of sensation.[5] I would like to add that exploring the creative habits of artists performing in virtual worlds such as Second Life – or, better said, avatars who perform as 'artists' – is key to a multimodal discussion on aesthetics from the virtual and flickering capabilities of search engines as well as social media intersecting with virtual world technology. I estimate that the alternation between telepresence, expanded subjectivity, and hyper-mediated communication relies on a peculiar feature that I have referred to in the title of this chapter as the paradoxical condition of the *individually social*.

In this fashion, the term *absence*, both as a metaphorical and literal (yet flickering) folding/unfolding dimension of the *self*, becomes a decisive process stemming from intensive virtual environments and online 'multiplayer' networked experiences. These threads, particularly in the relocation of users beside themselves, projected in their virtual characterizations as avatars, 'triggers' self-reinventing epistemological 'paths' when 'negotiating' through remote presence within the triad of browsing–interacting–embodying virtual existence. D'Aloia calls it 'auto-empathy' (D'Aloia, 2009).

To illustrate this point, *Lacan Galicia* (my Second Life avatar), inspired by Gazira Babeli's artwork, utilizes *absence* as a mutable *repertoire* always dependent on a personal (my 'real' person) imaginary plot: that of embodying a character *à la individually-social flanêur*. This is the condition of being a virtual character who might lose her connection to Actual Life (AL), displaying pure random gestuality, mocking the all too conventional limitations of telepresence in AL by, for example, 'physically' embodying various common Second Life delays, rendering times (*rezzing* in Second Life lingo), disarticulation of 'humanoid-gestures' through scripting and body language,[6] and so on. All of these traits reflect and underline the obscure origins of *Lacan* (according to my personal plot for 'his' character) as a castaway, a clandestine member of the Space Colony Necronom VI.[7]

Travatars: from auto-empathy to remediated avatars

Other topics around avatars and their relation to distributed aesthetics, distributed cognition, issues of design, and the conspicuous sociability built from the individual awareness of a virtual avatar's doubled selfhood are also discussed in my research and essays. Collectively, these have been proposed as a 'valid' yet remote mode of presence and meaning-making playing for the extension of our actual self. In my view, these subjects may contribute to imagining, understanding, and eventually researching a future 3D web. The study of avatar features, behaviors, and ethos in virtual environments – especially if one's *self* performs in avatar 'mode' – produces a doubly affective operation on perception and interaction domains in virtual worlds, taking place first at the level of the 'avatar-body': the means through which a resident or player becomes an *actant*. This represents, in semiotic terms, a 'position' in both physical and enunciational meaning. This happens because of the development of a particular sense of presence, that of 'being there' as 'another oneself', which implies an extension of the *actual* self. D'Aloia has developed this important idea: because the avatar is actually a symbol (in the semiotic sense), it represents a dual condition of the self, both reflexivity and intersubjectivity, so the 'fracture' between two different 'levels' of existence (the actual and the virtual) is just apparent (D'Aloia, 2009). In other words, the split between the physical body that remains in 'real' life and the virtual displaced in the metaverse is just symbolic, a semantic–syntactic operation. The 'player' is one individual living simultaneously in both real and virtual environments, but his/her self is not divided into two distinct identities. ' "Giving life" to an avatar means creating an extension to (rather than causing a fracture of) our body and our identity, and this kind of extended-Self is the reflective consciousness of the recalling of the Self, or the recognition of oneself as another oneself' (D'Aloia, 2009, p. 51).

The relationship between identities is performed through a 'dual actant' that renders identity and uniqueness in a *continuum*, so the recognition as 'oneself' does not neglect the relationship between the self (self as another 'oneself') in the virtual and the other self (otherness) in AL. However, in the virtual world environment (categorized by a semi-subjective visual frame), the dual actant also interferes with the nature of the relationship with Otherness. This point is especially important to my skeptic 'prediction' of 3D web *remediated* avatars, which I see as impoverished from the point of view of subjectivity and affectivity; the rich transference between selfness and otherness would be irremediably lost, what D'Aloia calls the 'intra-subjective front of a virtual relationship, wholly played out within the pole of Selfness' (D'Aloia, 2009, p. 52). In other words, from the particular 'subjectivity' unfolded by the interaction with avatars, it is possible to elaborate an elastic yet rich understanding of the intimate relationships among human beings, digital virtual selves, and aesthetic perception in collective experiences in virtual environments. It is necessary to dig more deeply into this idea when speaking of New Media Literacy, one that is dependent on the merging of technologies, methods, and perceptual *habitus* that would converge in the future metaverse as sketched above.

The idea of extending one's subjectivity into an augmented self 'as other' in virtual worlds takes epistemic ground because the incorporation of one's body into 'our' avatar is not just a psychological perceptual operation but, in essence, a narrative one. We create the conditions and the narratives for our digital incarnation to function as a real (virtual) self, making possible the inscription of 'reality' and 'life' onto that which is essentially artificial. Whether consciously or not, intentionally or not, our avatars act under a regime of subjective narratives or 'plots' around a former fiction, that of representing our self as one that is essentially another, with whom, however, we maintain more than a prosthetic relationship. Groys explains that, though virtually identical on the surface, their contextual displaying makes them necessarily different because digital images are not fixed entities; rather, they are fluxes of digital data that need to be 'staged or performed' while the image file (the original) remains non-visible, 'absent' so to speak, from the perceptual/symbolic plane (Groys, 2008). For Campanelli and Munster, although for different reasons, and to some extent for Ndalianis, the powerful autodidactic features that characterize such dynamic flow lead 'naturally' to the space of reciprocity. In other words, the possibility exists of exercising a compelling and contributing subjectivity immersed in the virtual collective formation of experiences, many of them arranged in informal yet highly functional networked patterns. In my view, the construction of contemporary media literacy departing from those patterns is a multilevel complex (yet naturalized) operation occurring along the lines of online (virtual) collective computing, social networks, blogs, wikis, and digital games culture. In this regard, Ndalianis underlines the key role of science fiction, cinema, and special effects in the process:

> As Bukatman (1998) has noted, since the release of Star Wars in 1977, not only has science fiction become paradigmatic of the cross-media and marketing possibilities of conglomeration, but the films narrativize the implications and effects of new technologies as well as implementing new technologies in the construction of the films' special effects. Science fiction and fantasy films, computer games, comic books, and theme park attractions become emblematic of changing conditions – cultural, historical, economic, and aesthetic – as played out across our entertainment media.
>
> (Ndalianis, 2004)[8]

I see in the emergence of these processes a redefinition of the relationship between narratives, original and copy. It is the inherent archival property of digital images (on the web, every visible element carries a locator or 'address' that needs to be sited and therefore archived) that comes to the foreground, effecting the inscription of 'reality' and 'life' on the artificial. This is particularly the case of an avatar's inventory list in Second Life, chat window records, and other networked tools that we would certainly miss in a standardized or *remediate* avatar version. Envisioned as the kind of avatars that are able to interact and travel between virtual worlds, *travatars* indeed (will) have the capability for crucial interplatform communication, but they may have relatively little to say when the subjective and auto-empathic capabilities blur. That is exactly what makes the use of avatars and our identification with them compelling and enjoyable as aesthetic exchange. From a media studies perspective, the interrelation of those factors seems to invoke and justify the investigation of merging social networks, web applications, and virtual worlds interaction.

Why unified, standardized avatar interaction is not necessarily better

In the end, if the metaverse goes the way of 3D geospatial browsing, avatars there may embrace two kinds of scenarios: one virtuous and luminous and the other dark and ominous. The former is a vision anchored in the optimistic belief that networked technologies and virtual reality applications, once unified, will allow anyone's avatar, independently of the platform, genealogy, and the ethos of the game or environment, to talk the 'same language' through idiosyncratic and formal transformations. That is to say, avatars become the *remediate* kind: 'uniformed' agents capable of manipulating and passing information and interacting across different virtual environment platforms and whose design of appearance, personality,[9] and subjectivity is still clearly conceivable and strategically under the user's control. That might be the vision of the *travatar*, an avatar able to travel amid interoperable virtual worlds, a term coined by Katrina Glerum.[10] Through these avatars it will be possible to make the metaverse a more simplified and homogeneous 'place' in which the complexity aggregated by the addition of highly efficient *sensor* and *effector* resources (the methods and forms in which avatars detect, recognize, and react to the 'environment') will nonetheless allow interfacing an enhanced three-dimensional web (Metaverse Roadmap, 2007). Transformed into a vast virtual geospatial collaborative and content-producing *continuum*, the metaphor of a future web in these terms would be difficult to rival in its optimism and reliance on a sort of smooth, direct techno-evolutionary sequence from the participatory to the collaborative web: a 'browsable' web of totally social networked *trust* and *smart* things that unfolds three-dimensionally in an infinite metaverse.

In the second scenario, the *ethically* recommended output would ideally require a massively applied metaverse operative system stemming from open source platforms. That seems quite unlikely today (and tomorrow). Even more disturbing is the possibility that the unfulfilled ethical concerns might lead to worrisome privacy invasion practices in the context of a 'war' of proprietary versus open source platforms trying to develop the top metaverse operating system. Also, having access to data-mining personal information from social media databases, cross-referenced through 'ubiquitous' and traveling (but depersonalized) avatars speaking *virtual environment's Esperanto* at interplatform and internetwork levels, might easily lead to the worst practices of invasive personal marketing, targeting, identity theft, surveillance (unnoticed and unwelcome) and, in extreme cases, non-reversible 'cognitive control'. This would turn massive digital users into virtually 'used' people, afraid or unable to securely collaborate within networks, effectively tearing apart the convergent growth post-Web 2.0 around the sociocultural and aesthetic dimensions intrinsic to transforming the experience of 'interfacing' the world through potent smart mobile objects that put the web, social and semantic networks, and new media in our hands 24/7. This would constitute the breakdown of what Anna Munster calls 'digital embodiment' envisioned as a true space of reciprocity within the incorporeal 'informatic universe' (Munster, 2006, p. 18).

According to Munster, the space of reciprocity is one of the invaluable properties of digital aesthesia, one of the essential and most important characteristics of (aesthetically) accessed (and shared) exchange through the digital virtual world's interaction, which is absent from mass media.[11] Campanelli also shares this concern, specifically in relation to the power of aesthetic processes to promote dialogue and non-solipsistic and monolingual cultural ways of approaching the techno-culture issues of today, an attack that Campanelli sees as the intrinsic violence of global contemporary communication: 'I believe that the constraints upon dialogue within both online and offline contexts constitute the principal blockage to the rising of a collective consciousness of Web dynamics and its spreading aesthetic forms' (Campanelli, 2010, p. 14).

From a distributed aesthetics perspective, these ideas embody a reliable articulation of technology, visual arts, subjectivity, and of sociality – a sort of paradoxical 'condition' noted in the title of this chapter: 'individually social', but the reverse is also true.

Essential questions for the preservation of dialogue and reciprocal spaces of collective interaction

As we may see, a collective consciousness of the web and the possibility of constantly reshaping our didactic literacy paths to new media are dependent on the familiar use of their potential and the preservation of dialogue and reciprocal spaces of collective interaction. This explains, at least to me, why avatars are so important in terms of representation of bodies and personalities and therefore identity and subjectivity on the future web. If the future of Web 3.0 turns out to be that of a 3D metaverse populated by *travatars*, into whom we are still able to project our identity and subjectivity, some essential questions arise: will they be the same as the ones we know and with which we interact today? Will they be different? What about other limitations like the ones predicted by Nielsen's Law (Nielsen, 1998),[12] inevitably posed by server, broadband connection, and optic/haptic rendering technologies? Are the standardization and seamless integration of virtual games and virtual worlds and their avatars good moves? Or will this result in our losing the refreshing, 'healthier' and more affective and psychologically powerful features of mature avatars such as those in virtual environments like Second Life?

If the 3D web of the future implies the use of both a metaverse browser and a metaverse operating system, then the metaverse can 'incarnate' the new dimensions of the informational space as a physical place: a place in which it is possible, and instantaneous, to access intimate contact with others, in which avatars (or *travatars*) are social *actants* and cultural–collaborative policymakers in an individually direct fashion but networked and socially projected, preserving subjectivity paths while at the same time using an enhanced network of layers of augmented reality apps and semantic tagging. The metaverse browser will need to be the right kind of tool for the job, the kind of tactical device that permits 'all our 3D access through one piece of software … enabling avatars and other information to pass seamlessly between virtual world platforms running a broad range of proprietary hardware and software' (Metaverse Roadmap, 2007). There is the belief that around 2016 an inter-communication platform will be adopted massively in most households, and in ten years time, a metaverse operating system will operate in most personal computers, performing virtualizations and plug-in modular architecture and able to run virtual environments (games and social worlds) between different platforms seamlessly. However, immersion and illusion are not dependable solely on more 'naturalistic' 3D representation, interplatform communicability, or unified protocols. Rather, affectivity, subjectivity, and the ability to generate both social and personal narratives are the true warrants of the augmentation of the body and human intelligence through virtuality. This is, in my view, an important message that artists working in virtual environments and using them as a medium can contribute to the collective construction of the future web.

Notes

1. Gazira Babeli is the avatar name of an important (ex) Second Life artist and member of *Second Front* (the pioneer performance art group in SL). This is an excerpt from 'A leap into the void: Interview with Second Front' by Domenico Quaranta, in *Rhizome/Discuss*. Accessed 8 June 2011, http://rhizome.org/discuss/view/24830/

2. In the collaborative initiative Metaverse Roadmap: Pathways to the 3D Web (2007), the metaverse is defined in terms of a global shift in modes of content creation, spectatorship, media access, and distribution of both 2D and 3D media technologies, encompassing to such an extent that 'every economic and social sector may get redefined in decades to come'. Accessed 26 April 2011, http://www.metaverseroadmap.org/roadmap_2.html

3. I am referring to the predominant current state of virtual games and virtual worlds platforms, unable to communicate and interact with each other and/or others.

4. Kittler, F. (1993) 'Geschichte der Kommunikationsmedien', in Hubner et al., pp. 169–88 (see 178), cited in Grau (2003, p. 8).

5. This is Deleuze and Guattari's description of the grouping of sensations into affectual moments that occur in aesthetic experience. See Deleuze, G. and F. Guattari (1994) *What is Philosophy?*, translated by H. Tomlinson. New York: Columbia University Press, cited in Munster (2006, pp. 173–4).

6. On certain occasions *Lacan* (my SL avatar) likes to adopt the posture of certain objects like chairs and other pieces of furniture, behaving accordingly, through the use of scripts in Linden Scripting Language.

7. See more at *Space Colony Necronomon VI* in SL, http://slurl.com/secondlife/Desperation%20Andromeda/193/204/348/

8. See more in Ndalianis, A. (2004) 'The Baroque and the Neobaroque, Postclassical, Modern Classicism, or Neo-Baroque? Will the Real Contemporary Cinema Please Stand Up?', in *Neo-Baroque Aesthetics and Contemporary Entertainment*. Cambridge: MIT Press. Accessed 17 May 2011, http://web.mit.edu/transition/subs/neo_intro.html

9. In my reading of Velleman, I interpret the avatar's identity as relying on a particular sense of 'selfhood' developed through digital manipulation and filtered by an amplified and mutable subjectivity. The identity is negotiated and shaped through the exchange between avatars and people in both the actual and the virtual worlds, to form a 'personality' to such an extent that they may have impact in actual reality (Velleman, 2008).

10. '5a. Vision Statements, Technology and Science', in *Metaverse Roadmap: Pathways to the 3D Web*, Roadmap Inputs. Accessed 12 June 2011, http://www.metaverseroadmap.org/inputs2A.html#visionstatements

11. Munster (2006) affirms that a theoretical–analytical perspective from media studies is indispensable for an informed (current) digital aesthetics view. What she means as a space of reciprocity is an opposite view from media studies to the traditional one centered on communication; one that can show how new media not only change other forms of former media, but also change and reorganize our taxonomies and epistemologies on

media. Munster would probably situate SL's case within the boundaries of the 'tremendous potential' for the production of alternative digitalities 'to the extent to which a distributed aesthetics simultaneously engages new experiences perceptually and socially' (p. 172).

12. Nielsen's law [of Internet Bandwidth] has charted a doubling of premium-access internet bandwidth every 21 months since 1983. This trend predicts that fiber-to-the-home initiatives, like today's Verizon FiOS (20/5 Mbps), will deliver over 300 megabits per second of wired bandwidth to typical premium users in 2016, allowing download of a two-hour video in two to three minutes (impulse buy/on-demand).

References

Bartlem, E. (2005) 'Reshaping Spectatorship: Immersive and Distributed Aesthetics', *The Fiberculture Journal*, 7: distributed aesthetics (FCJ-045). Accessed 26 May 2011, http://seven.fibreculturejournal.org/fcj-045-reshaping-spectatorship-immersive-and-distributed-aesthetics/

Bukatman, S. (1998) 'Zooming Out: The End of Offscreen Space', in Lewis, J. (ed) *New American Cinema*. Durham: Duke University Press, pp. 248–74.

Campanelli, V. (2010) *Web Aesthetics: How Digital Media Affect Culture and Society*. Amsterdam: NAi Publishers Rotterdam and Institute of Network Cultures.

Chapman, C. (2009) 'The Future of the Web: Where We Will Be in Five Years', *Noupe the Curious Side of Smashing Magazine*. Accessed 8 June 2011, http://www.noupe.com/design/the-future-of-the-web-where-will-we-be-in-five-years.html

D'Aloia, A. (2009) 'Adamant Bodies: The Avatar-body and the Problem of Autoempathy', *E|C Computer Games between Text and Practice, AISS-Associazione Italiana di Studi Semiotici*, Serie Speciale, III, 5, pp. 51–6. Accessed 21 October 2009, http://www.ec-aiss.it/monografici/5_computer_games.php

Grau, O. (2003) *Virtual Art. From Illusion to Immersion*, translated by Gloria Custance. Cambridge: MIT Press.

Groys, B. (2008) *Art Power*. Cambridge: MIT Press.

Lichty, P. (2009) *The Translation of Art in Virtual Worlds*, Leonardo Electronic Almanac, 16, 4–5, Leonardo Information. Accessed 21 May 2010, http://www.leonardo.info/LEA/DispersiveAnatomies/DA_lichty.pdf

Metaverse Roadmap: Pathways to the 3D Web (2007) A Cross-Industry Public Foresight Project A Project of Acceleration Studies Foundation, 2009. Accessed 26 April 2011, http://www.metaverseroadmap.org/roadmap_2.html

Mukerjee, P. (2009) *From the Real to the Virtual*, Praxis Business School, Calcutta, Slide presentation in Slideshare. Accessed 26 May 2011, http://www.slideshare.net/prithwis/imagineering-virtual-worlds-presentation

Munster, A. (2006) *Materializing New Media. Embodiment in Information Aesthetics*. Hanover: Dartmouth College Press, University Press of New England.

Ndalianis, A. (2004) *Neo-Baroque Aesthetics and Contemporary Entertainment*, Cambridge: MIT Press. Accessed 17 May 2011, http://web.mit.edu/transition/subs/neo_intro.html

Nielsen, J. (1998) *Nielsen's Law of Internet Bandwidth*. Accessed 17 March 2010, http://www.useit.com/alertbox/980405.html

Toledo Ramírez, F. G. (2011) 'Because I Am Not Here, Selected Second Life-Based Art Case Studies: Subjectivity, Autoempathy and Virtual World Aesthetics', Western University, Working Paper.

Velleman, D. J. (2008) 'Bodies, Selves', *American Imago*, 65, 3, pp. 405–26.

6
Virtual Worlds as Radical Theater: Extending the Proscenium

Anthony M. Townsend and Brian E. Mennecke

The idea of the computer as theater is not new; it is a comfortable metaphor first explored explicitly by Brenda Laurel in her book *Computers as Theater* (Laurel, 1993). Laurel's idea is that the computer (or, more specifically, the computer-generated environment) functions in ways that are analogous to a theatrical performance and that better computer application design would be informed by understanding how theatrical spaces and performances are designed. The intuitive appeal of this idea is overwhelming; we 'watch' the computer in the same way as we watch the television or the screen in a movie theater, and, as a conduit of entertainment content, we watch the computer precisely as we watch these other media. Certainly, films presented on the computer have the same aesthetic sensibilities as do the films presented via DVD or Blu-ray on the television or in digital theaters; so the computer as fundamental theater is difficult to dispute. Or is it?

Laurel's work was specifically metaphorical; as Goffman did sociologically (Goffman, 1959), she used a dramaturgical approach to explain metaphorically how communications passed across the interface and how the user interpreted them. The television *theater* and the movie *theater* contain very little, if any, of the processes of theater; both of these media merely terminally convey theatrical productions from elsewhere. And, for the computer user watching a streaming film from Netflix, the computer too is only a theater terminal, and, like the television and the movie theater, it offers only a final representation of the theatrical process.

In the *Poetics*, Aristotle provides a foundational definition of what theater (at least tragic theater) is for, arguing that, through the process of involving the spectator in a dramatic presentation, it arouses in the spectator pity and fear, which are then expiated in a cathartic resolution of the spectator's strong feelings. Aristotle describes this as both a personal and a social good, in that it allows (or encourages) spectators to rid themselves of dangerous passions before they create real social and personal problems. Frankly, if we end our discussion with Aristotle, we could probably accept that all dramatic representations via film, television, or computer monitors are theater. Aristotle's spectator was actively engaged but was not a part of the drama, merely a spectator who was acted upon by the dramatist's device. The only caveat to this is that Aristotle described an experience with live actors, albeit separated from the audience by the physical structures of the theater itself. The camera makes the actors more intimately available to the audience and probably allows a more powerful impact from the combined efforts of the actor and the dramatist. Taken together, the experience of film and 'traditional' theater is similar enough to accept in parity in the light of our broader discussion of virtual world as theater.

Of course, in the many centuries since Aristotle observed and analyzed the processes of theater, there have been considerable changes in how theater is understood and how we deliberately use the theater to manipulate the audience. Further, the accepted/expected role of the audience has changed as well, and all of this gives us some solid bases for understanding what makes the virtual world experience such a powerful medium. Virtual worlds, like contemporary theater, become transformative experiences beyond traditional theater and film, creating far more potential for personal and social change than any traditional media.

Contemporary theater and virtual worlds

It can be argued that the 'theater' in 'movie-theater' is really an appropriation of the term that describes the process of making the movie, not of its eventual presentation in a movie arena. The term *theater* has, in the 20th century, commonly come to refer to the space where we gather to watch something. Prior to film, the theater actually was theater in the stricter sense, since all of the processes of theater actually took place in the building with the audience members. This may appear to be a quibbling point, and an observant reader would note that, although the processes of the production of the film or television show take place elsewhere, the theater still contains all of the elements at the time of viewing... so the television set, the movie screen, and the computer monitor are all really theaters in an expanded sense. But there are entirely other forms of theater that film, television, and even proscenium – confined 'live' theater – do not encompass, and we need a term to differentiate these forms.

One of the many ways in which we can divide types of theater is by the ability of the audience member to change his or her perspective on the action of the piece. In conventional theater forms the spectator has a fixed perspective, whereas in non-traditional forms the spectator can move about. This simple distinction is critical to the role of the spectator; by moving and willfully changing his or her perspective on the action, the spectator assumes a control of the experience that was previously abrogated to the director. For lack of a better descriptor, we will use the term *active theater* to describe theater where the spectator/participant can effect this type of change and refer to the traditional theater as *passive theater.*[1]

The development of the deliberate *active theater* begins with Antonin Artaud in the early part of the 20th century (Artaud, 1958). Among Artaud's many contributions to theater, his most profound contribution was, in fact, his idea of a *theater of cruelty,*[2] wherein the spectator became a participant in his or her own theatrical experience. Although Artaud never realized the full force of his idea, it did provide the bases for reinterpretations of the idea that became powerful active theater models. Artaud advocated an immersion of the spectator in the theatrical spectacle.

> The spectacle will be extended, by elimination of the stage, to the entire hall of the theater and will scale the walls from the ground up on light catwalks, will physically envelop the spectator and immerse him in a constant bath of light, images, movements, and noises.
>
> (Artaud, 1958: p. 125)

Theorist/director Richard Schechner built on Artaud's ideas in the early 1970s with a movement loosely defined as environmental theater (Schechner, 1973). Schechner brought the audience into the performance space itself and created an immersive environment that included both actors and spectators, fully eliminating the separation of the proscenium. In doing so, he also eliminated the comfort and detachment that the proscenium provided to the spectator. In Schechner's theater, the spectator reacted to the actor as a present other, which created an intimacy with the theatrical action unmatched in any other form of theater experience. The parallels between this spectator-in-the-action theater and virtual world participation should be obvious; although the actual presence within the virtual world is mediated by the computer, the spectator/participant is immersed and present with others in the action.

Computers become theater rather than presentation terminals when the theatrical processes themselves, mediated by the computer interface, immerse the spectator/participant in some form of action. We assert that virtual worlds *are* active theater experiences and that theory about theater and spectator applies directly to these mediations. Virtual worlds all share four characteristics with contemporary theater that we believe make virtual worlds true theater experiences: (1) they have a bounding narrative or theme, (2) they have characters, (3) they require a suspension of disbelief, and (4) importantly, they share the participation of the contemporary spectator/participant.

Character

Characters in contemporary active theater are frequently not locked into a script. Depending on the activity of the spectator/participant, the timing and context of an actor's response may radically change from one performance to the next. The key to the character's continuity and reaction is the internal embrace of the character on the part of the actor. This internalization then allows the actor to respond in character, regardless of what the context presents. Spectators/participants in virtual worlds assume characters as well, sometimes simple projections of 'themselves', and sometimes with elaborate in-world characteristics, for example, in World of Warcraft. In a virtual world, it is not *as if* the spectator/participant became his or her character... he or she *becomes* the character. It is not a metaphorical becoming but a transformative becoming, just as it is for the actor in an active theater presentation. Schechner refers to the transformations of shamans, of ritual tribal transformations that are similar to transformations that take place in active theater for both spectator and actor. This may be a bit extreme, but those who have acted will usually agree that character is not all that easy to slip on or off, and the experiences one has as a character inevitably become part of the experience of the actor.

This is a critical observation when we consider virtual worlds; the spectator/participant assumes a character and then has experiences as that character. This is not the observation of passive theater but the real and immediate experience of the spectator/participant. This means that the experiences in virtual worlds have considerably more power to affect the spectator/participant, not only in character, but in their non-character life as well. In active theater everyone, actor and spectator/participant, experiences the reality of the action, both within their roles and in their non-character life as well. This is the basis of the exceptional power of active theater to transform. As a form of active theater, virtual worlds have these same visceral effects on the spectators/participants, and we would expect to see that 'life

lessons' experienced in virtual worlds would translate into the specta-
tor/participant's non-character life as well.

Narratives

All theater has a narrative, which is to say the circumstances of the
interactions of the characters. Even an improvisational troupe assumes a
circumstance as the basis of its interactions. In active theater the narrative may be quite durable, for example, a production of Brecht's *Mother
Courage*, or it may be very context specific, for example, a guerrilla theater action that has a theme, such as anti-war, but which is then played
out according to place or audience. With virtual worlds, the narrative
may be as specifically defined as in World of Warcraft, where the narrative defines the context and character potentials as well as the actions
that will be engaged.

In a virtual world such as Second Life, the narrative is only as weak
or as strong as the spectator/participant wishes; membership in some
groups may have a very formal thematic structure, while in others there
may be little more narrative than found at a cocktail party. Strength
of narrative does not affect the importance of character and character
participation, but it does create boundaries where the narrative is very
particular. One of the most dissected characteristics of narrative that we
see is the difference between game-themed virtual worlds and socially
themed ones. Analyzed as theater, this distinction lacks importance.
Regardless of the narrative structure, the spectator/participant's experience is a function of his or her intensity and the particular context
of his or her character actions. Whether participating in a fight to the
death or participating in a conversation about the meaning of life, the
spectator/participant's experience may be equally transformative, albeit
defined by actions that outwardly appear to be quite distinct. We see
the role of narrative in virtual worlds as an attractant, in that the initial
impulse to participate is probably based on interest in what roles and
interactions the spectator/participant may assume.

Suspension of disbelief

Rationally, we recognize active theater as an artifice, and we know that
virtual worlds are artificial. Nonetheless, in order to experience them
as spectators/participants, we need to temporarily accept their reality,
or, more precisely, suspend our disbelief of the artifice itself. Aristotle
notes the need to accept the fiction of the drama while viewing it in
order to achieve the catharsis that supports acceptance of the moral
order. Aristotle argues that character consistency and a logical flow of

action and consequence keep the audience from confronting the artifice of the stage and allow them to remain connected to the action of the drama. In the active theater of virtual worlds, our spectators/participants probably need this consistency to remain in character and truly in-world.

That is not to say that there is never a place to break the fourth wall[3] and cause the spectators/participants to be reminded that they are participating in a drama. In virtual worlds there are accidental interruptions, in that there are instances of technical malfunction as well as instances of out-of-world bookkeeping or other physical necessities that draw the participant's attention away. All of these serve to remind the spectator/participant that he or she is participating in an artifice. And, to some extent, these disruptions of disbelief may enhance the quality of the experience of the action. Bertolt Brecht's interpretation of the suspension of disbelief was the concept of *verfremdungseffekt* (Brecht, 1991), in which the dramatic experience encourages enough emotional distance from the spectator to allow him or her to retain a critical view of the action and its consequences, thereby creating a more transformative experience. While we would question the deliberate inclusion of *verfremdungseffekt* in the administration of virtual worlds, it may explain how they continue to capture the spectator/participant in spite of their sometimes substantial barriers to suspending all disbelief.

Spectator/participant

Throughout our discussion thus far, we have (somewhat self-consciously) referred to the *spectator/participant* and not the audience member, viewer, or simply spectator. By this point, we hope that the reader has accepted our term, and perhaps even attached some intention to it. The spectator/participant is not audience in the classical sense, even though he or she has chosen to attend a particular active theatrical experience. Ranciere noted that traditionally the audience is made passive by the impossibility of their affecting the action, which in turn affects their full absorption of the meaning of the action: '... it is the opposite of acting: the spectator remains immobile in her seat, passive. To be a spectator is to be separated from both the capacity to know and the power to act' (Ranciere, 2009; p. 2).

Sadly, the spectator role is primary in most contexts. DeBoord notes that the social production of spectacle is the primary method of disseminating and enforcing the values of control of the broader society (DeBoord, 1983). To DeBoord, spectacle is a managed form that has its greatest impact on the most passive of spectators. To effect this passivity, we make ever more comfortable movie theaters, complete with reclining seats and, in some 'extreme' theaters, bar and food service at one's seat, or more personal spectacle venues by streaming the spectacle to the home, the car, or the cellular phone. The passively apprehended spectacle is unavoidably ubiquitous.

As such, the possibility of the spectator/participant is radical in that it disrupts the passive absorption of the spectacle. Ranciere seconds this requirement to break free from the passive:

> What is required is a theater without spectators where those in attendance learn from as opposed to being seduced by images; where they become active participants as opposed to passive voyeurs.
>
> (Ranciere, 2009; p. 4)

With active theater, we realize this radical potential and stand at the threshold of emancipation and human growth and of the ability to disassemble the codes of the spectacle and enact them through active engagement in the performance. So, the obvious question is whether this is what virtual worlds are all about; is this why participants choose to engage resources, time, and attention with what appears to an outside observer as merely a game?

Lost opportunities

From the perspective of a social radical, the greatest disappointments are the technologies that have the potential to emancipate[4] and transform the human condition and then fail to do so. The process of failure is repetitive regardless of the technology. First, there is a public disinterest in emancipatory action, and then the technology is purposed to the enforcement of social control. Emancipation is a process of confrontation, particularly for the middle classes, whose members must examine and then reject their consumerist fascinations and see the subjugation imposed by the objects around them. This is unsettling, as it disrupts one's material comfort as well as one's sense of social stature and meaning. The second part of the failure occurs when either the State or capitalist institutions realize the opportunities to use the new technologies to advance public virtues.[5] From the printing press onward, every new technology offers the promise of emancipation. The printing press remained emancipatory longer than any other technology, possibly as a function of literacy rates, and allowed the public gestation of ideas leading to some very powerful revolutionary movements, for example, the American, French, and Bolshevik revolutions. Today, however, while there are certainly emancipatory works being published, the vast bulk of publication focuses on gossip, prurience, and escapism. Radio, television, film, and the passive theater have largely lost any sense of emancipatory purpose and in many respects are captured by either capitalist or Statist interests.

Historically, the active theater has retained its interest in the emancipatory. Beginning with Artaud and following through Grotowski, Schechner, and the numerous contemporary acting companies and performance artists that continue these traditions, there has remained an explicit commitment to emancipatory action. Outside virtual worlds, the active theater has admittedly bad attendance but strong goals; within virtual worlds, there are millions of spectators/participants but there is no unifying or transcendent purpose. Virtual worlds have evolved into phenomenal escapist fantasies,[6] where the spectator/participant can be a wizard, have a pair or more of extra spouses, and live in a virtual mansion...all while the real person behind the character lives alone in a walkup studio apartment.

No titan of capitalism could have imagined a more useful 'opium of the people' than a virtual world; as we have noted, it uses the well-developed tools of the theater to seduce and entrance the spectator/participant, giving them feelings of purpose and action, while keeping them from confronting their real lives or questioning their purpose in the capitalist life cycle. In fact, in many virtual worlds, capitalist consumption is synthesized as well and provides an important (and addictive) visceral thrill.

The anti-capitalism of virtual worlds

Interestingly, there *is* a tension between the virtual world and capitalism. Most virtual worlds do not yet offer many opportunities to consume in a way that supports capitalist interests. Every hour spent in a virtual world is a (hopefully) satisfying hour that an individual has spent away from the consumption of products and services present in their physical environs. Further, if they have carried away from their experiences a sense of well-being, they may not need to consume objects that (they are assured) will imbue them with that same satiating sense. Really happy, satisfied, and complete people do not need as many consumer objects in their lives to reify their sense of purpose and identity. So in this sense, the virtual world, wholly lacking any emancipatory intent, may emancipate people from the consumerist society around them. However, if the virtual world is an impediment to actual consumption, capitalist interests will discover a way to create real consumption from virtual experience. This is inevitable and brings with it many dangers for users.

Two factors make capitalist interest[7] in virtual worlds problematic. First, the power of the experience derived from active theater makes the spectator/participant vulnerable to manipulations of the in-world action, and second, the spectator/participant offers an advertiser a very disambiguated subject upon which to prey. Regarding the first problem, deliberate product celebrations introduced into powerful virtual environments can make *object desire* one of the outcomes of the in-world experience that is carried out of world. Regarding the second problem, the spectator/participant's character reveals much about their out-of-world self... not directly, but there are projections of themselves into their characters, and those characters have hours of captured actions, decisions, and dialogue to probe for opportunities to tailor advertising.

While our focus is primarily on immersive virtual worlds like Second Life or World of Warcraft, less immersive virtual environments like Facebook or Google+ paint a picture of how the engagement offered by virtual worlds can be used to attract and enrapture consumers and derive disambiguative data from them. Facebook and similar social networks are, on the one hand, empowering because they can be used to connect individuals from far-flung geographic or social environs. Behind this empowerment, though, the identities and profiles created on these sites are rich with data that are used to propagate the cycle of consumerism. As social networks and virtual worlds move on a path towards convergence, the distinctions between the nature and mode of virtual and real-world consumerism will fade. Consider Zynga Inc.'s recently reported financial statement, in which its net income of almost $100 million (on almost $600 million of revenue) was almost entirely from the sale of virtual goods (Wingfield and Cowan, 2011). The games that are offered by Zynga are free upfront, but spectators/participants can purchase and trade virtual goods, which accounts for the impressive revenue derived from this form of online gaming. While Farmville and similar social network games are currently unique relative to immersive virtual environments, the parallels are striking and point to the fact that the sale and trade of virtual goods represent an important 'new ground' for consumerism online.

An emancipatory program

Let us assume that virtual worlds will continue to grow in popularity. Our task then becomes the ignition of purpose in this form of active theater. We do not expect that the owners of current virtual worlds will suddenly determine a need to imbue their spaces with deliberately emancipatory themes or scenarios of social justice, at least not without prodding or intrinsic motivation.[8] Our goal would be to offer attractive alternatives that fully embrace the social goals of historic active theater. Within these environments, narratives and scenarios would be developed that allow the spectator/participant to join meaningful action contexts, such as spending time as a sweat shop laborer or as a dust bowl farmer. Not all of our scenarios would be necessarily dull or unpleasant; spectators/participants could take on roles such as a CEO confronting challenges in corporate ethics or assume the role of a very attractive and intelligent woman struggling to overcome the sexualization of her workplace. Of course, there are many examples we could draw on of existing virtual and near-virtual world scenarios where such constructive role-playing takes place. For example, players in Second Life routinely assume the 'role' of entrepreneurs and thereby learn about capitalism; they often change the sex, appearance or racial characteristics of their avatars and walk in the shoes of the oppressed or maligned, or face their deepest fears or stereotypes by confronting their phobias or biases through enacted therapies or educational activities. We are not treading ground here that has not been tentatively explored already in these and other virtual worlds. What we are saying is that we see an important framework for understanding why and how these endeavors operate and point to other opportunities whereby the confrontation of spectators/participants with the meaning of objects in their lives can be used to help them explore whether and how object meanings are manipulated to encourage consumption.

In addition to providing purposeful venues, we also see a need to teach individuals about the theater and its connection to virtual worlds. Learning about theater and acting teaches us not only how the artifice works but also how to maintain a perspective that allows us to be both appreciative of it and liberated from it. Again, theater is enacted in virtual worlds in many forms, whether by reconstructions of medieval theater halls or modern venues.[9] For most people, the opportunity to play a part is a recent phenomenon, and they are unprepared to do it with the detachment necessary for it not to have a disproportionate effect on their real lives. Part of the actor's training is learning to take off the role, and we believe that this would have significant benefit for the spectator/participant as well. Of course, as others have noted recently,[10] the future of virtual worlds like Second Life will not follow the same consumerist path as other virtual environments like Facebook; rather, the role of virtual worlds will be to enable the exploration of alternatives through participation in enacted experiences, which moves the user from the role of spectator to the powerful position of participant.

Notes

1. *Passive* (our definition) only refers to the perspective control ceded by the spectator. The spectator is an active participant intellectually and emotionally, even sitting in a dark cinema.
2. It is important to note that by cruelty Artaud referred to the cruelty of his unvarnished and intense theatrical experience, which he believed stripped the audience of its cognitive protections from the raw personalization of the theater experience.
3. 'Breaking the fourth wall' is a theatrical term that refers to an actor's stepping out of character or addressing the audience directly.
4. We follow Horkheimer here, who defines emancipation as the program 'to liberate human beings from the circumstances that enslave them' (Horkheimer, 1982). Programs of emancipation are not limited to critical theoretical positions but are a mainstay value of a variety of perspectives on social justice and the human condition. The emancipatory purpose, in the arts and theater specifically, is to cause the subject to confront their true reality (or the true reality of others) through an undistorted lens and to then re-evaluate purpose with this knowledge. Another way of approaching this is through a realism perspective (c.f., Lukacs, 2002) where we strip away the fabulous elements and portray characters and circumstances in their natural and often tragic situations. Both of these orientations come to essentially the same outcome vis à vis the spectator.
5. Recall that the original purpose of drama, according to Aristotle, was to reinforce among the spectators an appreciation for public virtues. 'Public virtues', though, are determined by those in charge and are not necessarily the philosophical *goods* but rather are the correct social attitudes that maintain the interests of the powerful, usually through maintaining a stable social order or hierarchy.
6. We are fully aware that there are virtual environments for education and business, or even emancipatory socialization, but we believe that the broader purposes of the majority of virtual worlds have devolved to the fantastic and escapist.
7. By capitalist interest, we refer to the broader capitalist interests of producers of goods and services for sale in the real world, not directly to the capitalists that are invested in the virtual world as a basis of direct income.
8. This is not to say that virtual environments are not already emancipatory in many dimensions. For example, EVE Online is in many respects one of

the least restrictive and, at least with regard to the economic and sociological aspects of the game, most emancipating environments. A player in EVE
Online can take on any number of roles, engaging in activities as diverse as
fleet commander, fighter pilot, courier, miner, sales broker, or pirate. A miner,
for example, might spend hours engaged in mundane work to extract raw
materials from asteroids. While such work might appear to be dull and con-
scriptatory, it may not only empower the user within the game to engage in
other more pleasant or enriching acts but it also might teach, for example, a
young person about the importance of patience, diligence, or resourcefulness
in a way that might help them to succeed in their real-world endeavors.

9. See, for example, the Rose Theater in Second Life, http://secondlife.com/
    destination/1913, which boasts extensive space for opera, live performances,
    and other forms of theater.
10. See the recent post by John Lester (aka, Pathfinder Linden) about the future
    of Second Life, http://becunningandfulloftricks.com/2011/02/14/virtual-
    world-endgame-collapsing-the-metaphor/.

References

Artaud, A. (1958) *The Theatre and its Double*, translated by Mary Caroline Richards.
    New York: Grove Weidenfeld.
Brecht, B. (1991) *Brecht on Theatre: The Development of an Aesthetic*. Frankfurt am
    Main: Suhrkamp Verlag.
DeBoord, G. (1983) *Society of the Spectacle*. Detroit: Black and Red.
Goffman, E. (1959) *The Presentation of Self in Everyday Life*. New York: Anchor
    Books.
Horkheimer, M. (1982) *Critical Theory*. New York: Seabury Press, p. 244.
Laurel, B. (1993) *Computers as Theater*. Indianapolis: Addison-Wesley Professional.
Lukacs, G. (2002) *Studies in European Realism*. New York: Howard Fertig.
Ranciere, J. (2009) *The Emancipated Spectator*. London: Verso.
Schechner, R. (1973) *Environmental Theater*. New York: Hawthorne Books.
Wingfield, N. and Cowan, L. (2011) 'Virtual Farms, Rich Harvest', *The Wall Street
    Journal*, 2 July 2011.

7
Virtual Worlds and Indigenous Narratives
James Barrett

Introduction

The narrative traditions of the Aboriginal Australians have the potential to contribute to the understanding and development of participatory and spatially defined narrative systems such as those found in virtual worlds. The relevance of Aboriginal narrative systems is based on the participatory first-person perspective often found in virtual worlds where embodied agents interact with places and spaces. The representation of place and space are powerful elements in narrative (Bal, 1997; Casey, 1993; Ryan, 2011). Virtual online worlds, or 'three-dimensional augmented reality interfaces which are becoming an increasingly prominent feature of twenty-first century computing' (Wankel and Malleck, 2010, pp. 1–2), include space and place in the creation of narratives. Likewise, the narrative systems of the Australian Aborigines that are collectively referred to as the Dreamtime are extremely developed and complex multimedia networks that rely on place and space. In both virtual worlds and the Dreamtime, performance and participation are part of the creation of narratives. In each, individual contributions to narrative creation are based on participation. In a transcultural examination of narrative, we can repurpose vocabularies for what are often described as new media narratives of the digital age according to older multimedia, performative, and participatory modes. Appropriate strategies can be developed for authoring narratives using virtual worlds, and more compelling and inclusive environments can become a reality.

This paper is a brief examination of four Aboriginal Australian narratives, which raises comparative issues in relation to their structures and those of virtual worlds. The construction of space and place in each of these narratives includes the embodiment of characters as participants. By embodiment I mean any figure that takes up the dimensions of time and/or space in the development of narrative. Movement and the characteristics of location are central to the development of narrative action and events. Along with participation by the keepers of the narratives, the characters in each take on the attributes of their settings and become integrated with actual places. This integration results in representations of space and time that contribute to social and cultural identity. Integration of people with place and space, based on embodiment and performance and mediated by language, sound, and the visual, is also possible with virtual worlds. Locations become part of an emergent narrative in virtual worlds that real people move through as avatars. In doing so, virtual worlds include communities that share spaces under conditions where social cohesion can develop (see also Mancini et al., 2003).

From the following readings of the Aboriginal narratives, a number of possible influences are explored briefly in relation to three-dimensional, virtual online worlds. Examples from virtual worlds are considered in terms of their relationship to space and place. Navigation is central to understanding the similarities between how space and place function in Australian Aboriginal narratives and in virtual worlds. In the Aboriginal narratives characters are pushed in particular directions by actions based on surroundings, such as fear and flight in the event of a fire or the expectation of combat in an enemy's territory. By moving through a space marked out with the meaningful features of a place, a narrative emerges according to the perspectives of the moving embodied agent (character, player, avatar, or user). In this way, places and their features frame characters both in the Aboriginal narratives and in the digital settings of online virtual worlds. This integration between locations and agents leads to places becoming bound together with characters through narratives in inhabitable systems or landscapes. Locations relate to each other and build into an environment, through which characters move and interact with each other and their surroundings.

Space, place, and narrative

Access to culturally important narratives in many Aboriginal traditions comes from taking up or being granted a position in the structures of the narrative and participating in it. Taking up these positions is usually marked by initiations and coming-of-age ceremonies. In this context, narrative can be understood as an articulation of power, where the narrator/creator holds sway over the production of narrative and the agency of those who are permitted to share in it. In the construction of narratives, the power relations expressed are negotiated according to community values and are very place-specific. The narrative is part of the identity of a group (the custodians of it) and is passed on via initiation procedures at particular points in the life of an individual, within the contexts provided by the group over time. These group contexts are realized, created, and imposed through the inhabiting of socially defined and produced space. In these contexts, space is not encountered but is the frame for all things produced, including social values and relationships. As Lefebvre argues, '(social) space is not a thing among things, nor a product among other products: rather, it subsumes things produced, and encompasses their interrelationships in their coexistence and simultaneity – their (relative) order and/or (relative) disorder' (Lefebvre, 1991, p. 73). Social space (and that is the only form of space communicated in narrative) materializes the same interrelationships between things as ordered or disordered, and according to the cultural and social values that can be associated with narrative as a textual mode.

Navigation is guided by the characteristics of place in both the Aboriginal narratives and virtual worlds. Edward S. Casey comments on the strong connections between place and narrative when he writes,

> Memorable journeys consist of events in places. Hearing of such journeys, we come to know places with as much right and as much insight as we know the time in which they have transpired. Narration hereby lives up to its own origin in *gnarus*, knowing. In learning of narrated times and places – times-of-places and places-of-times – we acquire a distinctive form of local knowledge.
>
> (Casey, 1993, p. 277)

Place is a determinate of subjectivity for Casey and is based on the human communicative experience of location and its attributes. Places are read, in a combination of the qualities and perspectives experienced. The places provide the settings for actions and events taking 'place' within their structures. In this capacity, narrative is indivisible from the place in which it is set. Place affects narration in at least two ways: first, it provides a focus for the possibilities of navigation and response, and, second, it addresses its audience according to the images that make up the fabula in the narratives, those raw elements that make its structure as 'the abstracted events in the order of their presumed "occurrence" ' (Rimmon-Kenan, 2006, p. 13). As Jenny Sundén argues, representations of place are explored in digital texts, and meaning is assigned to them at both interpretive and experiential levels, or, in her words, 'to become through navigation' (Sundén, 2006, p. 291). The places represented in the Aboriginal narratives and virtual worlds are markers of identity, frames for language genres, and reference points for dialogue and events. As in the Aboriginal narrative, the principles of participation, embodiment, voice, agency, improvisation, copresence, and creativity are critical to how virtual worlds operate as narrative environments.

Narrative as indigenous knowledge

The narrative-based knowledge systems that are termed in English 'Dreamtime' were given that name by the British-born anthropologist Baldwin Spencer in 1896 in relation to what he understood of the Arrernte culture of the Central Australian desert (Silverman, 2001, p. 212). The term persists today and is now used by many Aboriginal people to describe how the

> actualized transiency in the present, and the perduring life of the world is carried by ephemeral life forms. All living things are held to have an interest in the life of living things with whom they are connected because their own life is dependent upon them. Care requires presence not absence [and] those who destroy their country destroy themselves.
>
> (Rose, 2001, p. 106)

Embodiment and agency are intrinsic to the concept that 'care requires presence not absence' in place. This relationship to land and place is often expressed in the single word 'country'. In the different Dreamtime law systems, the individual is bound within complex networks of relationships and responsibilities to the land area and community from which they come, often via context-dependent family relations and the history of both these and their 'actualized transiency in the present'. How these relationships develop through a person's life is expressed in visual, spatial, linguistic, and sonic arts. These arts represent an extremely advanced system of place and space-based mediation, which has proven to be a sustainable and vital force for social maintenance of traditional Aboriginal cultures. Australian Aboriginal narrative systems begin with the body. An individual is built into a narrative depending upon the social regulations that are applicable and the individual/s for whom the narrative is intended and from whom it comes. In Aboriginal narrative, the concept of embodiment is generally one of continual regeneration when the forces represented in the narrative are in harmony, and when these forces are disturbed the consequences are usually dire. The emergence of individual social and cultural identity is the result of the drawing out of life from the Dreamtime, a continual mythical present that regenerates all things.

The Aboriginal narratives

According to the Ngarinyin people of the western Kimberley region in Australia's northwest, 'the spirit children, *anguma*, which are about the size of a finger, are attached to the long green weed, *jala*, which grows in the water holes' (Redmond, 2001, p. 123). After the father has dreamed of the child, he will 'often carry the spirit-child wrapped up in his own hair for up to a couple of years' (Redmond, 2001, p. 123). Of course, the Aboriginal people have understood the process of conception (something doubted by early anthropologists), but they believe, like Buddhists, that sentient life does not only reside in flesh. The clan position of the parents and their blood relationship to each other determines the narratives the child-to-be will have access to and be a holder of. This in turn determines what range of 'country' the child will be bound to and ultimately responsible for. Identity is based on these concepts and provides insight into the intractable link many Aboriginal people still have with their land or 'country'.

In the central Australian desert, when an Aboriginal mother feels the first kick of the unborn child within her, she notes the place in 'country' where she is when it occurs. The law and Dreamtime narratives related to the area and the relationship of the parents contribute to determining the narratives/knowledge in which the child will share. The spirits associated with the child determine the identity of the child in the group. Such a process is illustrated in the narrative of the yellow goanna (a large sand lizard) child:

> A man dreamed one night of the power of the essence of a species of yellow goanna, while hunting the next day he was invisibly assisted by this power and he captured a large goanna. As he approached his camp his wife saw that he had someone with him, but the mysterious companion vanished before he arrived. The meat that the man brought back was really a gift from the spirit power of the animal and his wife was made ill by eating it. The day after, the wife noticed

the same mysterious stranger standing on a rock. He held a small bullroarer [whirling sound-making instrument], which he threw at her and she felt a small pain as it struck her above the hip. The woman's husband together with his father-in-law deduced from these experiences that she was to conceive a yellow goanna child.

(Maddock, 1991, pp. 161–2)

This narrative refers to the beginnings of a human life and that the person-to-be is assured a position in the community. The transition between the dream, the land, and the body of the woman (specifically her hip) indicate that the relations between each and what they signify are mediated by language and by the body, place, and space.

The identity of an Aboriginal individual cannot be separated from the narratives they are given to keep and the country from which they come. Uni Nampijinpa is a keeper of the Warlukurlangu (Fire Dreaming) narrative from the Warlpiri Jukurrpa (Dreaming). In this ancient narrative, a father deceives his two grown sons into believing he is blind so they go out each day from their camp and hunt meat for him. The hunt is difficult and they move about the country in growing desperation to keep the old man supplied with meat. Meanwhile, the old man watches the sons go out each day and when they are far enough away he takes his own spear and goes hunting as well. Often when the old man was at the camp alone he would hear 'the one that talks' – a baby kangaroo, one of his totem animals that lived on 'the south side towards a place called Kirrkirrmanu' (Uni, 1994, p. 29). The two sons killed the sacred animal of the old man and took the meat back to him. He did not realize it was the meat of the totem animal and ate it. That night the old man 'went out into the open. The old man sat down. Then he listened for it. Still nothing'. After listening for two nights he realized the sons had killed the sacred kangaroo and he became so angry he 'cut a stick. He began to concentrate his thoughts in the manner of a sorcerer, to harm them. He sent fire to await them, like you might light with a firestick, when they returned from hunting' (p. 31). As the sons returned from the hunt they saw fire everywhere. 'The two who had been born in that place, in their own home, kept putting it out and putting it out but it burnt on and on' (p. 33). They fled a long way and the narrative passed out of the Warlpiri country into the Pitjatjantjara people and their country. They continue the narrative with the sons trying to return but 'they staggered along in agony trying not to brush against the places they had been burnt. They returned. They came past Pakajumanu. There they stopped exhausted. That place belongs to men. That is a sacred place' (p. 35). This narrative is performed as a dance, told as a narrative in song, and is the subject for the visual arts in images, which serve the dual purpose of both map and narrative for those who are initiated into interpreting the codes. The Warlukurlangu dance includes elaborate body paint and decorations and the use of sacred objects.

The Warlukurlangu narrative contains patrilineal laws concerning the duties and behavior of sons towards fathers and vice versa. *What Happened at the Place of Fire* speaks of the rules concerning hunting and maintaining sustainable levels of food by regulations. The narrative contains complex descriptions of clan boundaries and important places as well as directions for movement synchronized with the seasons. For the initiated clan member, *What Happened at the Place of Fire* renders the depicted area a marked territory in the same sense as a mapped region but with an added participatory dynamism not possible in a static map. The equivalent of the local and the global is represented in the boundaries and paths of the narrative. The fact that the narrative runs over into another people's country shows that the Dreaming tracks follow lines of geographical features described in the creation narratives and coordinate relations between groups according to the rules articulated in the narrative. One group, such as the Warlpiri, keeps a certain part of a narrative that relates to their interactions with the parts of country that they manage. The neighboring group keeps their part, and so on and so on.

Another narrative, of the flying fox clan from Western Cape York, is a law story connected to a specific place and therefore similar to *What Happened at the Place of Fire*, even down to the detail of involving two brothers and punishment for a breaking of the law. Both these stories and the yellow goanna story describe a metamorphic form of embodiment that is in constant flux. Arthur Koo-ekka Pambegan Jr (b. 1936) is a senior member of the Wik Clan, an Elder of the Winchanam people, a senior song man, and the keeper of the *Flying Fox Dreaming* for Chegem, his home country, on the Small Archer River of Western Cape York. The *Flying Fox Dreaming* is a sacred story and is represented as a spoken narrative, song, dance, body paint, and wood carved sculpture, all of which were taught to Arthur by his father. Arthur began performing the *Flying Fox Dreaming* in 1962, the first time with his father. Pambegan Jr is not the author and makes no claims to be such. Pambegan Jr says of his work as an artist and keeper or holder of the *Flying Fox Dreaming* that, 'My father showed me and my brother. But you must never stop. I am going to pass it on to my son, and my son will pass it on to his children for the future. We can never stop because this is our life – keeping us alive. [...] They are our clan designs, not to give away, not to die away' (Denham, 2003, p. 67). The caretaker status of participants and creators of the *Flying Fox Dreaming*, whereby it cannot be given away or cease, can be related to its performative nature. The narrative does not reside in a single place or document but is distributed about in its caretakers (the initiated), combined with the places in country to which it belongs. The narrative is performed when the initiated gather in the correct place at the correct time for its performance. This web carries people, places, and animals along through the generations in a living information nexus.

To summarize, the Aboriginal Dreamtime narratives emanate from the body in space, time, language, and forms, beginning when the individual is in utero. From these few brief examples, some idea can be gained of how co-creation, mediation, and spatiality function in the Australian Aboriginal Dreamtime narratives. The body is a site for mediation between the world/s and cognition. The pregnant mother of the *Yellow Goanna Dreaming* narrative begins inscribing meaning onto the child-to-be at the same moment she understands she is pregnant. These narratives are 'multimedial' representations in sonic, plastic, graphic, and vocal forms. The representations of the narrative are not fixed in time in the same way as writing or a pre-digital imagery is (in the sense of pastness); instead, they are passed on as living entities that belong to the country as much as do the people who live there. As Arthur Pambegan stated, 'We can never stop because this is our life – keeping us alive' (Denham, 2003, p. 67). The narrative is the reality of daily life and this is the narrative that is lived. With this in mind, transcendence of ordinary states of being, which is a common element in fiction, even as the concept of possible worlds, is largely disqualified under traditional Aboriginal narrative systems, as they do not transcend daily life; rather, they nurture it and make it both real and mythical. In the words of Deborah Bird Rose, the Dreamtime is 'actualized transiency in the present, and the perduring life of the world is carried by ephemeral life-forms' (Rose, 2001, p. 106). The context implied by transiency in the present is a dynamic, living, language-based multimedia that functions to maintain reality.

Virtual worlds

Embodiment is implied in online virtual worlds and can be compared to the Dreamtime narratives. In the digital media discussed here, embodiment can be described in terms of distributed physical presence in space. For example, 'I' am both here at the computer keyboard and participating in a guild raid in *World of Warcraft*. As a result, a clear distinction between fiction and non-fiction cannot be applied to the situation. Like the reality in which most of us live, virtual worlds are procedural, in that they observe real-time sequences of interaction and causality. Virtual worlds are also persistent, with the reality of the work continuing without a single avatar having to be present – when my avatar rejoins the world, things have changed in my absence. Within the virtual world, actions follow each other and feedback is immediate in an ongoing order of cause and effect. Finally, virtual worlds carry symbolic systems of meaning that go beyond the written and spoken language forms of stand-alone print, audio, or visual media. Physical gestures, spatial arrangements, significant objects, dialogue in real time, and remixing are present in virtual worlds. The totalizing nature of representation in virtual worlds is similar to the life art of the Aboriginal Dreamtime. In each, the movement by characters through space is the motivation for co-creative narratives rather than the passing of time. A narrative does not begin and end in either of these traditions; rather, it is participated in and 'closed off' at various times. Places are made through encountering them in narrative settings. Just as identity and reality form and develop in the flux of the Dreamtime, virtual worlds are constantly producing ontologies. This is not a single strand or linear progression, but complex networks of dialogues and appropriations where human agency and communication push the tools in multiple directions simultaneously, all centered on the presence of agents in narrative structure.

The avatar, or the virtual agent embodied in the space of the virtual world, is a central component of narrative. Baylor summarizes the structure behind embodiment with virtual agents, such as avatars in virtual worlds, in the following way, 'anthropomorphic virtual agents can serve as powerful technological mediators to impact motivational outcomes such as self-efficacy and attitude change. Such anthropomorphic agents can be designed as simulated social models in the Bandurian sense, providing social influence as virtual "role models" ' (Baylor, 2009, p. 1). Some of the values that are instilled in virtual role models are constructed from narrative associations in navigation, body, place, and landscape. For example, by altering the body image of an avatar, the perception of the person(ality) operating it can also change, with one study questioning whether 'participants with taller avatars would be more confident and be more willing to make unfair splits than participants in shorter avatars' (Yee and Bailenson, 2007, p. 21). The participants in the tall condition were significantly more likely to offer an unfair split than participants in the normal and short conditions. At the same time, 'participants in the short condition were significantly more likely to accept an unfair split than participants in the normal and tall conditions' (Yee and Bailenson, 2007, p. 21). The short and tall avatars are examples of meaning in virtual environments that have the potential to be harnessed within the participatory first-person narrative perspective of an embodied agent. Further implications are that virtual worlds through narrative can change perceptions, attitudes, and practices for people in social spheres of interaction.

Place and landscape

The representation of three-dimensional space in digital virtual worlds features the integration of the character with the place, whereby characters are driven into action and take on characteristics determined by the places they occupy. This is illustrated by how players negotiate landscapes in Massive Multiplayer Online Games (MMOGs) and Multi User Virtual Environments (MUVEs). Bjarke Liboriussen extends the concept of the visual space of virtual worlds as an image and brings to the experience of players the concept of landscape, where 'players exhibit the transcendent behavior typical of landscape experience in the personal mode' (Liboriussen, 2008, p. 149). Landscape in this case is the experience of the occupied environment, be it virtual or physical, along with the interactions that occur within them and the results thereof. Liboriussen goes on to argue that places join together in meaningful wholes for those who occupy landscape in MMOGs. Liboriussen explains that imagination and perception are mixed in 'places [that] are spatial wholes, and a landscape is the organization emerging when a number of such wholes are coordinated at a higher, mental level' (Liboriussen, 2008, p. 152). The higher mental level includes the narrative interpretation of places as meaningful structures in the virtual world. The qualities of these places, such as zones of conflict, natural oases, or haunted architectures, contribute to the narrative possibilities realized in characters when they are in those places.

The reactions to the activities of the Velvet Strike (VS) collective, which spreads 'sprays' or in-world graffiti in the online version of *Counterstrike*, a MMOG, indicate that players are expected to remain 'in character' when engaging with places. The VS website features abusive comments from players of *Counterstrike*, such as 'You and your boss are dumb and you deserve to die' (*Flamer Gallery*). These comments center on the idea of breaking the narrative agreement between the landscape, the player characters, and the conflict-defined nature of the game space. VS states on its archive site for hate mail, *Flamer Gallery*, that

> A flood of 'interesting' and sometimes hilarious hate mail and flames has come our way since VS launched in June 2002, (especially from some gamer sites and articles that misrepresented our views – let me state here clearly, and only for myself, A.M.S. does not support censorship nor does she oppose violence inside computer games).
>
> (*Flamer Gallery*)

What departs from standardized play in relation to the actions of VS is the alteration of the landscape. VS draws attention to virtual worlds as immersive spaces that are coordinated networks of meaning as wholes, in a similar fashion to landscapes. If any part of the whole is disturbed according to player expectations, the experience of the world is compromised for all. The death of the sacred kangaroo in the Warlukurlangu narrative and the old man's telepathic awareness of it is another example of the whole disturbed by the loss of a part within it. When the old man 'went out into the open. The old man sat down. Then he listened for it. Still nothing' (Uni, 1994, p. 31). The old man knows there is a part of the whole missing. The fabric of the narrative through which he knows himself has been torn.

Navigation as narrative

Movement through structured landscapes provides the forms for narrative in both Aboriginal narratives and virtual worlds. Each contains elements of a narrative structure unfolding in landscape simultaneously, based on responses to spatial features, navigation, gestures, and exploration and the places that unite these spaces. Digital space, as an authored environment, relies on a system of spatial narratives. In this way, 'spatial narratives can evoke pre-existing narrative associations; they can provide a staging ground where narrative events are enacted; they may embed narrative information within their *mise-en-scène*; or they provide resources for emergent narratives' (Jenkins, 2004, p. 123). With spatial narratives, the narrative is born of the engagement with the space and its features as a 'staging ground' for performance. Objects, landscapes, and other natural features, and the bodies that interact with them, are assigned meanings within the frames of the pre-existing narrative associations. Place defines how the features of spatial narratives function as narrative environments by providing a hierarchy and conceptual network for interpretation. Place organizes the elements of a space into understandable relationships. In relation to place, Jenny Sundén clarifies a storied place as that which 'alludes as to the ways narratives can be carefully structured places to explore, and inhabit' (Sundén, 2006, p. 281). Narration in the traditional sense does not occur in the Dreamtime narratives and virtual worlds. While there is a telling subject in the written adaptation of the Aboriginal narratives outlined above, the teller is a keeper of the narrative, as Arthur Pembagen Jr notes, and the telling is just one aspect of it. A dancer, a painter, or a singer could also enact the same narrative, not as an adaptation but in the transmedial sense of crossing platforms in the same narrative. The landscape itself holds the narrative and the initiated read the signs in country and explain their meanings as a history and as an instruction manual in a form of cognitive mapping.

The widespread use of maps in *World of Warcraft* indicates the role navigation plays in the narrative elements of the virtual world. Maps in *World of Warcraft* are standard in the game program and have also become part of player culture through the creation of maps as add-ons. Extra features used in play that appear on the screen are known as Heads Up Displays (HUDs). These maps often come with plug-ins, and players can customize them to their needs. The function of the maps with regard to responding to the virtual world is to provide 'Functional realism, used in much the same way as one would use a map in the real world [...] It also contributes to the sense of the game as world by locating the player spatially and temporarily (space has to be traveled in real time and is revealed chronologically, with some minor exceptions)' (Krzywinska, 2008, p. 133). The maps in *World of Warcraft* organize both the playing and the interpreting of the game on an equal footing and are centered on the embodied presence of the player. While not all elements of space and time are related to narrative, the sense of 'the game as world' that the maps provide for players situates them, via their avatars, in the whole that is the landscape of the game. As Liboriussen argues, the attention of the players is directed by the game, not towards the image/s from the perspective of a viewer, but to its networks of interrelated places, characters, settlements, and topology, with the avatar as a nomadic inhabitant (Liboriussen, 2008). The player character is essentially integrated into the landscape, its narratives, and the gaming experience, via the maps.

The multimedia forms related to the Warlukurlangu (*Fire Dreaming*) narrative and the *Flying Fox Dreaming* for Chegem depict landscapes that are transversed as networks of meaningful places. Similar sets of relationships exist in the construction and rendering of virtual world spaces. For example, territory is given identity in *World of Warcraft*. An area of danger or an enemy is associated with a location within the spaces of the game. In a quest task from the Thottbot online database, a series of locations and their relationship to each other are provided, such as 'These plans show the night elf forces at An'daroth, which we already knew, but also at An'owyn, a more remote ley-line nexus to the southeast' (*Thottbot*). Player characters and landscape are entwined with movement in this quotation, particularly with the reference to the concept of the ley-line nexus. Such topography makes movement through landscape a meaningful activity beyond just getting between two coordinated points on a map. Every point along the way of travel is given significance in the landscapes of *World of Warcraft*. Meaning as the transversal of places can be found in other virtual worlds, sometimes based on money and the ownership of virtual property, but more often on the narrative components of the world.

Conclusion

The study of narrative over cultures can be used to introduce sustainable practices into the changing ecology of representation that results from digital media development. The narrative tradition of the Australian Aborigines Dreamtime lexicon is one possible source of such inspiration. The above short readings of a few of the narratives from this vast storehouse of human knowledge demonstrate that embodiment, space, and place can function over enormous periods under representational regimes very different from those inherited from the age of industrial print culture. This very different system of material representation results in changes for human subjectivity and values (economic, social, cultural). Owning a narrative, which is connected inextricably to a tract of country or a single natural feature in a seasonal time cycle, presents challenges for transmission in anything that resembles the subject/object-orientated, market-driven, proprietary system that dominates the official knowledge economies of the world. If we are to meet the challenges presented to us by the spatial and place-bound affordances of digital media, such as virtual worlds, we need to look to alternative models of narrative creation, dissemination, and preservation. If treated with the respect they deserve, the song cycles and place narratives of the indigenous Australians can provide us with models, independent of content (which is often sacred and should not be exploited), for new and sustainable systems of knowledge creation through narrative.

References

Bal, M. (1997) *Narratology: An Introduction to the Theory of Narrativity*. Toronto: University of Toronto Press.

Baylor, A. L. (2009) 'Promoting Motivation with Virtual Agents and Avatars: Role of Visual Presence and Appearance'. *Philosophical Transactions of the Royal Society*. Accessed 21 August 2010, http://rstb.royalsocietypublishing.org/content/364/1535/3559.full.pdf+html

Casey, E. R. (1993) *Getting Back Into Place: Toward a Renewed Understanding of the Place-World*. Bloomington: Indiana University Press.

Denham, P. (2003) 'Not to Give Away, Not to Die Away: An Interview with Arthur Koo-ekka Pambegan Jr.', pp. 62–68 in *Story Place: Indigenous Art of Cape York and the Rainforest*. Allen, L. (ed.) Brisbane: Queensland Art Gallery.

Jenkins, H. (2004) 'Game Design as Narrative Architecture', in Wardrip-Fruin, N. and Harrigan, P. (eds) *First Person: New Media as Narrative, Performance and Game*. Cambridge: MIT Press.

Krzywinska, T. (2008) 'World Creation and Lore: World of Warcraft as Rich Text', in Corneliussen, H. G. and Rettberg, J. W. (eds) *Digital Culture, Play, and Identity: A World of Warcraft Reader*. Cambridge: MIT Press, pp. 123–43.

Lefebvre, H. (1991/1974) *The Production of Space*. Translated by D. Nicholson-Smith. Malden: Blackwell.

Liboriussen, B. (2008) 'The Landscape Aesthetics of Computer Games', in Günzel, S., Liebe, M., Mersch, D., and Möring, S. (eds) *Conference Proceedings of the Philosophy of Computer Games*. Potsdam: Potsdam University Press, pp. 144–56.

Maddock, K. (1991) 'World Creative Powers', in Charlesworth, M., Morphy, H., Bell, D., and Maddock, K. (eds) *Religion in Aboriginal Australia*. Quoted in Robert Lawlor, *Voices of the First Day: Awakening in the Aboriginal Dreamtime*. Rochester: Inner Traditions, pp. 161–2.

Mancini, D., Turner, J., and Harrison, F. (2003) *Avatara* (Film). Vancouver: 536 Productions.

Redmond, A. (2001) 'Places that Move', in A. Rumsey and J. F. Weiner (eds) *Emplaced Myth: Space Narrative and Knowledge in Aboriginal Australia and Papua New Guinea*. Honolulu: University of Hawai'i Press, pp. 120–39.

Rimmon-Kenan, S. (2006) 'Concepts of Narrative', in M. Hyvärinen, A. Korhonen, and J. Mykkänen (eds) *The Travelling Concept of Narrative Volume 1*, Digital Repository: University of Helsinki. Accessed 30 June 2011, https://helda.helsinki.fi

Rose, D. B. (2001) 'Sacred Sites, Ancestral Clearing and Environmental Ethics', in A. Rumsey and J. F. Weiner (eds) *Emplaced Myth: Space Narrative and Knowledge in Aboriginal Australia and Papua New Guinea*. Honolulu: University of Hawai'i Press, pp. 99–120.

Ryan, M.-L. (2011) 'Space', in *The Living Handbook of Narratology*. Hamburg: University of Hamburg. Accessed 30 June 2011, http://hup.sub.uni-hamburg.de/lhn/index.php/Space

Silverman, E. K. (2001) 'From Totemic Space to Cyberspace: Transformations in Sepik River and Aboriginal Myth, Knowledge, and Art', in A. Rumsey and J. F. Weiner (eds) *Emplaced Myth: Space Narrative and Knowledge in Aboriginal Australia and Papua New Guinea*. Honolulu: University of Hawai'i Press, pp. 189–214.

Sundén, J. (2006) 'Digital Geographies: From Narrative Space to Storied Places', in J. Falkheimer and A. Jansson (eds) *Geographies of Communication*. Gothenberg: Nordicom, pp. 279–96.

Thottbot Website. Accessed 21 August 2010, http://thottbot.com/q9163

Uni, N. (1994) 'Warlukurlangu: What Happened at the Place of Fire', in Yimikirli (ed.) *Warlpiri Dreamings and Histories*, Collected and translated by P. Rockman Napaljarri and L. Cataldi. Manchester: Harper Collins, pp. 23–37.

Velvet Strike. *Flamer Gallery*. Accessed 30 June 2011, http://www.opensorcery.net/velvet-strike/mailgallery.html

Wankel, C. and Malleck, S. (2010) *Emerging Ethical Issues of Life in Virtual Worlds*. Charlotte: Information Age Publishing.

World of Warcraft. Blizzard Entertainment 1994–2010. Accessed 30 June 2011, http://eu.battle.net/wow/en/

Yee, N. and Bailenson, J. (2007) 'The Proteus Effect: The Effect of Transformed Self Representation on Behavior' *Human Communication Research*, 33(3), pp. 271–90. doi:10.1111/j.1468-2958.2007.00299.x

8
The Immersive Hand: Non-verbal Communication in Virtual Environments

Smiljana Antonijević

Hardly anything has become a more popular expression of liking in contemporary online communication than the Facebook 'thumbs up' logo. And, just as the development of the first emoticons in the mid-1980s had, not coincidentally, been related to a smiling face, the same applies to the present-day Facebook illustration. Both of these popular visuals rely on non-verbal communicative cues – a facial expression and a hand gesture – to convey meaning in online interaction.

The importance of integrating non-verbal cues in computer-mediated communication (CMC) is twofold. First, non-verbal expression is the primary communicative ability a person develops, and it remains a key communicative capacity throughout a person's adult life, comprising up to two-thirds of communicative behavior in dyadic interaction (Ekman and Keltner, 1997). The way we understand, persuade, teach, inform, encourage, or hate each other is rooted in our non-verbal abilities. Second, non-verbal expression is one of the human communicative capacities most substantially affected by the development of CMC and virtual environments. To immerse oneself into virtual space, to augment the boundaries of a physical place, to blur the line between the virtual and the physical – all these concepts imply, in essence, transformations in the way various non-verbal stimuli are exchanged, employed, and interpreted in virtual environments. Therefore, in order to grasp increasingly ubiquitous online interaction and its potential socio-cultural implications, it is important to understand non-verbal communication (NVC) in virtual environments.

This chapter begins with an overview of key aspects and functions of NVC in physical and virtual environments. Next, it turns to addressing some of the design principles involved in the development of virtual non-verbal acts. Finally, this chapter explores the future of digital NVC with regard to affective computing, touching upon possible socio-cultural implications of these developments.

Non-verbal communication: the physical, the social, and the virtual body

Non-verbal communication is a broad field that encompasses various perceptual stimuli, created by both people and the environment. Non-verbal information can be conveyed through a variety of semiotic systems, such as architecture, clothing, or the body. Kendon's (Ekman and Friesen, 1981, p. 3) definition focuses more specifically on human interaction, positing that NVC refers to 'all of the ways in which communication is effected between persons when in each other's presence, by means other than words'.

Being so broad, the field of non-verbal communication is commonly differentiated into several code-systems, such as *proxemics* (communicative use of space), *kinesics* (communicative use of the body movements), *haptics* (communicative role of touch), *physical appearance* (communicative use of body endowments, e.g., body shape and size, skin and eye color, and body adornments, e.g., clothing, makeup, tattoos), *oculesics* (communicative eye behavior), *chronemics* (communicative role of time), *objectics* (communicative use of artifacts), and *vocalics* (communicative aspects of voice, such as tone, accent, and loudness). A specific code-system consists of biosemiotic signs – physiological reactions, such as blushing, that function as signifiers in human interaction, although they operate beyond a person's control (Sebeok, 2001). Such signs constitute a significant component of NVC, as well as of affective computing, as we will see below.

Non-verbal code-systems work together in achieving various communicative functions. A non-verbal act can substitute, repeat, augment, illustrate, accent, and/or contradict a verbal message. Conversely, it can be unrelated to the verbal utterance (Ekman and Friesen, 1981).[1] In an interactive event, non-verbal cues play an important role in managing conversation and in facilitating message production, processing, and comprehension. Non-verbal cues also function as potent signifiers in communicating relational themes, for example, group inclusion vs.

group exclusion, and in communicating situational dimensions of an interactive event, for example, private vs. public.

The broad range of functions that non-verbal behavior assumes start to operate from the earliest days of a person's life, as NVC represents the first communicative ability infants develop. Being such a fundamental interactive capacity, NVC is also the entry point to a person's socialization and enculturation. Before a person learns to talk, write, or create avatars, he or she uses the primordial means of communication, the body, learning the non-verbal communicative norms of his or her culture. Non-verbal communication is thus considered a meeting point of nature and culture, or, in the words of Mary Douglas, a meeting point of the physical and the social body (Douglas, 2003 [1970]).

With the development of interaction in virtual spaces, NVC becomes even more complex. It develops into a meeting point of nature, culture, and technology, that is, into a meeting point of the physical, the social, and the virtual body. The possibility of non-verbal expression in virtual spaces has been an important area of investigation since the early days of CMC research. For instance, in *The Network Nation*, Hiltz and Turoff (1978) noted that for novice users the experience of CMC could be a kind of culture shock because the non-verbal channels are missing.

In subsequent research, two main approaches have been developed with regard to NVC in text-based CMC. One is the 'cues-filtered-out' approach, which determines that the lack of non-verbal cues in CMC results in narrowing of communicative abilities of online interactants, while the Social Information Processing theory argues that users adapt their language and style to communicative situations in which non-verbal cues are unavailable (Walther and Granka, 2005, p. 37). Also relevant for an understanding of NVC in virtual environments is the research on emoticons (Riva, 2002; Rivera et al., 1996; Walther and D'Addario, 2001) as well as the early works of Donna Haraway and Allucquere Rosanne Stone (Haraway, 1991; Stone, 2000 [1992]), which inspired, respectively, a series of studies in 'cyborgology' and the analyses of representation of the human body in virtual environments.

The emergence of multiuser, 3D virtual environments shifted the researcher's attention to avatar-based non-verbal expression. Research in computer sciences provided useful insights into the process of designing software solutions for non-verbal communication in multiuser, 3D virtual environments (Erickson and Kellog, 2000; Fabri and Moore, 2005; Guye-Vuilleme et al., 1999). In the field of social sciences, studies addressed issues such as the role of non-verbal cues in identity formation (Talamo and Ligorio, 2000), non-verbal communication as a source of user experimentation (Brown and Bell, 2004), persistence of non-verbal communicative norms in virtual environments (Yee et al., 2007), practices of looking in virtual environments (Irani et al., 2008), and the role of avatar bodies in social interaction (Schroeder, 2011).

Both computer science and the social sciences research have thus been fine-tuning our understanding of NVC in virtual environments. One of the areas in which these two research fields come into close contact is the area of computer systems design, which brings to the forefront ambiguities of computational and socio-cultural aspects of interaction in virtual environments. In the next section, we will focus on the design principles underlying NVC in virtual environments.

Designing an immersive hand

Interaction in virtual environments involves three equally important components: a new media object, that is, a programmable numerical representation composed of digital code (Manovich, 2001, p. 27), a new media object user, and a new media object designer. A dialectical process unfolding among these actants generates the complexity of interaction in virtual environments (de Souza, 2005).

At the outset of this process, the designer identifies a problem situation that a new media object should solve. The designer then analyzes user needs and expectations related to the identified problem and the projected object as well as the user's estimated socio-demographic characteristics. Once these tasks are completed, the designer creates a new media object. User interaction with the object is the next phase of the process. Through this interaction, the user first decodes the designer's message encoded in the object and then employs it, which is the peak of the dialectical process among the object, the user, and the designer (Ibid.).

The same dialectical process can be observed in designing non-verbal aspects of user interaction in virtual environments. Non-verbal communication in virtual environments represents a constant interplay between the designer's decisions related to options made available to users regarding their non-verbal behavior and the user's ability to reconcile the physical, social, and technological requirements imposed on their virtual bodies.

To understand this interplay better, let us take a look at one example of new media object design in a multiuser virtual environment, *Second Life* (SL). The object we shall analyze here, the Romantic Flirt Bench, offers users flirt animations that correspond to their mood.[2]

In a previously described dialectical process, the problem this object aims to solve is the lack of flirt-related non-verbal cues in user interaction. To achieve that goal, the bench provides a series of non-verbal acts built into its script, which users' virtual bodies automatically start to perform when seated on the bench.

These non-verbal acts, built into the script, are equivalent to non-verbal cues that Kendon found typical of face-to-face courting interaction in contemporary Western cultures. For instance, the Involvement and Disengagement subphases of the 'kissing round' ritual are clearly recognizable in the series of non-verbal acts built into the script. Further, the female avatar seated on the bench initiates both subphases while the male avatar adjusts his non-verbal acts accordingly, which is again a simulation of contemporary Western courting ritual, often dependent on female solicitation cues (Kendon, 1990; Moore, 1985).

Through such modeling of user non-verbal behavior, the analyzed new media object becomes an intellectual artifact that encodes a particular communicative solution to a particular problem. This solution, however, is deeply rooted in contemporary Western cultural assumptions about gender roles (e.g., the female manages a courting ritual while the male adjusts), the principles of sexual attraction and mating (e.g., a courting ritual is necessarily heterosexual), and the particular non-verbal codes and cues through which courtship is expressed (e.g., the forward lean as a female solicitation cue). In this way, the flirt bench also becomes a metacommunicative artifact that conveys a particular understanding of communicative processes and signification systems in SL user interaction.

Virtual non-verbal acts thus stand as epistemic tools juxtaposed with user agency. Agency is understood here as the socio-culturally and technologically mediated capacity to act; the term epistemic tool is conceived as a specific complement of the more widely used term epistemic object. While epistemic objects generate new questions (Rheinberger, 1997), the term 'tool' is used here to refer to the fact that computer-mediated non-verbal acts 'provide answers,' that is, endorse a specific understanding of non-verbal communicative practices and processes.

A digital non-verbal act assumes the character of an epistemic tool through the process of double objectification. First, a digital non-verbal act is objectified through the use of scientific models of face-to-face communicative practices. As the Romantic Flirt Bench example shows, NVC in virtual environments is often modeled upon findings in NVC scholarship. Yet scientific models of non-verbal behavior are heuristic representations of communicative practice, and, as Bourdieu persuasively argued, those models misconstrue practice by transforming this dynamic process into a fixed object of inquiry (Bourdieu, 1977 [1972]). As a consequence, scientific models of practice never account for all the instances of practice that can and do happen in situ, and a practical activity never actually assumes the form represented in a scientific model.

The second instance of objectification emerges from the transformation of physical activities into numerical, digitally coded representations of those activities. Put differently, a non-verbal act becomes transformed into a new media object. This transformation has two major consequences. First, non-verbal behavior assumes the attributes of a new media object, yielding to its epistemic, representational, and operational principles. For instance, continuous, analogically coded, and transient non-verbal behavior turns into a series of digitally coded, discrete, and persistent units. Second, agency becomes divided between the user – an executor of a non-verbal act – and the computer programmer – a designer of such an act. This dual character results in the coexistence of two discourses in virtual non-verbal behavior – the design discourse and the user discourse.

Through those two discourses, a virtual body simultaneously operates as a subject and as an object of communication. Within the user discourse, user agency feeds the actions of a virtual body, making it a subject of communication. Within the design discourse, agency rests with the computer system, transforming the virtual body into an object of communication, that is, into an item of algorithmic manipulation controlled by the computer system. Within the user discourse, the virtual body augments the user's physical body and acts in a way called for by an interactional situation. Within the design discourse, the virtual body is acted upon in a way called for by the system epistemology and pragmatics.

Such an interplay between computer systems on the one hand and user bodies on the other becomes particularly prominent when we probe possible further directions in virtual non-verbal behavior, which is closely associated with the concept of affective computing.

Towards the affective web

Among the authors researching digital technologies and communication, affect is often identified as 'the next big thing' in networked computing (Baldoni et al., 2008; Becker, 2006; Kambil, 2008; Picard, 2000, 2010; Woolf et al., 2009). Two main lines of predicted development include a kind of semantic web focused on affective content on the one hand and integration of digital technologies and emotion through the use of affective computing on the other. These two directions are closely related, not just in terms of their common orientation on affect but also as a kind of sequential progression towards what might be termed 'artificial emotional intelligence'.

The idea of emotionally intelligent computers is not new, but with recent developments it has assumed more user-centered focus than before. Earlier initiatives have mainly been focused on loading autonomous agents with sets of predefined emotional and behavioral features abstracted from human experience; this precoded emotionality was intended to serve as the source of an agent's reaction to user input, and to make agents more believable interactants in human–computer interaction (HCI) (Bates, 1994).

In such approaches, non-verbal cues are used as an enhancement of agents' precoded emotionality. For instance, Fabri et al. argued that NVC of human-like agents is the essence of their capacity for human behavioral resemblance, as with that capacity 'it [an agent] becomes a genuine representation of the underlying individual, not only visually, but also within a social context' (Fabri et al., 2002, p. 2). Precoded emotionality enhanced with the use of NVC has also become an important aspect of multiuser, 3D virtual environments, such as *Second Life*, where both avatars and agents have more or less sophisticated pools of predefined non-verbal acts (Antonijević, 2008).

More recent approaches rely on extracting affective attributes of actual human behavior rather than on arbitrarily selecting such features from 'theories of affective practice' (to paraphrase Bourdieu). As previously mentioned, one approach refers to a set of semantic web techniques focused on affective data. This method derives from a larger body of research in computer sciences focused on developing algorithms for extracting, analyzing, and synthesizing affective data from various sources, including textual and multimodal web sources (Douglas-Cowie et al., 2007). These data and applications can be used in a variety of settings, such as commercial (Dass and Chen, 2007) or cultural (Baldoni et al., 2008).

Another approach is related to affective computing and technological advances in the areas of sensory and wireless devices. The core idea surrounding this area of study is to enable emotionally sensitive HCI, in which technology can capture, record, and recognize user affect and respond in an emotionally sound way. Similar to affective computing are affective interaction and technology as experience lines of research, which focus, respectively, on affect as socio-culturally constructed and/or as one element in the holistic HCI experience (Boehner et al., 2005; Gaver, 2009; McCarthy and Wright, 2004).

These approaches differ from earlier methods in emotionally intelligent computing primarily because they refocus attention from applications to users. As Picard notes, 'computers do not need affective abilities for the fanciful goal of becoming humanoids; they need them for a meeker and more practical goal: to function with intelligence and sensitivity toward humans.' In order to achieve this kind of emotional intelligence, affective computing relies on devices that provide data about user physiological and psycho-emotional states transmitted through various non-verbal cues, such as facial expressions, gestures, body temperatures, galvanic skin responses, and so on (Picard, 2000, p. 248).

Thus gathered affective computing data can be put into use in various domains. One of them is affective e-learning, in which intelligent web tutors recognize student affect through the input from sensory devices and adjust instruction accordingly. For instance, if pattern recognition software spots a student's facial movements associated with frowning coupled with fidgeting and looking around, the tutor infers that the student is confused and that a pedagogical action is required (Woolf et al., 2009). Another application is affective self-reflection through the use of a system that collects different types of user input, such as time-stamped biosensor data, text messages, and photos, all of which comprise a user's affective diary, providing an opportunity to record one's experiences and reflect on them in a more holistic way (see: http://www.sics.se/interaction/projects/ad/). Computational tracking of non-verbal cues can also assist people with autism to develop better functioning in their socio-emotional experiences (Kaliouby et al., 2006) as well as the general population to better handle stressful situations (Healey and Picard, 2005).

As previously mentioned, the non-verbal code-system of haptics is also widely used in affective computing. Virtual haptics relies on tactile and kinesthetic force receptors, which provide information such as pressure, temperature, softness, and wetness, as well as on microgeometric and microtexture receptors that, respectively, encode the shape of objects and provide texture information, allowing users to feel virtual objects and to interact with them in virtual environments (Robles de la Torre, 2009; Salisbury et al., 2004). This type of virtual non-verbal communication has been increasingly used in areas such as surgical simulation and medical training, computer-assisted design, sign language recognition, military training, cultural heritage, and virtual museums (McLaughlin et al., 2001; van der Meijden and Schijven, 2009).

All these examples demonstrate the extent to which NVC becomes central to both user–user and human–computer interaction in networked environments. Although these environments started off as 'body-free' communicative spaces characterized by the lack of non-verbal cues, they are progressively turning into arenas in which the importance of non-verbal cues not only meets but potentially even transcends the significance of non-verbal behavior observed in physical space. For instance, it is possible to imagine networked environments in which direct 'body reading', that is, the detection and interpretation of galvanic skin response, facial expressions, and other non-verbal cues, will become a powerful enhancement of, and in some areas maybe a replacement for, written and/or spoken discourse. As the above-mentioned example of e-learning shows, web tutors are already able to infer psycho-emotional information by interpreting student non-verbal cues rather than by engaging in verbal exchange. With further developments in tracking and recognition systems focused on kinetic, haptic, vocalic, and other non-verbal code-systems and with developments in affective computing in general, it is sound to envision virtual environments as interactive spaces saturated with, and reliant upon, non-verbal cues.

The emotional and other communicative nuances conveyed in high-fidelity, high-resolution, and low-latency systems will transform user interaction in virtual environments. Additionally enhanced and fine-grained technologies of immersion and augmentation will also bring changes in terms of user interaction both with other users and with the environment itself. Furthermore, user psycho-affective states that become increasingly observable through technologies such as face and speech recognition and eye tracking will be a rich field of interdisciplinary study. Finally, further developments in ubiquitous computing, ambiance intelligence, and geolocation will all expand the scope and range of the domain of virtual non-verbal behavior and the need for understanding of that domain.

These developments, however, are not without important challenges. For instance, tracking, recognizing, and/or modeling human non-verbal acts produced with extensive use of contextual cues and socio-cultural codes are a big challenge for computer science. The same applies to tracking and modeling complex sequences of naturally occurring behavior with rich interaction dynamics (Salah et al., 2010). Moreover, interpreting user non-verbal cues and inferring underlying affective states often provides inconsistent and contradictory results due to the idiosyncratic and context-dependent character of these cues (Ward and Marsden, 2004).

In addition to the technological issues, a set of socio-cultural issues will emerge, too. For instance, privacy concerns will assume a new dimension and require new regulations once user non-verbal and affective traits become recordable and searchable. Closely related to that are questions related to research ethics, where researcher and designer decisions determine which non-verbal cues will be recorded and how, how these cues will be interpreted, who will be able to access the results, in what way the results will be used, and so on. Issues of multiculturalism could come to the forefront, too. Non-verbal behavior is highly culture-dependent, so developing culturally appropriate approaches to NVC in the global, and presumably globalized, networked spaces might emerge as a significant challenge. The politics of technology design will also develop new shades when faced with the requirements of non-verbal and affective virtual environments. Finally, non-verbal communication itself could experience transformations. Just as written and spoken discourses underwent changes in the encounter with digital technologies and CMC (Crystal, 2006; Gurak and Antonijević, 2008), non-verbal discourse could also face a set of important and difficult to predict changes. For instance, the repertoire of non-verbal code-systems might broaden (or shrink) so as to accommodate new or transformed code-systems that might arise in virtual environments. Similarly, both non-verbal 'display rules' and their mechanisms (Ekman and Keltner, 1997) could assume a different character when faced with the principles of Transformed Social Interaction (Bailenson et al., 2004).

An immersive hand is certainly part of the future of virtual environments, but it is yet to be seen what this future will bring. For computers to learn to do what we feel, rather than what we say, we will first need to learn more about our affective side as well as about expressing it via an immersive hand.

Notes

1. Verbal and non-verbal utterances originate simultaneously, as elements of a single cognitive process (see McNeill, 1992), with verbal and non-verbal discourses making an active communicative interrelationship in an interactive event.
2. See https://marketplace.secondlife.com/p/AA-Romantic-Flirt-Bench/280085? id=280085&slug=AA-Romantic-Flirt-Bench

References

Antonijević, S. (2008) 'From Text to Gesture Online: A Microethnographic Analysis of Non-verbal Communication in the Second Life Virtual Environment', *Information, Communication, and Society*, 11, 2, pp. 211–38.

Bailenson, N. J., Beall, A., Blascovich, J., Loomis, J., and Turk, M. (2004) 'Transformed Social Interaction: Decoupling Representation from Behavior and Form in Collaborative Virtual Environments', *Presence*, 13, 4, pp. 428–41.

Baldoni, M., Baroglio, C., Horvath, A., Patti, V., Portis, F., Avilla, M., and Grillo, P. (2008) 'Folksonomies Meet Ontologies in ARSMETEO: From Social Descriptions of Artifacts to Emotional Concepts', in Borgo, S. and Lesmo, L. (eds) *Formal Ontologies Meet Industry*. Amsterdam: IOS Press, pp. 132–44.

Bates, J. (1994) 'The Role of Emotion in Believable Agents', *Communications of the ACM*, 37, 7, pp. 122–5.

Becker, B. (2006) 'Social Robots – Emotional Agents: Some Remarks on Naturalizing Man-machine Interaction', *International Review of Information Ethics*, 6, pp. 37–45.

Boehner, K., dePaula, R., Dourish, P., and Sengers, P. (2005) 'Affect: From Information to Interaction', *Proceedings of the 4th Decennial Conference on Critical Computing*, pp. 59–68.

Bourdieu, P. (1977 [1972]) *Outline of a Theory of Practice*. Cambridge: Cambridge University Press.

Brown, B. and Bell, M. (2004) 'Social Interaction in "There" ', in Dykstra-Erickson, E. and Tscheligi, M. (eds) *CHI '04 Extended Abstracts on Human Factors in Computing Systems*, Vienna, Austria, pp. 1465–8.

Crystal, D. (2006) *Language and the Internet*. Cambridge, UK: Cambridge University Press.

Dass, S. and Chen, M. (2007) 'Yahoo! for Amazon: Sentiment Extraction from Small Talk on the Web', *Management Science*, 53, 9, pp. 1375–88.

de Souza, C. S. (2005) *The Semiotic Engineering of Human–Computer Interaction*. Cambridge: MIT Press.

Douglas, M. (2003 [1970]) *Natural Symbols*. New York and London: Routledge.

Douglas-Cowie, E., Cowie, R., Sneddon, I., Cox, C., Lowry, O., McRorie, M., Martin, J. C., Devillers, L., Abrilian, S., Batliner, A., Amir, N., and Karpouzis, K. (2007) 'The HUMAINE Database: Addressing the Collection and Annotation of Naturalistic and Induced Emotional Data', in A. Paiva, R. Prada and R. W. Picard (eds) *Affective Computing and Intelligent Interaction*. Berlin, Heidelberg, New York: Springer, pp. 488–500.

Ekman, P. and Friesen, W. V. (1981) 'The Repertoire of Non-verbal Behavior', in A. Kendon (ed.) *Non-Verbal Communication, Interaction, and Gesture: Selections from Semiotica*. New York: Moutoun, pp. 46–105.

Ekman, P. and Keltner, D. (1997) 'Universal Facial Expressions of Emotion: An Old Controversy and New Findings', in Segerstrale, U. and Molnar, P. (eds) *Non-verbal Communication: Where Nature Meets Culture*. New Jersey: Lawrence Erlbaum Associates, pp. 27–47.

Erickson, T. and Kellogg, W. (2000) 'Social Translucence: An Approach to Designing Systems that Mesh with Social Processes', *ACM Transactions on Human Computer Interaction*, 7, 1, pp. 59–83.

Fabri, M., Moore, D. K., and Hobbs, D. J. (2002) 'Expressive Agents: Non-verbal Communication in Collaborative Virtual Environments', *Embodied Conversational Agents at AAMAS '02*, Bologna, Italy.

Fabri, M. and Moore, D. (2005) 'The Use of Emotionally Expressive Avatars in Collaborative Virtual Environments', *Proceeding of Symposium on Empathic Interaction with Synthetic Characters*.

Gaver, W. (2009) 'Designing for Emotion', *Philosophical Transactions of the Royal Society*, 364, 1535, pp. 3597–604.

Gurak, L. and Antonijević, S. (2008) 'Digital Rhetoric', in Lunsford, A. and Aune, J. (eds) *The Sage Handbook of Rhetoric*. London, Thousand Oaks: Sage, pp. 497–508.

Guye-Vuilleme, A., Capin, T. K., Pandzic, S., Thalamann, N. M. (1999) 'Non-verbal Communication Interface for Collaborative Virtual Environments', *The Virtual Reality Journal*, 4, pp. 49–59.

Haraway, D. (1991) 'A Cyborg Manifesto Science, Technology, and Socialist-Feminism in the Late Twentieth Century', in Haraway, D. (ed.) *Simians, Cyborgs and Women: The Reinvention of Nature*. New York and London: Routledge, pp. 149–81.

Healey, J. and Picard, R. W. (2005) 'Detecting Stress During Real-world Driving Tasks Using Physiological Sensors', *IEEE Trans. on Intelligent Transportation Systems*, 6, 2, pp. 156–66.

Hiltz, S. R. and Turoff, M. (1978) *The Network Nation: Human Communication via Computer*. Cambridge and London: MIT Press.

Irani, C. L., Hayes, G. R., and Dourish, P. (2008) 'Situated Practices of Looking: Visual Practice in an Online World', *Proceedings of the 2008 ACM Conference on Computer-supported Cooperative Work*, pp. 187–96.

Kaliouby, R., Picard, R., and Baron-Cohen, S. (2006) 'Affective Computing and Autism', *New York Academy of Sciences*, 1093, pp. 228–48.

Kambil, A. (2008) 'What Is Your Web 5.0 Strategy?', *Journal of Business Strategy*, 29, 6, pp. 56–8.

Kendon, A. (1990) *Conducting Interaction: Patterns of Behavior in Focused Encounters*. Cambridge, NY: Cambridge University Press.

Manovich, L. (2001) *The Language of New Media*. Cambridge: MIT Press.

McCarthy, J. and Wright, P. (2004) *Technology as Experience*. Cambridge: MIT Press.

McLaughlin, M. L., Sukhatme, G., and Hespanha, J. (2001) *Touch in Virtual Environments: Haptics and the Design of Interactive Systems*. Upper Sidle River: Pearson Education.

McNeill, D. (1992) *Hand and Mind: What Gestures Reveal about Thought*. Chicago and London: University of Chicago Press.

Meijden, van der, O. A. J. and Schijven, M. P. (2009) 'The Value of Haptic Feedback in Conventional and Robot-assisted Minimal Invasive Surgery and Virtual Reality Training: A Current Review', *Surgical Endoscopy*, 23, 6, pp. 1180–90.

Moore, M. M. (1985) 'Non-verbal Courtship Patterns in Women: Context and Consequences', *Ethology and Sociobiology*, 6, pp. 237–45.

Picard, R. W. (2000) *Affective Computing*. Cambridge: MIT Press.

Picard, R. W. (2010) 'Emotion Research by the People, for the People', *Emotion Review*, 2, 3, pp. 250–4.

Rheinberger, H. J. (1997) *Toward a History of Epistemic Things*. Stanford: Stanford University Press.

Riva, G. (2002) 'The Cognitive Psychology of Computer-mediated Communication', *Cyber Psychology & Behavior*, 5, 6, pp. 581–98.

Rivera, K., Cooke, J. N., and Bauhs, A. J. (1996) 'The Effects of Emotional Icons on Remote Communication', *Proceedings of the CHI '96 Conference Companion on Human Factors in Computing Systems*, Vancouver, British Columbia, Canada.

Robles De La Torre, G. (2009) 'Virtual Reality: Touch/Haptics', in B. Goldstein (ed.) *Encyclopedia of Perception*, Vol. 2. Thousand Oaks: Sage Publications, pp. 1036–8.

Salah, A. A., Gevers, T., Sebe, N., and Vinciarelli, A. (2010) 'Challenges of Human Behavior Understanding', *Springer Verlag*, 6219, pp. 1–12.

Salisbury, K., Conti, F., and Barbagli, F. (2004) 'Haptic Rendering: Introductory Concepts', *IEEE Computer Society*, March–April, pp. 24–32.

Schroeder, R. (2011) *Being There Together: Social Interaction in Shared Virtual Environments*. Oxford: Oxford University Press.

Sebeok, T. A. (2001) *Global Semiotics*. Bloomington: Indiana University Press.

Stone, A. R. (2000 [1992]) 'Will the Real Body Please Stand Up? Boundary Stories about Virtual Cultures', in Bell, D. and Kennedy, B. M. (eds) *The Cybercultures Reader*. London: Routledge, pp. 504–29.

Talamo, A. and Ligorio, M. B. (2000) 'Identity in the Cyberspace: The Social Construction of Identity Through On-line Virtual Interactions', *1st Dialogical Self Conference*, 23–26 June, Nijmegen, NL.

Walther, J. B. and D'Addario, K. P. (2001) 'The Impacts of Emoticons on Message Interpretation in Computer-Mediated Communication', *Social Science Computer Review*, 19, 3, pp. 324–47.

Walther, J. B., Loh, T., and Granka, L. (2005) 'Let Me Count the Ways', *Journal of Language and Social Psychology*, 24, 1, pp. 36–65.

Ward, R. D. and Marsden, P. H. (2004) 'Affective Computing: Problems, Reactions and Intentions', *Interacting with Computers*, 16, pp. 701–13.

Woolf, B., Burleson, W., Arroyo, I., Dragon, T., Cooper, D., and Picard, R. (2009) 'Affect-aware Tutors: Recognising and Responding to Student Affect', *International Journal of Learning Technology*, 4, 3/4, pp. 129–64.

Yee, N., Bailenson, J. N., Urbanek, M., Chang, F., and Merget, D. (2007) 'The Unbearable Likeness of Being Digital: The Persistence of Non-verbal Social Norms in Online Virtual Environments', *CyberPsychology and Behavior*, 10, 1, pp. 115–21.

9
Discovering the 'I' in Avatar: Performance and Self-therapy

Alicia B. Corts

The famous theatre director Peter Brook wrote, 'In the theatre the slate is wiped clean all the time. In everyday life, "if" is a fiction, in the theatre "if" is an experiment' (Brook, 1968, p. 175). For those of us who research theatre and performance, the concept of taking on a role, wiping the slate clean and taking on a new personality is not foreign or unusual; on the contrary, it is our specialty, our daily experiment. With that in mind, it seems appropriate to consider the ways in which theatre studies can illuminate issues within the metaverse, specifically in the way identity is shaped, reformed, and challenged.

The discussion of identity creation and play in virtual worlds has mainly focused on the creation of the avatar and the physical body (Savin-Baden, 2010; Suler, 2002; Taylor, 2002; Wolfendale, 2006). While some have mentioned the performance of the avatar within the virtual space, the emphasis of most studies has been on the construction of the body and its implications for the user. While this area of study also deserves attention from the research community, an avatar's activities within the virtual space seem just as critical to a full understanding of how identity is being reshaped and questioned. In theatrical language, the blocking of a character is just as critical to the role as the costume and makeup. From the extraordinary to the mundane, virtual performances point to how residents of virtual worlds interact with other users as well as their own virtual selves. Could these performances help us understand how identity changes over time? In this chapter, I propose that using theatre performance theory and key concepts from drama as therapy can help us see the power of virtual worlds to question and investigate identity. Specifically, I believe that ritual performances are being re-enacted in the virtual world, often with personal and possibly healing results.

To help guide the discussion, I would like to introduce my avatar, Airtsela Charisma. I often read research on virtual worlds with Airtsela in mind, since I am intimate with her creation. Of course, I paid close attention to how I formed her body and how people would view her. For example, we share the same eye color, similar hair color, and a slightly shorter than average frame. Airtsela's appearance differs from Alicia's, but where I find the most discrepancies between my first and virtual identities is in the way each person performs within the given world. It is as though we share a common brain, but the environment and the body that brain inhabits produce different behaviors. Just as an actor slips on the skin of a character within the mise-en-scene of a play, I am quite capable of slipping on Airtsela when I log into the virtual world.

It is important to note the flirtation of the previous paragraph with a Cartesian duality. I am certainly not suggesting that the first life body of the user is not important, or that the brain is the sole center of consciousness. Rather, as N. Katherine Hayles argues, it is vital to remember the body within a culture where information has become disembodied (Hayles, 1999). Airtsela is information: she is made up of bits of data that come together on my computer screen. Alicia's body, however, has the ability to control those bits of data. It may appear that the body of Alicia is erased in favor of Airtsela, but it is clear that a connection between the two still exists.

Part of the reason avatar performance has been overlooked has been the lack of rigorous thought on the subject of identity itself and the connection between mind and body. For example, the production of identity in the virtual space has led some theorists to label avatar identity as an erasure or multiplication of the self (Birringer, 1999; Sandler, 1998). Are we disconnecting our brains from the bodies that control them to enter the virtual space, thus erasing our primary identity? Can we simply log off from our first life selves when we decide to enter the virtual world? It is not as though I turn off Alicia when I log on to a virtual world, nor does it seem plausible that I am cloning or producing other personalities that are totally separate from my primary identity. Airtsela is, in many ways, like Alicia, but she operates as an extended self, within the confines of the original body but with an extension of the identity (Belk, 1988; Hermans, 2006). Actors are well aware of how this concept works. As they build a role, they begin a dialogue with the characters they are molding, yet these characters spring from their own memories and experiences. The character is, in essence, an extension of their self, one that can be examined and dissected at a distance.

Mark Meadows provocatively describes the avatar as an identity container, and it appears that those within the metaverse challenge the outer boundaries of their first life identities through their choices within the virtual space (Meadows, 2008). How do these identities interact with the user on the other side of the screen? If we consider how these avatars are performing in the virtual space, I believe we can begin to understand how the dialogue sheds light both on avatar identity as well as on the primary identity of the user him/herself. The study of the performance itself opens the door to these inquiries. For example, David Goldblatt's work in ventriloquism can be very useful in understanding how the computer user and the avatar engage in an identity dialogue. He suggests that the ventriloquist and the dummy engage each other, and, while one may seem more dominant at any one point, there is a give and take between both a single identity and a dual personality (Goldblatt, 2006). For example, when we watch someone like Edgar Bergen onstage, we see him as two people: as himself and as Charlie McCarthy. Yet, in the performance, Edgar Bergen is the performer and the performed, able to look upon his alternative self and engage with it. In fact, even though he was the one controlling Charlie, Bergen was noted to have said, 'I am really jealous of the way Charlie makes friends' (Bergen, 1984, p. 25). That statement seems extraordinary. Edgar Bergen is Charlie McCarthy, so how could he be jealous of his own personality? Because Charlie McCarthy is an extended self of Edgar Bergen, he was able to step back and comment on his alternate identity with a degree of distance. Similarly, the virtual world resident is able to stand back and see a new version of his or her identity, one that has been called the idealized version of the person (Bessiere et al., 2007). Just as Bergen could note his extended self's social abilities with some longing, we can create in the virtual world a version of our identity that glosses over the flaws in our first life.

When we look upon this multiplied version of our self, what can we learn from how he/she interacts with the other residents and the environment of the virtual space? What kinds of conversations can we have with our avatars through performances within the virtual world? When I look at Airtsela, I can see that she has many of the qualities that I wish I possessed, and I can see these qualities demonstrated through the way she performs within her social group. In many ways, there are times when I feel like Edgar Bergen, conversing with this digitized dummy who has so many of the qualities I lack. In fact, if I were to have a conversation with Airtsela about this issue, I am fairly certain it would go something along these lines:

Airtsela: (Offering me a chair near the fire) Alicia! So lovely to see you. Do sit down.

Alicia: (Standing awkwardly in the middle of the room before attempting to sit gracefully) Thank you. Sorry I'm a little late.

Airtsela: No problem! I'm just so glad you made it safely.

Alicia: How is it that you can be so unruffled in these circumstances?

Airtsela: Me? Unruffled? Why, whatever could you mean? (Slicing a piece of impossibly perfect homemade peach pie for Alicia)

Alicia: But the house, the decorating, what you're wearing... it's all so organized and put together.

Airtsela: (Motioning towards the ball gown she's wearing) This old thing? Why, it's just an outfit I threw on at the last minute!

Airtsela is remarkably organized and nonjudgmental. On days when I have barely been able to haul myself out of bed and brush my teeth, she is already dressed, her house is immaculate, and she would never dream of snapping at the driver who cuts her off on the way to the office. I want to be her, and I certainly strive for the kind of sweetness and light that Airtsela represents. I find, however, that my performances in first life are often so full of stress that I react badly. Can I learn from Airtsela's performances? She has seen her share of dramatic situations in the virtual world, but she somehow manages to distance herself and make the right choice. It is through these trying moments that Alicia, as the controlling identity, becomes aware of the difference between the two identities. Sherry Turkle talks about the way that computer windows have decentered our selves, which makes the computer the border between our digitized and actual selves (Turkle, 1995). That border, however, gives us the space to examine the performance on each side of the divide and objectively determine which performance best fits our lives.

As a user distances himself from his primary identity, the separation can be great enough to allow an objective look at the primary identity and the problems and challenges encountered. Through these encounters, we are able to experience frustrations without the consequences that are necessarily entailed with similar performances in real life. Kendall Walton points out that play can be play because of the way it encourages us to try new things without fear of consequences, and many of the performances in the virtual world reflect this attitude (Walton, 1990). I would never dream of riding a motorcycle in first life, for example. The possibility of an accident prevents me from trying one, as well as the knowledge that my coordination in first life is very poor. In the virtual world, however, Airtsela owns a motorcycle and regularly rides across a sim in a most reckless fashion; she has even been known to try to drive straight up the side of a mountain. If we consider this performance in terms of identity, it would be simple to suggest that perhaps I wish to explore a more reckless side of my identity, and some researchers have suggested that such a violent virtual driving habit might lead to dangerous first life driving (Anderson and Dill, 2000). I think this analysis barely scratches the surface of what it is possible to learn from the dialogue between my motorcycle-riding avatar and my calm, rational, safe-driving first life self. To suggest that reckless driving would transfer into first life only looks at one person in the identity equation: the avatar. It does not consider how the user and the avatar interact to reconstruct or question areas of identity. It may be, for example, that I have no desire to drive recklessly in first life, but I recognize the release of letting go and driving without a care in the world. On the other hand, I may simply wish to explore the landscape in a unique way, and, since it does no harm to me or to the sim itself, it is a harmless form of daydreaming. Walton presents the idea of props, which are objects that propel us into a state of imagination. In the case of virtual worlds, the avatar can be used as a prop that pushes us into a state of imagination about what life could be like without the restrictions placed on us within the first world. In other words, when I let Airtsela play on a motorcycle, I am using that representation of myself as a way of daydreaming about what could be possible in my first life, then objectively deciding whether or not Airtsela's decisions are worthwhile.

We have always had this ability to daydream and tell stories, but what the virtual space presents us with is the ability to create representations or props that propel our imagination in ways which go beyond what we can do in first life. J. L. Moreno, the founder of drama as therapy, referred to the ability to transcend the natural order as performance within surplus reality, a space where a person could play the role of anyone or anything (Moreno et al., 2000, p. xiv). By freeing yourself to play these roles, Moreno believed that a person could achieve *ecstasis*, or standing outside oneself, an ideal state for self-reflection. This idea puts my own motorcycle riding into a different frame. Perhaps I was watching another version of myself to learn from her mistakes. Moreno's examples suggested more than just learning better driving behavior. He details the story of an actress who was verbally abusive to her husband offstage but who was sweetness incarnate when playing opposite him onstage. By having her play a character that reversed that situation and was cruel to her husband onstage, Moreno was able to guide her to the self-revelation that her behavior was unacceptable. While the actress did not take an extreme character (Moreno suggests that God or a tree would be possible roles to play), it demonstrates that playing a role can produce the curious effect of being able to look at your life objectively. By combining Goldblatt's ventriloquism theory with Moreno's surplus reality, we come to a startling conclusion: the virtual space could be not only a space where identity can be questioned, but a place where real therapy and healing can begin as well. If that theory proves true, what are avatars within the metaverse able to learn about themselves? What performances show us areas where healing is taking place in virtual worlds?

My examples about Airtsela have so far been quite frivolous. She is the perfect domestic woman who can look perfect and yet still manage to find time to ride motorcycles all over the virtual world (presumably in a fabulous gown and diamonds). I think Alicia can learn some very interesting lessons from Airtsela, but for other users of virtual worlds the performances take on a much more serious connotation. One curious outgrowth of this phenomenon of avatar identity, for example, is the ritualization of certain common performances within the virtual world. Victor Turner describes ritual as a three-step process in which a person separates from the rest of society, enters a liminal space, then finishes with a new inscription of identity and a re-entrance into society (Turner, 1982). Turner's theory of ritual is closely connected to social drama. When a breach occurs in the social fabric, it is followed by a crisis, at which point ritual performance can be used to redress the breach and reintegrate society (Turner, 1990). Rituals are used to resolve issues of misfortune, illness, or personal crises that afflict a person during the course of their life. Because these performances have the ability to address specific social issues that are not dealt with in society at large, they can help the suffering come to grips with their position and re-enter society in a healthy way. Many societies have these rituals in place, yet in the West the pace and structure of our lives do not necessarily allow for such performances, which can often leave people in need of resolution to issues that place them outside society. For example, performances of virtual birth point to women who are seeking to reclaim certain titles, such as mother, wife, and lover, from particularly bad memories in first life. In this way, I believe the virtual world, and its ability to simulate Moreno's surplus reality, carries the ability to help people overcome traumatic memories.

Let us take Sierra Sugar as an example. On her blog, Sierra talks about how her first life pregnancy was traumatic, fueled by an unhealthy relationship with her partner (The Sweet Life of Sierra Sugar, 2007). She did not feel as though she could be called a good mother or wife, and when she met her partner, Thor, in Second Life, she saw it as a chance to reclaim her designation as the kind of mother she wanted to be. Accordingly, she made the decision to become pregnant in the virtual world. By simulating the ritual of birth from conception to delivery, Sierra felt as if the performance allowed her to claim her position in society as a wife and mother. Sierra Sugar allowed her user to dialogue about what it meant to be a perfect wife and mother, following Goldblatt's theory of how a ventriloquist can engage with his/her dummy in a dialogue about identity. In addition, Moreno's surplus reality is evident in the freedom Sierra had to create a ritual that perfectly matched her need to experience pregnancy again. Finally, the ritual aspect of the performance produced the conditions that allowed Sierra to reinscribe the label 'mother' to her life. Sierra needed the pregnancy ritual, but identity can be explored through many different kinds of performances. First life rituals like death, marriage, and illness are performed in virtual worlds, and researchers may be able to use these performances to further their work in identity theory and therapeutic techniques, as well as in performance theory.

If the virtual world can serve as a surplus reality capable of providing insights into our identity, perhaps these rituals like pregnancy are a way of exploring who we are in first life. Will these new performances change the way we view ourselves? How will the metaverse change the labels placed on us by society? And, most importantly, can the virtual world act as a source of healing? These questions offer exciting areas of research, not only into the nature of our identity but into ritual performance and its implications as well. As Peter Brook might suggest, what virtual world performance suggests is a space of play, not an absentminded play of childhood but a focused work that creates the ideal self:

> In everyday life, 'if' is an evasion, in the theatre 'if' is the truth. When we are persuaded to believe in this truth, then the theatre and life are one. This is a high aim. It sounds like hard work. To play needs much work. But when we experience the work as play, then it is not work anymore.
>
> A play is play.

(Brook, 1968, p. 175)

What does our play look like in the metaverse? The full story of these performances has yet to be fully told, and it offers a rich area for researchers to mine in future years.

References

Anderson, C. and Dill, K. E. (2000) 'Video Games and Aggressive Thoughts, Feelings, and Behavior in the Laboratory and in Life', *Journal of Personality and Social Psychology*, 78, 4, pp. 772–90.

Belk, R. W. (1988) 'Possessions and the Extended Self', *Journal of Consumer Research*, 15, 2, pp. 139–68.

Bergen, C. (1984) *Knock Wood*. New York: Random House.

Bessiere, K., Seay, A. F., and Kiesler, S. (2007) 'The Ideal Elf: Identity and Identity Exploration in World of Warcraft', *Cyberpsychology & Behavior*, 10, 4, pp. 530–5.

Birringer, J. (1999) 'Contemporary Performance/Technology', *Theatre Journal*, 51, 4, pp. 361–81.

Brook, P. (1968) *The Empty Space*. New York: Touchstone.

Goldblatt, D. (2006) *Art and Ventriloquism*. New York: Routledge.

Hayles, N. K. (1999) *How We Became Posthuman: Virtual Bodies in Cybernetics, Literature, Informatics*. Chicago: University of Chicago Press.

Hermans, H. J. M. (2006) 'The Self as a Theater of Voices: Disorganization and Reorganization of a Position Repertoire', *Journal of Constructivist Psychology*, 19, 2, pp. 147–69.

Meadows, M. A. (2008) *I, Avatar: The Culture and Consequence of Having a Second Life*. New York: New Riders.

Moreno, Z. T., Blomkvist, L. D., and Rützel, T. (2000) *Psychodrama, Surplus Reality, and the Art of Healing*. London: Routledge.

Sandler, K. (1998) *Reading the Rabbit: Explorations in Warner Brothers Animation*. New Brunswick, NJ: Rutgers University Press.

Savin-Baden, M. (2010) 'Changelings and Shape Shifters? Identity Play and Pedagogical Positioning of Staff in Immersive Worlds', *London Review of Education*, 8, 1, pp. 25–38.

Suler, J. R. (2002) 'Identity Management in Cyberspace', *Journal of Applied Psychoanalytic Studies*, 4, 4, pp. 455–9.

The Sweet Life of Sierra Sugar (2007) 'A Journey Through SL Pregnancy Blog Entry', 15 November 2007, http://sierrasugar.blogspot.com/2007/11/journey-through-sl-pregnancy.html

Taylor, T. L. (2002) 'Living Digitally: Embodiment in Virtual Worlds', in R. Schroeder (ed.) *The Social Life of Avatars: Presence and Interaction*. New York: Springer, pp. 40–63.

Turkle, S. (1995) *Life on the Screen*. New York: Simon and Schuster.

Turner, V. (1982) *From Ritual to Theatre: The Human Seriousness of Play*. New York: Performing Arts Journal Publication.

Turner, V. (1990) 'Are There Universals of Performance?', in Schechner, R. and Appel, W. (eds) *By Means of Performance: Intercultural Studies of Theatre and Ritual*. New York: Cambridge University Press, pp. 8–18.

Walton, K. L. (1990) *Mimesis as Make Believe*. Cambridge, MA: Harvard University Press.

Wolfendale, J. (2006) 'My Avatar, My Self: Virtual Harm and Attachment', *Ethics and Information Technology*, 9, 2, pp. 111–19.

10
Reflections and Projections: Enabling the Social Enterprise

Steve Mahaley, Chuck Hamilton, and Tony O'Driscoll

The early days

We escaped flatland together, me, Chuck and Tony

For me it was when I first touched those unfamiliar keys on the keyboard that activated this new thing called an 'avatar', and I began to realize that I was in a new land – that I could approach and distance myself from people and objects. In creating my first avatar, I was faced with choices – choices that made me ask new questions about how I would present myself in a new context. The cursor blinked for several minutes as I pondered my new name. 'Ace.'

Ace Carson.

I am an educator and designer of education by trade and by profession. Over the months following my initial step into 3D virtual worlds in 2005, I realized that this new world allowed me to do things I could not do using conventional approaches and technologies. Suddenly I could build environments that were faithful replicas of real work and learning spaces. Or, more interestingly, I could create the tropical island to which I could invite educators, coaches, and participants to experience something altogether new. Together.

So that's what we did. 3D Teaming is an approach that incorporates the use of 3D immersive worlds as a critical part of a learning process. Duke CE collaborated with IBM and Dr. Robin Teigland at the Stockholm School of Economics to develop this model. As with all Duke CE designs, we had to identify the key learning outcomes for the selected audience – and in this case it was a set of global managers who were seeking to improve the performance of their distributed teams. We narrowed down the field of focus to three things: (1) clarifying team purpose, (2) practicing clear communication, and (3) testing assumptions.

Never before had we conducted such an event, and as such there was a rather steep learning curve for all involved. With the building and communication tools available in Second Life, we quickly moved past creating a replica of a real-life situation and opted to create an environment that felt new and, yes, slightly exotic: a beach front with a small island just offshore. We developed an orientation area on the island and held two 'office hours' for participants to help them practice with navigation, object manipulation, and communication tools. We forwarded detailed instructions, topical reading material, and pre-event surveys to the attendees. We prepared coaches and held rehearsals with them. And we sourced the virtual components of the experience itself – bridge construction pieces, flags, colored hats, presentation panels.

7:30 am New York. 12:30 pm London. 8:30 pm Tokyo. 9:30 am Bangalore

Participants arrived from around the world. The session was introduced by a faculty member standing in the sand next to a presentation panel. The coaches were introduced and the participants were given their colored hats to wear (to designate their teams), and then the fun began. Each team set out to build a bridge together to the island offshore. As they did this, the coaches noted aspects of team performance related to the three points of focus. There was celebration when they all made it across the bridge, and then discussion and debriefing with all. Key insights and 'ah-ha' moments were voiced as participants made the connections.

And, before they left, a picture was taken in front of the flags of the nations they all represented (Figure 10.1).

Standing there on the beach at the end of the event with avatars mingling, one participant was overheard saying to another, 'It's nice to finally meet you!'

And *that* revealed the promise of this new world.

In my initial pilot work in a number of immersive virtual environments, and with junior employees to senior managers, the response was overall extremely positive. In one instance we deployed a 3D immersive game that put junior employees and new managers in a scenario in which they had to appease an upset customer. At the end of the collaborative, problem-based, coached, and measured event in the immersive world, a participant commented that the experience was better than what they had experienced face-to-face during 'orientation week'. This new technology afforded a level of abstraction and a sense of common

Figure 10.1   3D teaming participants

challenge that gave the participants permission to focus less on embarrassing themselves in front of others, and more on offering ideas and taking on the risky scenario.

Yes. There seemed to be new advantages to these new immersive spaces. Chuck calls them 'affordances'.

On affordances

One of the most valuable lessons we learned about virtual work and tools through immersive environments was that these wonderful new spaces were good for particular things but not all things. In other words, immersive spaces *afforded* us some opportunities that we need to leverage today, and with time we fully expect more *affordances* to emerge.

When considering affordances of immersive virtual environments at IBM, we first looked at those traits that evoked similar affordances in the real world. The power of immersive environments stems from the fact that they leverage familiar patterns and modalities, for example, moving, pointing, gesturing, and talking, but also allow systematic violations of constraints that normally prevail in reality, for example, gravity. Therefore, we can observe both native affordances (particular to those environments chosen for a solution) and constructed affordances (those recombined features or wholly new design elements) that we design into the environment. The relationship between native and constructed affordances is complex – in almost all cases, each affordance is supported by several native affordances, connected and combined in different ways.

Though space in this chapter does not allow full explanation of each of the following ten affordances (a book in and of itself), we believe that understanding these affordances can be a core differentiator in the use of virtual social world spaces for collaboration, learning, and work. The following top ten affordances were identified as we leveraged various virtual environments, and we include actual dialogue examples extracted from conversations in these spaces to support each particular affordance:

Presence and reputation – complementary affordances (observed as both native and constructed) used to support connection, group affinity, and remote teams, especially with teams that would otherwise be very loosely connected.

> *I see you are here often and people rate you highly.*

Space or **scale** – complementary affordances (observed as both native and constructed) where a designed place requires greater space and scale than normally afforded in either a classroom or via legacy presentation mediums such as projected presentation documents or webinar forums.

> *From 200 feet up I can see that this is a really big space, something I missed while I was crawling around inside that molecule.*

Practice and simulation – types of affordances (both native and constructed within virtual spaces) that can be applied to help learners develop a better understanding of concepts, build confidence, or expand/contract time and scale. People naturally create learning simulations and have been doing so as part of play and work for centuries.

> *Let's walk through this simulation and see if you get what I'm talking about.*

Blending of place – an affordance that is observed natively within most immersive spaces, which can be significantly enhanced by the construction of additional design elements. As discussed earlier, place plays a special role in the definition of a virtual space. Blending many places can give the participants the feeling of being in multiple places at the same time, or the feeling of a common virtual geography running parallel to the real world we share every day.

> *On this street you can see real backdrops from a typical street in Beijing as well as see comparable objects from the Americas.*

Co-creation and collaboration – native and constructed affordances that are observed in many virtual social spaces and significantly enhanced by co-presence within immersive environments. Inherent functionality in user-defined immersive environments (in some but not all environments) allows participants to manipulate and expand an environment with their coworkers.

> *Let's move this block left about 10 feet and change its parameters. I'll move it and you click on it and edit its properties.*

Observable behavior and performance – native and constructed affordances that can be applied in both individual and group settings within a virtual space. Virtual spaces inherently allow the third party observer to lurk or watch activities from numerous vantage points. With additional design, observers can monitor and measure group participation on another level.

> *See how people are moving into that quadrant, they are voting with their feet and that is obviously their preferred spot.*

Self and anonymity – native and constructed affordances that are widely observed in immersive environments and leveraged for a variety of purposes. These affordances are best observed through personal participation, when the feeling and self-identification experience is evident. Linked to the notion of presence and reputation, *self* is designed in part by the environment and to a greater extent by the individual.

> *Hello, Rasta40 – because you have chosen to present yourself as a "furry", I gather you wish to keep your identity private?*

Enrichment of the experience – immersive environments are rich interactive spaces. Such environments offer highly converged media spaces combining many tools and affordances together to create that enriched experience. Participants' attention to the screen is normally very high, even in the simplest of spaces, as participants describe the experience as 'so much going on'. Enriching the user experiences requires that the designer understand the native and constructed affordances available for the selected environment and how to control this experience.

Tony, there is so much going on here, I'm afraid to look away or risk getting left behind. No multitasking allowed I guess!

Mass connected innovation – both a native and constructed affordance that considers what can occur when mass collaborative environments are meshed with the collective action of large numbers of people working together. The affordances discussed above reveal that virtual environments can present an opportunity for people to come together to see and manipulate elements that might otherwise not be able to be shown. Leveraging any amount of space, at any scale, across multiple geographies, perspectives with iterative design is a formula that enables unexpected innovation to occur.

It's hard to say why, but I feel like the crowd supports us here, everyone is on call, on demand or close to it. If you like I'll poll my communities and get you some immediate feedback on your idea.

Universal visual language – both a native and a constructed affordance that speaks to the highly visual qualities of the immersive spaces. Highly visual virtual landscapes can be visually stunning, highly realistic or highly conceptual, yet somehow always familiar to a wide cross-section of users. Observation of many virtual world designs reveals that less written language is needed to explain how to use a space or object. The metaphors used in virtual spaces often reflect real world elements, allowing participants to be both avatar and browser, walking or flying through designs with little additional instruction.

Watch what happens when I launch this office simulation.... Once I've provided the chairs and table, people naturally walk over and take a seat. This happens the same way in nearly every geography.

Challenges we face

Today the world is a fragmented place. We use a disconnected set of tools to instant message, talk by voice, see each other, share screens, collaborate on work products ... and simply 'be' together. The 3D spaces are fragmented as well – multiple viewers, different platforms, walled gardens of very specific applications. While the 2D world has seen a variety of platforms developed that integrate multiple methods for data contribution, personal profiles and collaboration, none provides the variety of affordances outlined above.

There remains a wide variance in the availability of hardware, software, and bandwidth that can handle the more data-intensive 3D spaces. Many organizations have a significant level of variety in the levels of service they can provide their people in different geographies. And there are serious considerations from members of the IT, security, and legal departments that need to be factored in to the eventual provisioning of these new spaces – especially those that might be shared outside the firewall.

And, once the 3D space is available, there is a good deal of work that needs to be done to orient key stakeholders to the value proposition of such spaces, and certainly in the field of learning and development, to train educators in how to think 'outside the box'. One of the worst things you can do is replicate mediocre training techniques in an immersive environment. We have to work with our educators and staff to understand the possibilities and leverage the affordances these spaces provide.

The issue, we believe, is NOT with whether or not a 3D context can be leveraged to create meaningful and memorable learning experiences but HOW we can overcome the technological hurdles required to develop a worldwide platform that everyone can leverage to engage in these meaningful experiences. And, while we observe the maturation of the 3D technologies, we know that things are also changing in the business world.

What has changed for businesses

If you look at the overarching social trends impacting the way we learn and work today, as compared with just five years ago, you will observe the following four dramatic shifts. These shifts mark our move towards a social business culture. Immersive environments have shown us the first big integration opportunity for this new culture. Whether any of the current immersive spaces have perfected this integration point remains a matter of debate, but it is clear that organizations have been forever changed. The most dramatic shifts we observe are discussed below.

Wider internet adoption, with far less expensive connection tools – Access to the internet and the wealth of its resources has grown substantially in just the past five years. The total number of internet users rose to over 2 billion users in 2010 from just over 1 billion in 2005, with a penetration rate of 30 per cent worldwide.[1] This growth in demand, combined with literally thousands of new, often free, platforms (e.g., Skype, Twitter, Foursquare, Facebook), buoyed the producer/consumer community while also demonstrating that true virtual work was not only a possibility but a part of the everyday.

The demonstration of inexpensive and well-coordinated production – The tangible and measurable emergence of tools, techniques, and inexpensive modes of production for the creation of many different things is a powerful opportunity. This production was shown to be either wholly virtual (creation of an entire online meeting space) or part of the process of creating something for real world consumption (such as the Toyota Scion mod culture).

The possibility of a visible and level playing field – A virtual/physical place where the cross-geography, cross-culture amateurs and professionals could mingle, co-create, produce, and consume. At the same time, people could also leverage their crowd strength to teach, lead, and interact in a many-to-many model. While some social networks work towards this same model, few match the connective quality of immersive spaces.

Evolution and efficient organization of community – A community of communities with strong voices in everything from purchasing decisions and world governance to health care tips. Well-organized and moderated communities continue to wield power and influence, ensuring that 'the crowd voice' is now enabled as part of any important strategy. We have learned that like-minded connectedness is not only possible but highly desirable.

The summary impact of these trends is beginning to be felt within organizations as they begin to adopt social media and leverage new technologies to optimize the performance of their teams and employees and to more rapidly address the issues they face. We are seeing the dawn of a new era – that of what Tony calls the *social enterprise*.

The social enterprise

Welcome to the era of the social enterprise. We have made the transition from connecting to information ON the web to connecting to others THROUGH the web to collaborating and co-creating as avatars WITHIN the web. As we move into an era where enterprise becomes increasingly focused on effectively and efficiently aggregating its capability around fruitful profit-generating endeavors to create differentiated value, there is now essentially a requirement that the people within and outside the firewalls increase serendipitous social interaction. The higher the sociality within and across enterprises, the higher is the likelihood of coalescence around endeavors that make a difference.

We have to come to the realization, as do most early adopters in a new technological paradigm, that this is not about the 3D technology in and of itself but about the possibilities that this technology holds to enable the social side of our connectedness around the globe. The promise of virtual environments to establish motivation and leverage affordances in new and different ways to drive collaborative sensemaking and learning is unprecedented, but it has stalled out technologically.

In many ways the dawning of social media and the notion of the race to create the next generation social enterprise suffers from the same curse. It is full of possibility while at the same time fraught with technicalities that impede it from achieving its fullest potential through scale.

Given this *social enterprise movement*, we would do well to reframe what we have learned to date about the affordances of 3D as a core component of an overarching social enterprise strategy and not as a medium and movement in and of itself. Based on our initial immersion, we must ask ourselves, 'What can 3D do that other social technologies cannot in increasing the sociality coefficient across the enterprise ecosystem?'

Is 3D the integration layer for the last social mile of organizational performance? Could it unleash the cognitive surplus (Shirky, 2011) that lies largely dormant within the existing social networks?

At one end of the spectrum, some argue that the web's ubiquity allows us to surf the shallows of the internet as we become increasingly alone together (Turkle, 2011); our view is that there is an alternative that can allow us to collectively indwell within the Immersive Internet as opposed to passively connecting to it. At the end of the day, the integration of social media and 3D will allow us to create sensemaking contexts that will enable us to more rapidly tackle the great issues the world is facing today. See, for example, the response through social media during horrific earthquakes, tsunamis, and floods or the use of such media to unlock amazing social and political change in North Africa – AND the creation of virtual spaces in 3D as part of that effort.

A postcard from the future

The unique qualities and affordances that 3D immersive spaces bring will become the integrative layer for all sorts of social communication and collaboration tools within and across organizations. What was previously an unwieldy and fragmented distribution of tools will now have a 'home' – that third place where what started as a simple conversation can quickly evolve into rapid, real-time sharing, where individuals enter immersive spaces they initialize on the fly. 'Here, let me show you' becomes eminently doable wherever we happen to be.

To achieve this, we do not need new technology so much as new thinking. This begins with the recognition that both the Immersive Internet and Social Enterprise movements are stalling out, not because of the possibilities they present discretely but because of the lack of our ability to scale them collectively. It is only with the addition of the glue of 3D affordances that the true promise of the Social Enterprise will be achieved.

We need to reframe the affordances that 3D brings, not as differentiators for learning but as enablers of sociality. The physical space we live in is nothing but a giant integrator of surface contexts that allows us humans to interact and solve problems together with very limited technical overhead. The real benefit of 3D may be in the affordance that it provides to allow avatars to have real-time co-agency around data surfaces that allow us to collectively make sense of information faster together. Imagine if we could do that within the web. Envision 3D as the ultimate integration layer that brings the incredible promise of the social enterprise into focus.

Well, we can – and we should – and it all begins with placing the Immersive Internet as the core integrating technology for the social enterprise.

We'll see you there.

Note

1. Website Optimization.com, http://www.websiteoptimization.com/bw/1103/

References

Shirky, C. (2011) *Cognitive Surplus: How Technology Makes Consumers into Collaborators*. New York: Penguin Group.
Turkle, S. (2011) *Alone Together: Why We Expect More from Technology and Less from Each Other*. New York: Basic Books.

11
Added Value of Teaching in a Virtual World

Inger-Marie Falgren Christensen, Andrew Marunchak, and Cristina Stefanelli

Introduction

It is unfortunate that we often think of virtual worlds in education as a forced application of technology rather than an opportunity to test new theories and educational methodologies or as a way to step into our collective and individual knowledge in a way that we have never been able to do before. Although virtual worlds have been around for many years, their real potential and use for educational purposes has only recently been made evident through affordances involving the replication of teaching environments and museums, art galleries as well as potentially hazardous environments such as laboratories. According to the article 'Serious Virtual Worlds',

> the lines between virtual worlds, games and social networking are blurring significantly leading to the assertion that over the next five years the majority of young people under 18 will have avatars and be using these kinds of applications daily and therefore have different expectations about how education may be delivered to them.
>
> (de Freitas, 2008)

While major research studies on the benefits of virtual worlds in terms of participation, learner control, educational standards, and quality assurance are still underway, the development of education in virtual worlds in the next five to ten years has the potential to radically change not only how we learn but also the face of education.

Initially, this chapter discusses the impact of virtual worlds on education in the next five to ten years. Then the chapter illustrates how teaching and learning could actually take place in a virtual world in the near future by describing and discussing a fictional educational program for secondary schools. Following this scenario, the chapter discusses the challenges involved in implementing such an educational program.

Nowadays, teachers involved in virtual worlds face similar barriers as the educators who pioneered web-based, distance-learning programs. The focus remains on educational methodology and processes as ways to improve learning outcomes, and few resources are spent on investigating the technical aspects of e-learning platforms, standards, and the myriad of technical offers.

In a time when our modern educational system is under fire for being disconnected from the real world, many secondary school teachers see virtual worlds as a tool that might help them to connect students to real-life education. Part of this enthusiastic approach comes from the unique characteristics of virtual worlds: they give students the ability to play, to practice, and to be creative and imaginative, and they add a practical dimension to teaching and learning activities, provide authentic situations, and make collaboration more meaningful. Virtual worlds move beyond real-life learning and, embedded in an appropriate pedagogical approach, seem to contribute to enhanced collaborative learning, learning by reflecting, and learning by doing as well as promoting learner autonomy and social empathy (Pivec et al., 2011).

On the other hand, virtual world technologies are not without their obstacles. There are many platforms from which to choose, and there are hardware as well as internet requirements to meet. It can be a time-consuming process for a school, teachers, and students to get ready for education in virtual worlds. The ideal situation is for IT staff to work closely together with teachers and management in an effort to choose the virtual world that best suits their needs and to upgrade the computer equipment, and, most importantly, the competences of teachers.

The impact of virtual world technology on education in the near future

True to form, display devices function as windows to another environment. They afford users the ability to experience events within from a third-person perspective while remaining in comfortable isolation. It may seem strange, then, to consider that it is the goal of many virtual worlds to emulate the characteristics of a locale from which people seek to exclude themselves. The irony of the situation is made evident when we find ourselves attempting to recreate these environments in order to obtain mastery over them. Descending into the depths of a volcano or walking on the surface of the moon, such are the delights of virtual reality.

The visual medium has, throughout the history of mankind, been used to convey narrative(s) by way of form and shape. From Neolithic to modern times, the contrast between cave paintings and 3D cinema is evident though the underlying principle, in that a single image or frame is displayed at one time remains the same. The moving image, or animation, has done much to impact our culture. Images presented sequentially, in a linear fashion and at high speed, give life and movement to what, alone, is but a static picture. This practice has been extended via the use of real-time graphics processing, the stuff of which high-fidelity flight simulations and video games are made. This technology is defined by the ability of the computer to generate images at high speed while receiving input from the user, thus resulting in interactive on-screen content. Where, then, does the future lie?

Much of the future lies in establishing how to use this dynamic form for means other than entertainment, which, as an industry, has spurred its growth and prevalence in society. There is a generation gap characterized by the disproportionate amount of interest invested by the younger users of the medium as opposed to those who are older and creating the medium. Those people for whom real-time 3D remains a mystery must devote the required time to gain familiarity with the medium or forego the opportunity to contribute and share in its wonder. This prospective audience can be likened to an untapped resource for which the commercial sector must provide the means to make the technology accessible. It is likely, therefore, that the current trend of experimentation and research into interface devices will continue and, in so doing, provide new affordances by way of interactivity and immersion. Global broadband speeds continue to rise, and with them an increase in the number of cloud computing services that, in turn, create opportunities for streaming pre-rendered real-time 3D footage to the most humble of devices, be it a digital tablet or a phone.

Accessibility plays a pivotal role in education, and all students must be accommodated, whether they have hearing/visual impairments or otherwise. The greater the extent to which a user can become immersed in a 3D simulation (the constituent elements of which are graphics and audio), the more remains inaccessible to those without the means to experience it. It is therefore necessary to tread with caution and continue researching the subject. While the avatar, as a representational entity, provides a valuable tool for exercises involving role-play, caution should be advised regarding its potential to act as a source of distraction rather than as a tool/point of reference (as in the case of Second Life, when there are times a user might be overcome with an urge to change an attribute, such as the color of their clothing, thus breaking concentration).

Multiuser virtual worlds are not without merit, though they require more development time than a single-user environment. With this in mind, a business model needs to be considered before private companies are able to provide networked virtual platforms to educational establishments. This, with the current lack of standardization in 3D classroom-based learning, means that there will be many 'failed attempts'. Given the nature of the most prominent virtual world used for educational purposes (Second Life), it should be noted that it is a *general-purpose* multiuser 3D environment and that the use of it for a specific means is an exercise in improvisation.

It seems likely, then, with the proficiencies displayed by the younger users of virtual worlds, that the educators of tomorrow will have the understanding required to create bespoke simulations for classroom-based learning themselves. What is needed is a highly visual and intuitive authoring environment for such individuals to use. Given current trends in the gaming industry, pertaining to the introduction of 'indie developers' (independent professionals), this seems to hint at a future wherein high-caliber content creation will no longer be the domain of the overpopulated development team. Rather, the future of virtual worlds in education belongs to the creative entrepreneur for whom the disciplines of both art and science are not mutually exclusive but one and the same.

How will teaching and learning take place in a virtual world in the near future? Let's observe Vera on her first day at upper secondary school and find out.

Teaching with virtual worlds tomorrow

A fictional educational program for secondary schools

It's Vera's very first day at upper secondary school. Vera wants to specialize in design and languages, and therefore she has chosen 'Virtual World (VW) High', which brands itself on its innovative teaching and practical approach to both fields. Vera received an IM with practical details a couple of weeks ago, and she is now finding her way to the locale where the introductory session will take place. She doesn't have to worry about transportation, since she is going to the virtual campus of VW High in the 3D world called VEDU. So she logs on to her computer and clicks the link that will teleport her to the right locale. In VEDU, users are represented via a virtual figure, an avatar. Fortunately, VEDU has a useful feature: if a person already has an avatar in another 3D world, s/he can import it to VEDU. Vera has made use of this functionality. She already has a previously created avatar from the online game 'Catwalk' where she has been styling virtual models and designed virtual clothing for several years. She has grown quite attached to her 'Catwalk' avatar and simply couldn't imagine going to VW High as anybody else.

Let us pause here to consider the implications of using an already existing avatar and transferring this avatar from a gaming and entertainment environment to an educational context. The concept of an avatar is actually a curious thing. In a single-user (offline, computer-based) environment, a visible representational entity for the user is not a prerequisite for a meaningful experience. Interactions with programmable entities, be they doors or something more dynamic, by way of artificial intelligence can take place without the user having a removed sense of self. In such cases, only a first-person perspective is needed, allowing an extension of the user's senses into the virtual environment.

The situation is made complex in multiuser environments wherein multiple points of reference are required. In being able to see the position of another user, one can also be seen oneself. This mutual realization of exposure provokes a profound sense of self-awareness: one in which, it can be said, we realize we are 'naked' and must be clothed. In accordance with our own misgivings, it is often the case that users portray themselves in as 'perfect' a manner as they can in the time they may care to devote to this. Sadly, the ability to customize the appearance of an avatar acts as a means of expressing the unattainable beauty one may bear witness to in fashion magazines wherein photos of digitally enhanced models parade the catwalk, turning and posing in a pretense of fitting seamlessly into the natural order of things, provoking the human urge to engage in an act of mimicry. That being said, the affordances provided by an avatar are many. It is not uncommon for those with physical disabilities to use this entity as a means of expressing uninhibited locomotion, free from the confines of a wheelchair or whatever else one might feel restricted by (appearance or otherwise).

Indeed, the phenomenon of competing with our looks increases in potency as the level of customization deepens. What, at this point, is the contribution of the avatar? It is without doubt that, at worst, the avatar is a distraction from events occurring on-screen. The implementation of such entities requires consideration and justification, lest the prescribed experience be diminished. Whether or not it can act as a doorway to some form of psychosis is outside the authors' sphere of competence, though we would refer, affectionately, to such a condition as a 'dollhouse' complex.

The channels of self-expression are not limited to appearance but also include the manner in which a user behaves. In treating others with politeness, it can seem as though users may have a vested interest in learning more about the strange environment in which they find themselves, but not all is as it seems. In much the same way as bullying exists in real life, the digital equivalent of 'trolling' has an active presence in virtual worlds. The degree to which troublemakers are able to impact the experience of another user is defined by the level of interaction made possible by the rules governing the locale. Pushing the avatar of another user to a different location and attempting to disrupt the proceedings of a presentation are examples of 'griefing', that is, acting with intent to cause grief to others. Indeed, in open-ended environments 'policing' by the administration of the connected users is all but impossible and people are free to engage in any sort of conduct they choose. Such are the affordances provided by anonymity. This begs the question of whether or not users might act differently if, as an example, their social network profile held some sort of mutual relationship with their avatar. Having one's public-facing internet presence at stake would certainly provide pause for thought. Such an emotional investment is unlikely to be put at risk.

With the aforementioned unregulated behavior come questions of censorship. The content of a website can be categorized as suitable for an adult or under-age audience due to its static nature. The behavior of another user/avatar, on the other hand, is wildly unpredictable.

Teaching and learning activities in a virtual world

Scenario continued...

Back in VEDU, Vera has arrived at the introductory session and meets her fellow students and the five teachers who will take them through the initial year of the program. Vera activates the voice chat and says hello to everybody. Her greetings are returned. Then the formal introductions start and each teacher presents his/her topic. There's Mr Thompson who teaches Spanish. Vera really looks forward to the Spanish lessons. She loves to travel and would like to work abroad when she has finished upper secondary school. She is especially interested in the Latin-American countries, hence her choice of Spanish.

Mr Thompson explains the intended learning outcomes of Spanish, and Vera is a bit bored. Oral proficiency, written proficiency, culture studies. It sounds a bit dry and not very motivating. Will this mean endless hours of reading and swatting up on grammar? But then Vera pays attention. Mr Thompson has stopped listing learning outcomes and has begun explaining how the subject will be taught and what activities are in store. He now hands out teleports to everyone; they are about to visit their virtual, Spanish families with whom they will spend time during their lessons in oral proficiency. Vera teleports to an address in virtual Madrid and says hello to Mr and Mrs Gonzales and their daughter, Carmen, who is about the same age as Vera. For the next 15 minutes, Vera gets acquainted with the Gonzales family. She then teleports back to the introductory session and already feels a bit better at exchanging pleasantries in Spanish. Before she teleported back, she made plans for her next visit to the Gonzales family. She will go shopping with Carmen and meet some of her friends at the virtual mall. She is already very excited.

But what about written proficiency? Vera never liked writing school papers on the boring subjects proposed by teachers, and will she have to translate tiresome bits of text? No, not at all. Mr Thompson has moved on and is now introducing the virtual newspaper, the virtual fashion magazine, and the virtual ad agency from which students can choose for their written proficiency activities. The students will do a six-month traineeship at each organization in turn. What a challenge, Vera thinks, but I will really be able to achieve good writing skills in Spanish. It should be no problem getting a job in a Spanish speaking country when I finish my studies.

Next is Ms Brown who teaches Design. She, too, has a long list of intended learning outcomes but again follows a set of some very interesting teaching and learning activities. There are two parallel tracks in the design course. Track one is the study of design principles and analysis of how these principles are used in practice. Track two is a group design project. Each group will choose a theme and create a virtual design. The grand finale is an exhibition at the end of the semester. The best three designs win money prizes. Vera's mind wanders. Will she be doing a fashion design or should she choose arts, paintings, and sculptures?

Who would think that upper secondary school could be so fun and at the same time so challenging? Vera cannot wait to get started on the virtual activities and improve her Spanish. At the same time, she is very much looking forward to studying design and becoming more adept at implementing the design principles in practice.

In the proposed scenario, the delivery of teaching and learning activities occurs solely online. Virtual world delivery of education greatly enhances students' efforts with respect to achieving valuable competencies by providing a wealth of opportunities for young people to train practical skills. This motivates and engages the students in a way that traditional teaching in the classroom fails to do today. There is a gap between young people's use of media and the integration of it in teaching. Young people are used to playing an active part, and this must be mirrored in teaching and learning activities.

It is often difficult to learn something that is abstract and isolated from its actual context. Virtual worlds can provide this authentic context and thus make teaching and learning activities more meaningful for young people. This authentic 3D context also provides an immersive experience that enables students to use multiple learning strategies, which means that more students will benefit.

Virtual worlds can provide an exciting playground for students in the future. They consist of environments where students can obtain practical experience in collaborating with people on an international scale and thus improve both their language and communication and teamwork skills. There is a greater degree of autonomy when students practice their planning and project skills and are encouraged to take innovative approaches to problem-solving rather than learning their textbooks by heart. Such skills are relevant to their futures. The solutions to the problems the world is facing cannot be found in textbooks. Innovative approaches are needed, and the first step is to provide students with innovative teaching and learning activities. This practical and immersive angle to teaching and learning is what makes virtual worlds so interesting with respect to secondary education. It is a new teaching and learning arena for a new online age.

However, it remains to be seen whether a blended or exclusively online mode of delivery would be more beneficial to students. Given the complexities involved with coming to terms with a virtual environment, issues of support and accessibility are key. It stands to reason, then, that having support personnel in close physical vicinity is of paramount importance when making the initial foray into the medium. In an attempt to instill confidence in the provision of the virtual world, students need to have their questions answered quickly, lest they lose interest.

Scenario continued...

Back in VEDU, there is a ten minute break in the introductory program, and Vera quickly logs on to her preferred social network to share her thoughts and experiences with friends and family. She posts a few snapshots from her virtual visit to the Gonzales family and writes some excited remarks about her new school and the activities on which she is about to embark. Within a few seconds, she is chatting away with a couple of friends who want to know more.

Then a message pops up on her screen from VEDU – time to get back to her virtual class.

The challenges in reaching an ideal program

Before we can reach a stage where both teachers and students interact comfortably in a virtual world, there are several issues that need to be scrutinized. How does one make sure, for example, that students and teachers are who they claim to be? When a person is represented by an avatar, the question of who sits behind the computer screen is of key importance. This is more of a practical issue that can be taken care of through the issuing of usernames and passwords that restrict access to the virtual campus. Furthermore, to be proactive with regard to the issues of avatars, body ideals, and bullying, schools offering virtual world courses should carefully consider how best to guide and regulate student use of avatars and virtual world behavior. It is recommended to prepare a policy and implement relevant regulations, especially with the secondary school population of students, which is under age.

It also remains to be seen whether virtual worlds can create enough of a sense of presence to secure retention and avoid student drop-out more efficiently than asynchronous distance learning. However, with the rich possibilities for synchronous communication and the immersive aspect of virtual worlds, retention rates should be higher.

It is a challenge, though, to find out how the visually or hearing impaired can be catered for in virtual worlds where the learning experience is very much dependent on sight and hearing. Research is very much needed in this field.

There is also the equipment issue. Even today, in many schools, the hardware and internet connections do not support the use of virtual worlds. Students and teachers might not have access due to school policies and/or firewall issues or computer performance, and bandwidth may be lacking, causing the users to experience lag in-world and thus detracting from the overall experience.

Finally, teachers must be prepared to teach and organize learning activities in-world. This will pose quite a challenge for some teachers, and no doubt competence development is needed. Today, we have teachers who fully embrace IT-supported learning, but we also have many teachers who are reluctant to integrate it into their teaching. They fail to see the point and do not have the time or motivation to investigate possible uses. This calls for systematic and paid competence development of teachers, who need the time and skills to become confident enough to bring their students in-world. This is very much a question of IT skills, but it is also a question of becoming acquainted with different teaching methods that mean more freedom and autonomy for students and an alternative role for teachers, who will act more like coaches and supervisors than the traditional expert with all the right answers.

When integrating new technology into teaching, it is very tempting to simply transfer the teaching methods from the traditional classroom into the new technology. However, to fully realize the learning potential embedded in a new tool or technology, it is important to be innovative and find new ways to reach the learning objectives (Christensen, 2010; Lim, 2009). Lim's 'six learnings framework' (Lim, 2009) provides useful insight into the learning processes that virtual worlds can facilitate. The six learning frameworks involve the following learning processes:

Learning by Exploring. This involves exploring landscapes, objects, constructions, and communities in a virtual world. When Vera in our scenario above teleports to Madrid in connection with her oral proficiency lessons, she learns by exploring. Virtual worlds are excellent arenas for language teaching in that they provide a cultural framework that allows students to get acquainted with local cultures and habits. The language teaching thus becomes embedded in a meaningful context.

Learning by Collaborating. Virtual worlds provide ample opportunity for allowing students to collaborate to conduct problem-solving tasks in practice. This learning process is the basis of the group design project to which Vera is introduced on her first day at school.

Learning by Being. This type of learning can be facilitated in a number of ways. For example, students and teachers can engage in role-playing and become nurses, shop assistants, and so on, to practice real-life work processes and thus achieve valuable competences. Furthermore, most virtual worlds enable users to change the appearance of their avatars, thus giving them the chance to explore different looks and study the reactions of other avatars. In this way, young people can explore the assumption of identities. Vera in our scenario already has an avatar that has become part of her 'being' in a virtual world. Thus, it gives her comfort and security to be able to use this avatar at her new, virtual school. As mentioned above, the avatar also carries with it important discussions on body ideals, distraction from learning activities, and so on.

Learning by Building. This is about having the students construct objects and/or script them. These learning processes are especially suited to design and technology. Students can demonstrate their mathematical understanding and/or their insight into design principles and aesthetics. Vera's group design project also implies learning by building.

Learning by Championing. This involves organizing communication campaigns and other initiatives in virtual worlds that have the purpose of creating attention to and informing people about a certain cause. This type of learning process would be particularly relevant to social studies and health science.

Learning by Expressing. This is the final element in the six learnings framework. It is different from the other five elements in that it relates to a meta-level. The first five elements in the framework relate directly to learning activities in a virtual world; however, learning by expressing is the communication of students' reflections on what they have experienced in-world to an audience, often located outside the virtual world. This could be friends, family, and so on. When Vera blogs about her exciting day at VW High, she learns by expressing herself.

Conclusion

This chapter illustrates the ample educational potential of virtual worlds. Unleashing this potential, however, requires that teachers dare to be innovative and implement new teaching methods and technologies into the classroom. In order for this to happen, there are a number of challenges to overcome. The most important factors are, perhaps, making sure that teachers have the necessary competences to design and deliver teaching and learning activities in virtual worlds and that schools have the necessary IT equipment and internet connections. We are, at present, in a transition phase. Teachers today may not have a 'history' of playing online games and navigating virtual, multiuser environments. But teachers tomorrow will be comfortable with 3D multiuser environments and will also have the necessary knowledge and skills to implement these into the classroom. And the students? They are waiting for innovative, digital ways to help them learn the skills needed for their future work lives in a motivating and engaging way.

Acknowledgments

This chapter draws on the results of the EU project AVATAR funded with support by the European Commission under the Lifelong Learning Programme Comenius (Project number 502882-LLP-1-2009-1-IT-COMENIUS-CMP). We would like to thank all project partners, FOR.COM (Italy), FH JOANNEUM University of Applied Sciences (Austria), Burgas Free University (Bulgaria), University of Southern Denmark, Universidad Nacional de Educación a Distancia (Spain), University of Hertfordshire (United Kingdom), and SOPH.ia In Action Consulting (Italy), for their significant and essential contributions to the project.

References

Christensen, I. F. (2010) 'Empowering Teachers in Secondary School – Designing a Course on Virtual Worlds Teaching', *Proceedings Online Education*, Berlin, December 2010, pp. 86–90.

de Freitas, S. (2008) *Serious Virtual Worlds, A Scoping Study*, prepared for the JISC e-Learning Programme.

Lim, K. Y. T. (2009) 'Editor's Corner: The Six Learnings of Second Life – A Framework for Designing Curricular Interventions In-world', *Journal of Virtual Worlds Research*, 2, 1, Pedagogy, Education and Innovation in 3-D Virtual Worlds, pp. 3–11.

Pivec, M., Stefanelli, C., Christensen, I. M., and Pauschenwein, J. (2011) 'AVATAR – The Course: Recommendations for Using 3D Virtual Environments for Teaching', *eLearning Papers – Game-Based Learning: New Practices, New Classrooms*, 25, July 2011. Accessed 8 May 2012, http://www.elearningpapers.eu/en/node/107280, full text: http://www.elearningeuropa.info/en/download/file/fid/23296

12

Play and Fun Politics to Increase the Pervasiveness of Social Community: The Experience of Angels 4 Travellers

Maria Laura Toraldo, Gianluigi Mangia, Stefano Consiglio, and Riccardo Mercurio

Angels 4 Travellers and the rhetoric of participation

As every Friday evening at seven o'clock, we were chatting along the Naples waterfront, tasting a refreshing lemon ice-cream; it was a delicious ice cream from Chalet Ciro ice cream parlor. While I praised the ice-cream cone, Stefano was intent upon uploading an enthusiastic description of 'Chalet Ciro' on the Angels 4 Travellers platform, writing about the tastiness of the lemon flavor and the kindness of the parlor personnel.

The episode described above is an incipit to provoke reflection upon a specific aspect of social networks related to the playful component of networking activity and the perception of fun by its amateurs. Indeed, while some of us were uploading content onto the Angels 4 Travellers (A4T) platform, we dismissed from our minds that we were performing a creative act, devoted to the creation of content to be shared with our virtual 'friends'. Starting from this event, we became involved in reflection on how much virtual activity is done voluntarily and, certainly, with some degree of enjoyment, with the consequence that many virtual communities are becoming widespread thanks to the role of voluntary subjects.

The perception of fun activities related to the production of online content is described by Van Dijck, who argues that people's participation is often characterized by the perception of networking actions as hobbies among 'amateurs' that are encouraged by a spirit of community (Van Dijck, 2009). In this vein, the mixture of 'community' and 'creative expression' might on the surface seem to be grounded in some sort of enjoyment – does not the very idea of social networking on platforms such as Facebook and MySpace or on coproduction platforms such as YouTube or Twitter seem confined to the realm of leisure? Or will juxtaposition perhaps eradicate the boundaries in the work-life balance as a central feature of the era of soft capitalism (Heelas, 2002)? The pervasiveness of social networks was brought home to us when we realized that we were working on online content during our free time. It was during this relaxed chatting that we realized that our private sphere was being eaten up by spending time online to produce 'fresh' content.

Since the rhetoric of the 'old' media has become outdated due to its focus on the passive recipient, a new active participant has ideally surfaced in opposition, in a range of managerial and business discourses, described as 'someone who is well-versed in the skills of new media' (Olsson, 2009, p. 101). A newly empowered user – whose structuring trait revolves around creative expression, cooperative activity, and a playful attitude – has arisen as the participating subject of the numerous living web platforms (Tapscott and Williams, 2006) and virtual worlds. In this context, social networks such as Facebook, MySpace, and Twitter have acquired an undisputed role, helping people to make new friends and keep in touch with old ones (Dodson, 2006).

Web platforms, blogs, community sites, and other kinds of virtual interfaces are frequently depicted as venues for user active participation in various forms of coproduction. This follows a logic based on participants as 'operant resources', where they are framed as active contributors in relational exchanges and coproduction (Vargo and Lusch, 2004, p. 2).

The 'participative paradigm' derived from online collaboration has been clearly described by Tapscott and Williams in their well-informed account of a 'new world' of 'ever-connected people' that consists of the mass creativity of many 'web initiatives'. At the same time, the participatory role of users becomes the central dynamic for the creation of value, where the key competence for managers is 'the ability to integrate the talents of dispersed individuals and organizations' (Tapscott and Williams, 2006, p. 18). Similarly, the co-creation approach has been widely depicted in the marketing literature as a form of economic value. For instance, Cova and Dalli argue that value production is capitalized upon by consumers' interaction with one another through interpersonal relationships, where what is unintentionally produced is enthusiasm and social cooperation (Cova and Dalli, 2009).

What is perhaps more interesting in the 'participative paradigm' is that online collaboration is animated by a sense of fun, happiness to share, and the promise of new interactive experiences on virtual platforms. For instance, fun culture has received a great deal of attention in managerial studies (Costea et al., 2007, 2008; Fleming, 2005; Warren, 2002), where it has been unmasked as a tool in the service of organizational performance. Crafting fun experiences in the workplace and the management of play have acquired an important position as managerial practices that managers consciously seek to evoke as typically 'enjoyable extra employment experiences inside the organization' (Fleming, 2005, p. 286). In addition, a playful spirit in the workplace is deemed to be the primary source for enrolling the whole person (Costea, 2007) and enhancing his or her emotional well-being.

Due to recent developments of the web, the co-creation model has been critically discussed by Van Dijck and Nieborg, who dismantle the *'rhetoric of connectivity'* as a means for companies to extract value from 'networked active co-creators' (p. 863). Following this perspective, clicking, blogging, and uploading videos are, among other things, activities conducted by an 'army of amateurs who dedicate their time and energy to developing and sustaining a vast array of products and services' (Van Dijck and Nieborg, 2009, p. 860).

From this angle, the web includes as its primary raw material users' contributions. The promise for them is receiving recognition and, potentially, to seek their sense of self-worth by marketing themselves (Bauman, 2007) to other virtual subjectivities.

Recognizing many of the features above that describe the culture of fun, we will in this chapter consider a social community – A4T – by examining the user experience. By taking into account the playful techniques and the sense of fun perceived by its users, we will reflect on the implications for the web by looking at the mass of creative subjects that finally produce 'free' labor. Our argument, simply put, is that the *'architecture of participation'* (O'Reilly, 2005) surrounding the web is inextricably linked with the perception of enjoyable experiences deriving from networking activity through the mobilization of millions of voluntary subjects. To a large extent, A4T is rooted in this mass of creative subjects, as the site is kept alive through their labor and sociability (Terranova, 2004). In this vein, the 'free' labor generated by these subjects anticipates the form of immaterial labor of which the informationalized economy is composed, and which will be explored in the next part of our chapter.

This chapter is organized in the following way. Taking our cue from A4T, we will first reflect on whether social communities harness free time to work and to what extent participants are aware that their free time is somehow being exploited. In so doing, the notion of immaterial labor is outlined and its relevance to the social community explored. In this discussion we will consider how many virtual communities are flourishing and becoming widespread thanks to the activity of amateurs and their perception of fun. Finally, a reflection on the blurring of work and non-work activities and the unconscious dimension of doing work for web communities is provided. Implications for the future roles of users are discussed in relation to potential directions that 'rewarding criteria' might take.

Freedom, fun, and immaterial labor

In this section, we will investigate the recreational use of A4T, claiming that the labor done by unknowledgeable users is grounded in a deep sense of fun among participants. In extension, we argue that the voluntary participation of A4T users is achieved through a sense of freedom and a significant 'degree of enjoyment' perceived by being in contact with the community's visitors. Similarly, A4T seems to be a place for individuals to realize 'playful production of their own consumption experiences' (Zwick et al., 2008, p. 174).

It is a travel community of users who are willing to share itineraries, adventures, and other travel information with other readers eager to exchange opinions on places to visit and keen to make their journey authentic. From a small group of friends based in Naples (Italy) and joined by the idea of creating a community of friends or guiding Angels in every city, this travel community has rapidly grown since its establishment in 2009 and is now extending to other cities in the world, where people become Angels of their own city. The travel community enables people to participate and bring their expertise in archaeology, history, the arts, local market places, and the like. What is perhaps most interesting about A4T is the one-to-one relationship of the service; each traveler chooses his/her preferred guiding Angel by clicking 'ask for help'. If the request is accepted, the Angels will be charged with providing all useful information to the traveler in order to help him/her plan the journey and will meet with the traveler to guide him/her around the city. A4T is also aimed at attracting visitors by creating membership profiles. People can thus upload videos about their journeys, photos, and texts.

In this chapter, we will look at the A4T platform as a virtual venue where an unpaid mass of creative subjects produces 'free' labor, both in the sense of being unpaid and in the sense of being impossible to command in managing the value generation process (Terranova, 2000). In this sense, we want to reflect on the 'free' labor provided by social community users drawing from the concept of immaterial labor – a source of labor rich in sociability.

In fact, we find this concept useful for the purposes of our analysis when it is applied to online social communities. For instance, Coté and Pybus discuss the concept of '*Immaterial labour 2.0*' as an emerging kind of immaterial labor; specifically, they refer to the 'social and cultural components of labor' related to social networks like MySpace (Coté and Pybus, 2007). Moving from the theorization proposed by Maurizio Lazzarato (Lazzarato, 1997), MySpace is described as grounded in the cultural and communicative skills of its users, where 'the networked capacity is captured as a dynamic source of surplus value' (Coté and Pybus, 2007, p. 90). As observed, continually updating the users' profile on this social interface as well as sharing music, interests, photos, and the like among the community members is the central work undertaken by the users and is based on their cooperation and sociability.

According to Lazzarato's idea concerning the increasing significance acquired by communicational relationships in the post-industrial economy, the concept of immaterial labor has been theorized as an activity 'rich in knowledge' comprising intellectual skills for the production of 'cultural-informational content' (ibid., p. 136), which is constituted in the form of 'networks and cooperation' (Lazzarato, 1997). What is at stake in the theorization of immaterial labor is that labor produces immaterial goods in the form of knowledge, communication, or cultural content, while a constitutive part is referred to the affective labor involved. This latter concept has been subtly discussed by Emma Dowling, who highlights the intangible nature of this labor, put into practice through 'feelings of ease, well being, satisfaction, excitement or passion' in the work performed (Dowling, 2007). Accordingly, 'any type of affective work by definition is social in nature, whereby the worker produces forms of community that rely heavily on the worker's interpersonal skills learned in common with other people throughout their working and non-working life' (ibid., p. 125).

Echoing the suggestion that web platforms tailored to *collaboration* and *participation* are becoming the new ideological paradigm of modernity (Tapscott and Williams, 2006), some scholars (Zwick et al., 2008) have noted that the main source of value occurs today at the point of social communication, where the co-creation activity becomes a 'way of extracting "free" labor'. What is perhaps more interesting in this account is that the exploitation of consumers through coproductive activities is attained in voluntary forms whereby value is produced by social interaction in ways that allow creative new forms of life to continuously emerge (Zwick et al., 2008).

This last point draws our attention to an interesting implication related to the role of the virtual subject, who is expected to become an 'active subject' who brings his personality and subjectivity to the activities undertaken. Putting the user's needs, aspirations, tastes, preferences, and all the attributes that constitute (or that he/she perceives as constituting) his/her inner self at the core of cyberspatial reality means allowing him or her to construct an 'authentic' virtual subjectivity across social platforms (Coté and Pybus, 2007). These are thus experienced by its users as places where they can free themselves – in opposition to the frequent boredom of working life – by putting their creativity and affective capacities into enjoyable activities. Equally, the creative content generated by the web user is deemed to be an important, yet unacknowledged, resource for value generation and reproduction of the 'digital economy'. In this sense, as noted by Land and Böhm, measuring value is becoming one of the main problems in the era of creative capitalism (Land and Böhm, 2009). An interesting point is to what extent the immaterial components – including knowledge, communicative acts, and cooperation – make value immeasurable, and consequently in what way it can be measured as 'free' labor that is somehow exploited. In fact, we argue that the immaterial components of labor, specifically related to sociability and cooperation, have finally resulted in a form of 'free' labor, frequently performed with the expectation of having a more satisfying social life, to gain visibility, or simply to increase one's number of 'friends' from 100 to 5000.

In the digital economy, the concept of 'free' labor has been the subject of a well-informed essay by Tiziana Terranova, in which the connotation of 'free' is intended in the sense of being both 'not financially rewarded and willingly given' (Terranova, 2000, p. 6). Despite the difficulty in distinguishing necessary and surplus value coming from unpaid labor (Land and Böhm, 2009), evidence of this 'free' labor is given, for instance, by open source programmers, amateur web designers, and mailing list editors (Terranova, 2000).

To better explain the nature of this 'free' labor, we can reflect on the creativity that bloggers, users, and all the citizens of virtual platforms perform. In fact, as highlighted by Comor, the object of exploitation is precisely the user's intelligence (Comor, 2010). More to the point, the 'unpaid mass of creative subjects producing free labor' is depicted by Arvidsson, who states that creativity and the mental activity of users in contributing to the digital media are deployed as a form of labor that does not envisage any financial compensation (Arvidsson, 2007, p. 9; 2010).

In drawing attention to the contribution of unpaid digital labor, it seems interesting from our position to reflect on the reasons behind the user's willingness to contribute freely. Is financial recompense the only stimulus to agency? Or is people's participation motivated by the desire to gain recognition? Or might rewards in the form of the satisfaction in contributing to a project that enhances cooperation among people (Hesmondhalgh, 2010) be a 'fair wage' for such contributors? And what about the dichotomy between leisure and work and the pressure that bloggers would feel if they were earning money to post a blog, update a web page, or upload a video?

From free work to new forms of participation?

The core tenets of A4T are '*participation, immersion,* creation of *creative contents* by compiling a travel diary with impressions, photos and videos, and *connection* with a network of locals' (Angels 4 Travellers, 2011). The distinctive feature of this amateur travel community is that it relies on the active role of virtual subjects. These 'activate their knowledge, intelligence and immaterial qualities along the productive processes' (Terranova, 2000) with the aim of generating tourist information and creative content in the form of suggested experiences to have, genuine destinations to visit and trips worth undertaking.

As stated by *The Guardian* (Dodson, 2006), alongside MySpace and Twitter, travel communities are a new frontier in the social networking domain where travelers are encouraged to create content online and participate in discussion forums. Travel experiences are, in fact, prominent for their experiential content. From this perspective, travel planning is conceived as an experience in itself, which needs to be individually constructed by the traveler in order to get as much as possible out of the journey.

The A4T website is thus designed to provide an immersive engagement for its users where the recreational use of the platform is crafted to give a sense of fun and stimulate users' creative ideas. This is the form of creativity described by Arvidsson, who notes that creativity is nowadays mostly produced in relatively autonomous forms of social cooperation whose externality, represented by creative work, is appropriated as a crucial element in the information society's circuit value (Arvidsson, 2007).

The value derived from the production of creative content has been the object of a dispute, as reported by the newspaper *Le Monde* (Ternisien, 2011). A new wave of critics and dissatisfied writers is emerging on the scene; bloggers who provide content to the US number one information website – the *Huffington Post* – have started to request to be paid for the creative content provided. This is the phenomenon described as 'bloggers' tiredness', which the *Huffington Post* managers counter with the visibility argument. Indeed, visibility is one of the reasons put forward for sustaining free collaboration, in which unknown users have the opportunity to acquire a reputation by writing for popular websites. What seems to emerge here is a problem of consciousness of the 'free' worker about the creative content produced.

But can this fundamental tension between 'free' work and visibility acquire a balance in the reality of social media? How long will users be motivated to produce content with only the promise of visibility? Are we moving towards an era of more conscious users? Can the conscious volunteer, by unmasking the rhetoric of fun, enjoyment, and free expression, put himself forward as a subject claiming rights and a fair wage? And in what way will a more demanding user contribute to shaping an innovative criterion of remuneration? Could a creative 'proletariat' (Arvidsson, 2007) become in the long term a driving force in measuring value and in reconstructing a more generous form of labor compensation?

These and similar questions are opening the route to new forms of recompense. Mixing pay with voluntary work was envisaged by some web commentators, who tried to identify potential ways to reward online workers monetarily. For instance, *'pay for tasks that aren't fun'* is a criterion proposed by Andy Oram, but he also recognizes the difficulty of finding a common opinion on what is fun and what is not. Further, *'pay for extraordinary skills'* (Oram, 2010) is another way to pay participants, but the problem is that there is no clear line dividing the extraordinary and the ordinary in terms of the creative content provided.

Conclusion

This chapter draws on the concept of immaterial labor to reflect on the role of the virtual subject in the production of online creative content. Taking as an empirical case a travel platform – A4T – we prompted a reflection on the unpaid participation of digital laborers and to what extent the internet can eventually capitalize on this free labor.

Our reflection was guided by a wider underlying consideration, which is tied to transformations in value understandings, that is, what value is and according to what logic it is produced. We found, indeed, that new means of defining value are surpassing traditional political-economic conceptualizations. The explanation of value based on labor time no longer seems the only measure to determine value. Instead, we argue that new elements – being able to maintain a sense of community, sharing with others, and participating – are taking center stage when value issues are under analysis. In this light, we raised some points on how user immersion can be transformed into economic value and for whom this translation is proving to be advantageous.

In a context where companies seem to show an increased willingness to engage talent from beyond the confines of their offices (Belsky, 2011), it seems important to ask whether future rewards mechanisms are on the horizon and how the Immersive Internet could constantly engage its users.

References

Angels for Travellers (2012) http://www.angelsfortravellers.com/aft/site/it/index

Arvidsson, A. (2007) 'Creative Class or Administrative Class? On Advertising and the Underground', *Ephemera*, 71, 1, pp. 8–23.

Arvidsson, A. (2010) 'Speaking out: The ethical economy: new forms of value in the information society?', *Organization*, 17 (5), pp. 637–644.

Bauman, Z. (2007) *Consuming Life*. Cambridge: Polity Press.

Belsky, S. (2011) *Crowdsourcing is Broken: How to Fix It*, http://www.businessweek.com/innovate/content/jan2010/id20100122_047502.htm

Comor, E. (2010) 'Digital Prosumption and Alienation', *Ephemera*, 10, 3/4, pp. 439–54.

Costea, B., Crump, N., and Amiridis, K. (2008) 'Managerialism, the Therapeutic Habitus and the Self in Contemporary Organizing', *Human Relations*, 61, 5, pp. 661–85.

Costea, B., Crump, N., and Holm, J. (2007) 'The Spectre of Dionysus: Play, Work, and Managerialism', *Society and Business Review*, 2, 2, pp. 153–65.

Coté, M. and Pybus, J. (2007) 'Learning to Immaterial Labour 2.0: MySpace and Social Networks', *Ephemera*, 7, 1, pp. 88–106.

Cova, B. and Dalli, D. (2009) 'Working Consumers: The Next Step in Marketing Theory?'*Marketing Theory*, 9, 3, pp. 315–39.

Dodson, S. (2006) 'What is Travel Networking?', *The Guardian*, 30 September, http://www.guardian.co.uk/travel/2006/sep/30/travelwebsites.travellingsolo? INTCMP=SRCH

Dowling, E. (2007) 'Producing the Dining Experience: Measure, Subjectivity and the Affective Labour', *Ephemera*, 7, 1, pp. 117–32.

Fleming, P. (2005) 'Workers' Playtime? Boundaries and Cynicism in a "Culture of Fun" Program', *Journal of Applied Behavioral Science*, 41, 3, pp. 285–303.

Heelas, P. (2002) 'Work Ethics, Soft Capitalism and the Turn to Life', in Du Gay, P. and Pryke, M. (eds) *Cultural Economy: Cultural Analysis and Commercial Life*. London: Sage.

Hesmondhalgh, D. (2010) 'User Generated Content, Free Labour and the Cultural Industries', *Ephemera*, 10, 3/4, pp. 267–84.

Land, C. and Böhm, S. (2009) *'The New "Hidden Abode" Reflections on Value and Labour in the New Economy'*, Working Paper, University of Essex.

Lazzarato, M. (1997) *Lavoro Immateriale*. Verona: Ombre Corte.

Olsson, T. (2009) *'From the Ecology of Broadcasting to the Economy of Participation'*, Presented at Nord Media, Karlstad, 13–15 August.

Oram, A. (2010) 'Crowdsourcing and the Challenge of Payment', http://radar.oreilly.com/2010/05/crowdsourcing-and-the-challeng.html

O'Reilly, T. (2005) 'What is Web 2.0? Design Patterns and Business Models for the Next Generation of Software', http://www.oreillynet.com/pub/a/oreilly/tim/news/2005/09/30/what-is-web-20.html

Tapscott, D. and Williams, A. D. (2006) *Wikinomics: How Mass Collaboration Changes Everything*. New York: Penguin.

Ternisien, X. (2011) 'La Révolte des Blogueurs', *Le Monde Editions*, 15 April 2011, pp. 18.

Terranova, T. (2000) 'Producing Culture for the Digital Economy', *Social Text*, 6, 18, pp. 33–58.

Terranova, T. (2004) *Network Culture: Politics for the Information Age*. London: Pluto Press.

Van Dijck, J. (2009) 'Users Like You? Theorizing Agency in User-generated Content', *Media Culture & Society*, 31, 1, pp. 41–58.

Van Dijck, J. and Nieborg, D. (2009) 'Wikinomics and its Discontents: A Critical Analysis of Web 2.0 Business Manifestos', *New Media and Society*, 11, 4, pp. 855–74.

Vargo, S. L. and Lusch, R. F. (2004) 'Evolving to a New Dominant Logic for Marketing', *Journal of Marketing*, 68, 1, pp. 211–15.

Warren, S. (2002) 'Show Me How it Feels to Work Here: Using Photography to Research Organizational Aesthetics', *Ephemera*, 2, 3, pp. 224–45.

Zwick., D., Bonsu, S. K., and Darmody, A. (2008) 'Putting Consumers to Work: Co-creation and New Marketing Govern-mentality', *Journal of Consumer Culture*, 8, 2, pp. 163–96.

13
Framing Online Games Positively: Entertainment and Engagement through 'Mindful Loss' of Flow

Müberra Yüksel

> The illiterate of the twenty-first century will not be those who cannot read and write, but those who cannot learn, unlearn, and relearn.
>
> (Alvin Toffler)

Introduction

This chapter deals with online games, and in particular it wrestles with the idea that online gaming and immersion may be emancipatory due to their framing within interactive, decentralized, and self-organizing platforms. If the future of online games takes this route, then it may offer us the chance to move from the 'rule-driven' frames within which many standard video game users become isolated. Playing online games that are embedded in social media such as Facebook and Twitter is more than an individual competition against a computer as a 'rational perfect mirror'; it is both an interactive experience of a second self and a shared group action. It provides the highest degree of focus and concentration simultaneously with social networking. Online games have additional features that provide the user with rich, immediate feedback and that can induce high levels of immersion in the game as well as a feeling of control (Chiang et al., 2011). Thus, this new venue may encourage a state of flow, or an optimal experience from the positive psychology perspective (Csikszentmihalyi, 1991), along with a heightened interest in discovery and creativity if employed properly.

In this chapter, I will first discuss the idea of 'state of flow' and the major characteristics of this 'optimal autotelic experience'– that is, the intrinsic reward resulting from the activities involved in the games themselves. These include clear goals, immediate feedback, loss of a sense of time and self-consciousness, and an integration of the self with the activity (Csikszentmihalyi, 1991). I will then discuss the development of two different game genres – advergames and serious games – and how new media such as the Immersive Internet are enabling their development.

Inducing the 'state of flow'

The state of flow is a concept used by psychologists to describe a mental state in which attention is highly concentrated on a specific process, surrounding environmental information is screened out, and the person experiences a harmonious flow of his or her present experience (Csikszentmihalyi, 1991). The state of flow is known to create a state of well-being as well as increased perception and learning capacity.

In developing flow theory, Csikszentmihalyi used experience sampling methodology (ESM), in which research participants were asked to take notes on their experiences in real time. His research suggests that a player will exhibit different states based upon how challenged they are and the skills demanded of them, and that various combinations of skill and challenge lead to different states: anxiety, apathy, relaxation, or flow. A state of flow avoids states of either anxiety or boredom and is found in any activity, such as a game, where a balance is achieved between external complexity, or the challenge of the system or game program, and the internal model, or the skills a player develops for that particular program. Alternatively, players are likely to be apathetic when they lack challenge and need little skill, or relaxed and bored in situations where skill is needed but little challenge is presented. A player attains a more accurate internal model of the system through learning and virtual experience by trial and error. A state of flow can thus be induced by any activity that is very interesting to a person, for example, watching a movie, reading a book, playing a game. In fact, play is considered as one of the best inducers of the state of flow for children, and often also for adults.

Interaction with internet applications may induce a state of flow in specific circumstances, and numerous researchers have used the Flow Model through different qualitative and quantitative methods to explore various aspects of human online interaction (Chen, 2006; Chiang et al., 2011; Pearce et al., 2004). For example, empirical research on online gaming has demonstrated how, through flow, negative consequences such as addiction to such games can develop. Virtual worlds have also been described as a 'postmodern chronotope' where a loss of a sense of passing time and a loss of perception of space are simultaneous, circumstances that may induce the state of flow (Bakhtin, 1986). However, the findings to date are inconclusive, since controlling for addicted players is not possible and the effect of flow experiences on positive affect is not clear.

Inducing flow in advergaming: a theoretical framework

In the search for non-traditional marketing and business communication that emphasizes pull factors instead of push factors and the growing use of the internet and mobile devices, viral marketing and advertising blogs are attracting increased attention as a potentially inexpensive way of reaching targeted groups of consumers, and in particular youth. Behavioral targeting and mood matching are being used to deliver messages that engage audiences and ensure content is absorbed rather than merely recalled. When engaged in an online gaming session that is challenging, people prefer full engagement and concentration rather than doing simultaneous tasks like chatting. Moreover, people often do not choose between experiences but choose between memories of real or virtual experiences, a finding that may have profound implications for games, simulations, and even the mode of business. Consequently, advergaming has been found to be an effective way to communicate marketing and advertising content to people (Kahneman and Tversky, 2000). While similar to in-game advertising, advergames are not solely about product placement. Rather, they are about stimulating an unforgettable experience as a game player whereby the brand identity or value is covertly enhanced, which demands a different mental frame from all stakeholders (Kretchmer, 2005).

The need to develop new methods of internet advertising arose from the rapid decline in the late 1990s of the effectiveness of rich media banner advertising along with increasing spam of online direct marketing (Yuan et al., 1998). Advergames have been defined as online games that incorporate marketing and communication content. They are interactive games or have game characteristics that are centered on or associated with a brand or a product. Branding and products are incorporated into the game itself through either associative or demonstrative methods – meaning that a game can be used to demonstrate the use of a product or to associate the product with an activity or a lifestyle. The meaning of advergames is multidimensional, since they may be seen as a developing industry, a new advertising system, and a viral marketing tool as well as a form of entertainment.

While such games may hold huge potential (Sennott, 2004), most of the discussion and debate related to advergames is professionally oriented, despite the publicity created by this new advertising method (Bannan, 2002; Hartsock, 2004). Few academic studies have investigated the characteristics of advergames and their influence on consumers' perceptions and behavior (Hernandez et al., 2004; Nelson, 2002). While research does suggest that the most successful websites are those that offer interactive experiences and do not merely provide content, research on the flow experience of players or on distinguishing characteristics of effective advergames to date is limited (see Cauberge and De Pelsmacker, 2010).

As noted above, the existence and maintenance of the state of flow is a dynamic process that depends on the relation between the capabilities of the user – or player in the case of an advergame – and the level of difficulty proposed by the game. Furthermore, if the conditions of user motivation, user telepresence, and interactivity of the internet application are combined, we may begin to develop a model for inducing the state of flow within advergaming. Following on from Csikszentmihalyi, we can imagine there to be three possible simplified scenarios of the interaction between an internet user and an online advergame: frustration (leading to exit), boredom (leading to exit), and flow (leading to continued interest and immersion). When the capability of the player is lower than the level of difficulty of the advergame, the player will experience frustration and will abandon the game with a negative feeling. If the capability of the player is higher than the level of difficulty proposed by the game, a feeling of boredom is likely to result, having as a direct effect the exit of the player from the advergame environment. Finally, if the level of capability of the player and the level of difficulty of the advergame match, the state of flow results and reinforces the motivation of the internet user to revisit the site and to play the game again. However, the situation is more complex than that. Once induced, the maintenance of the state of flow requires a constantly evolving challenge for the player because his/her level of capability is likely to improve after playing the game a few times. This raises the problem of including in the game a progressive level of difficulty that can represent a dynamic challenge for the players.

All sorts of games provide useful tools for generating feedback for game players for experience-based learning. When constructed with different learning styles of individuals in mind, games can accelerate the learning process interactively by repeated experience and recall. The creators of advergames can take advantage of such tools to ensure a maintained state of flow.

Moreover, similarly to any other marketing communication tool, advergame designers must take into consideration (1) the personality of the advertised brand, (2) the profile of the targeted audience, (3) the characteristics of the medium – in this case the internet, and (4) the strategic objectives of the communication campaign. In summary, the creation of an effective advergame is considered as predominantly a creative design work – one that is continuously evolving as online sites become more interactive and immersive.

In my exploratory research on young people in Turkey, I have developed a number of key variables related to the inducement of the state of flow derived from the above model: (1) the *accessibility* of the advergame, (2) the *challenge* of understanding with respect to the rules of the advergame, (3) the *challenge* with respect to the competitiveness of the advergame, (4) the *relevance* of the advergame to the player, (5) the degree of *viral* (word-of-mouth) marketing of the advergame, and (6) the extent of *flow* achieved within the game. I discuss each of these in turn below.

> *Accessibility* depends on the ability to identify the hyperlink between the firm/product site and the game, registration that may be free or required, the specialized software and hardware requirements, and downloading and installation time.
>
> *Difficulty of understanding / challenge one* relates to the ability of the player to access and understand the explicit instructions/rules of the game as well as to commence and continue playing the game.
>
> *Competitiveness level / challenge two* depends on the number of players, the display of score lists, and the multiple levels of difficulty and whether or not the player can choose the level of difficulty.
>
> *Relevance* refers to how relevant the company, brand, or product that is the focus of the advergame is for the player.
>
> *Viral marketing* relates to the degree to which the player communicates about the company, brand, or product that is the focus of the advergame with friends, family, and others.
>
> *Capacity to induce and maintain the state of flow* depends on the multiple levels of difficulty and the possibility offered to players to choose a specific level of difficulty.

Advergames in developing economies

One empirical study in Turkey compared people who play games on the internet, people who use the internet but not for gaming, and people who do not use the internet at all (Youn et al., 2005). The study found that online gamers are the youngest group and have above-average education and income, but that non-gaming internet users enjoy the highest socio-economic status, especially among female adult consumers. Furthermore, online gamers are more impulsive and more open to the internet than the other groups. Online gamers also have the highest degree of novelty-seeking, risk-taking, and word-of-mouth communication. The study's findings also suggest that female adult consumers are expected to be a growing market in the gaming industry, and advertisers have an opportunity to reach female consumers using online games as the venue to promote their brands.

Further research has found that the primary reason why women play games online is to relieve or eliminate stress, while men are mainly attracted by the competitive factor of internet gaming. Women seem to prefer word and puzzle games while men are seemingly more interested in sports, combat, or casino games (Arkadium, 2012). One conclusion from the above studies and other related research is that advertisers need to direct their efforts towards designing gender-specific advergames to better accommodate female consumers (Youn et al., 2005).

From a marketing point of view, these games may be used for various reasons, such as (1) increasing the recognition of a company, brand, or product, (2) associating positive emotions with a company, brand or product, (3) initiating an action of viral marketing, (4) introducing and facilitating a promotional campaign, or (5) inducing a purchasing behavior, that is, increasing the volume of sales.

From advergames to serious games

In addition to in-game advertising, 'serious games' concerning social issues like healthcare, environment or education, city planning and business simulations concerning business ethics may be employed for enhancing multiple perspectives of individuals and their cultural understanding in developing economies. Likewise, exposing individuals to trade-offs between social responsibility and profitability along with ethical dilemmas/challenges would facilitate the development of creative solutions that would enhance their competencies. Through understanding and changing priorities or making difficult choices and coping with their consequent results in solo games, along with learning interactively by practice through teamwork in multiplayer games, active and optimal learning might be possible (see Bos et al., 2006; Mehalow, 2010).

Moreover, the flow experience as a component of online multiplayer games may be explored within the serious games context. For example, we may explore cross-cultural contexts to expand our comprehension of the demarcation between affirmative flow conditions based on perceived challenge–skill balance to enhance focusing, strategic planning, learning, remembering, and developing skills.

On the whole, games can be intrinsically motivating and can be adapted to different styles of learning, such as visual, audio, and kinesthetic means, since games encourage players to engage interactively and through peer-to-peer collaboration. That is why games are gaining significance in both academic and corporate settings, where both formative and summative evaluation are relevant as alternative methods. However, there is a tendency for the current institutions to undermine the value of play in the context of games both at schools and in the workplace. We are not paid to play at work, nor do we study at schools to have fun but to learn, and many schools and businesses are blaming 'addiction' on games.

The recent emergence of serious games as a promising frontier of education has introduced the concept of games designed for a serious purpose rather than pure entertainment. If blended with conventional training, serious games applications like simulations may provide another powerful means of knowledge creation, the transfer and sharing across numerous application domains through 'crowdsourcing' (Howe, 2008). Considering the positive impact of playing games on reducing stress and enhancing problem-solving, critical thinking, creativity, and teamwork, along with the increasing ability to interpret visual cues such as maps, graphs, and other visual displays of data that are underlined in positive psychology by Csikszentmihalyi, 'educational games' will be employed more in business as well as at universities in the future. Moreover, games may make learning fun and meaningful since they can be designed to bridge real-world relevance to theory with practice as a platform for collaboration through simulations. Ordinary life with its issues and incompatible trade-offs is gradually becoming the fantasy world of serious games; therefore, scientific and artistic curiosity will continue to be a potential usage of such on-line games that go beyond the representation of reality.

Conclusion

Computer games in general, and advergames and serious games in particular, have not been major objects of study despite an ever-expanding drive towards consumer culture and commercialization and the preference for 'advertising-as-entertainment'. Thus we need to start thinking deeply about and researching the issues involved with future iterations of the internet that involve advergames as a major genre. Promising areas of empirical research include (1) the relation between the characteristics of the game, the personality of the represented brand, the profile of the targeted audience, and the strategic objectives of the marketing campaign, (2) the influence of advergames on the perceptions, attitudes, and buying behaviors of both serious gamers and more casual game players, and (3) the relation between experiential and material purchasing decision of gamers. As the internet becomes more immersive, theories of flow and virtual marketing communication may be further probed if researchers can understand the reasons why people immerse themselves in various worlds and how they wish to play and interact there, as well as the circumstances that lead to consumer satisfaction through virtual purchases. Indeed, both purchasing and gaming experiences often involve both real and virtual activities. Even solitary virtual experiences may allow more self-involvement and immersion through possible flow. To be able to relate effective advergames to brand awareness, further studies may move beyond descriptive cases or exploratory analyses towards controlled experimental designs or experiential sampling methodology (ESM) based on Csikszentmihalyi's flow model to test the ability of advergames in virtual worlds to affect brand recall, attitude changes, and purchase intentions and actual purchases in the real world, so that comparisons between virtual and material purchases may be possible, and even encourage more conscientious consumers.

While new media technologies such as smart phones and tablets are transforming almost all aspects of our lives, advergames are changing business models towards continuous interaction with consumers. Meanwhile, serious games, through collaboration and engagement, may have affirmative impacts on understanding and solving business dilemmas and even human rights issues through social innovation (McGonigal, 2011, pp. 296–369).

By and large, advergame and serious game designers should consider various issues, such as limiting the time spent in the game, blending face-to-face interaction with online gaming, and using cooperative platforms or creative modes as much as possible. Otherwise, immersive use of games may turn into an escape route for killing valuable time instead of enriching it. That is why parental guidance for children up to 16 years old will be helpful, so that, in the initial stages of entering into gaming culture, they will gradually learn the rules and limits of gaming along with the ability to select the 'right' games. Consequently, raising parental awareness and enhancing digital citizenship and the relevant competencies must be given high priority (see Livingstone et al., 2011).

On the whole, I hope that the use of advergames, serious games, and other forms of digital games may raise the global quality of life and that sustainability through collaboration will be increasingly preferred in the coming gamer generation. The comfort zone of using popular competitive games that enhance only immediate gratification without any concern for global or social issues is a waste of the potential transformative power of both games and gamers. However, I am afraid that escapist entertainment will continue to overshadow serious games in the near future due to limited resources being invested in the relevant research. Moreover, it has also been claimed that the possibility of 'cyber-activism' of alternate reality games on human suffering and the rights of distant others may pave the way to 'false activity' or to 'ethical amnesia' due to compassion fatigue rather than forging an ethical community of human beings, since group identities of 'thick relations' rather than distant strangers often determine our responsible choices (Margalit, 2002; Oliver, 2010; Zizek, 2006). Despite these critical arguments, online games are no longer for isolated nerds, and serious games may well prove effective educational tools in the hands of gamers.

References

Arkadium   (2012)   Arkadium   Social   Gaming   Monetization   Research Report.   http://www.slideshare.net/ArkadiumInc/arkadium-social-gaming-monetization-research-part-1#btnNext Accessed December 14, 2012

Bannan, K. J. (2002) 'Let the Games Begin'. Accessed April 2012, http://www.oracle.com/oramag/profit/02-nov/

Bakhtin, M. M. (1986) *Speech Genres and Other Late Essays*. Austin: University of Texas Press.

Bos, N. D., Shami, N. S., and Naab, S. (2006) 'A Globalization Simulation to Teach Corporate Social Responsibility: Design Features and Analysis of Student Reasoning', *Simulation & Gaming*, 37, 1, pp. 56–72.

Cauberge, V. and Pelsmacker, P. De (2010) 'Advergames: The Impact of Brand Prominence and Game Repetition on Brand Responses', *The Journal of Advertising*, 39, 1, pp. 5–18.

Chen, H. (2006) 'Flow on the Net: Detecting Web Users' Positive Affects and their Flow States', *Computer in Human Behavior*, 22, 2, pp. 221–3.

Chiang, Y.-T., Lin, S. S. J., Cheng, C. Y., and Liu, E. Z. F. (2011) 'Exploring Online Game Players' Flow Experiences and Positive Affect', *The Turkish Online Journal of Educational Technology*, 10, 1, pp. 106–14.

Csikszentmihalyi, M. (1991) *Flow: The Psychology of Optimal Experience*. New York: Harper Perennial.

Hartsock, N. (2004) 'Advergames Newly Viable after All These Years', *E-Marketing IQ*. Accessed December 2011, http://www.emarketingiq.com/news/1409

Hernandez, M. D., Chapa, S., Minor, M. S., Maldonaldo, C., and Barranzuela, F. (2004) 'Hispanic Attitudes toward Advergames: A Proposed Model of Their Antecedents', *Journal of Interactive Advertising*, 5, 1, pp. 74–83.

Howe, J. (2008) *Crowdsourcing*. New York: Crown Publishing Group.

Kahneman, D. and Tversky, A. (eds) (2000) *Choices, Values and Frames*. New York: Cambridge University Press.

Kretchmer, S. (2005) 'Changing Views of Commercialization in Digital Games: In-game Advertising and Advergames as Worlds in Play'. In Proceedings of DIGRA Conf.. 2005. http://www.informatik.uni-trier.de/~ ley/pers/hd/k/Kretchmer:Susan_B=.html Accessed December 14, 2012

Livingstone, S., Haddon, L., Görzig, A., and Ólafsson, K., with members of the EU Kids Online Network (2011) *Risks and Safety on the Internet*: *The Perspective of European Children*. London: LSE, EU Kids Online, www.eukidsonline.net for updates on this ongoing project in 25 countries.

Margalit, A. (2002) *The Ethics of Memory*. Cambridge: Harvard University Press.

McGonigal, J. (2011) *Reality Is Broken: Why Games Make Us Better and How They Can Change the World*. New York: Penguin Press.

Mehalow, C. (2010) 'Teaching Sustainable Values through Serious Gaming', *Games that Can Change the World*. Accessed March 2011, http://www.triplepundit.com/2010/11/teaching-sustainable-values-serious-gaming/

Nelson, M. R. (2002) 'Recall of Brand Placements in Computer/Video Games', *Journal of Advertising Research*, 42, 2, pp. 80–92.

Oliver, S. (2010) 'Stimulating the Ethical Community: Interactive Game Media and Engaging Human Rights Claims', *Culture, Theory and Critique*, 51, 1, pp. 93–108.

Pearce, J. M., Ainley, M., and Howard, S. (2004) 'The Ebb and Flow of Online Learning', *Computer in Human Behavior*, 21, pp. 327–63.

Sennott, S. (2004) 'Advertising: The Latest Marketing Trend Makes the Consumer a Player Inside the Commercial', *Newsweek*, International Edition.

Yuan, Y., Caulkins, J. P., and Roehrig, S. (1998) 'The Relationship between Advertising and Content Provision on the Internet', *European Journal of Marketing*, 32, 7–8, pp. 677–87.

Youn, S., Mira, L., and Doyle, K. (2005) *Lifestyles of Online Gamers: A Psychographic Approach*. Accessed September 2011.

Zizek, S. (2006) *How to Read Lacan*. London: Granta Books.

14
Inhabitants of Virtual Worlds, Players of Online Video Games – Beware!

Antti Ainamo and Tuukka Tammi

Too much of a good thing?

Massively multiplayer online role-playing games (MMORPGs), virtual worlds, and online games that resemble them amount to a force that is both a force of light and a force of darkness. As a force of light, they provide for many a rich environment full of possibilities for recreation and entertainment, 'an increasingly central part of both American culture and of an emerging global culture...that...has the power to re-mold the 21st century at least as radically as cinema and television did the 20th' (Chatfield, 2010, Ch. 1). MMORPGs, as well as all other online games and virtual worlds that resemble their workings, are also spaces where real-world money can be made, with more than 80 current titles and many more under development, targeted at a player population that totals around 30 million worldwide. World of Warcraft, by Blizzard Entertainment in Irvine, California, was already in 2007 earning close to $1 billion a year in monthly subscriptions and other revenue (Dibbell, 2007). By 2012, it is clear that *nomen est omen* and the MMORPG business has become a massive phenomenon, burgeoning in size and scope around the world as we have known it, as well as in the virtual worlds where this new game species breeds. We are facing a global and all-encompassing immersive experience.

As a force of darkness, and as a source of despair, MMORPGs and other online games and virtual worlds leverage the fact that the recreation, entertainment, and business advantages are not all there is. These are games that are gaining power and influence over an increasing amount of people, taking hold of the psyche. In a typical MMORPG like World of Warcraft, each player leads his fantasy character on a life of combat and adventure that may last for months or even years of play. With that level of immersion, the need to spend money and time also invades the real world of a player. The originally 'casual player' becomes dependent on and, over time, addicted to playing. The business corporations derive their huge revenue by exploiting the addiction of immersed players and the immersion of casual ones.

In this chapter, we review ultra-new strands of evidence that extreme immersion by players in MMORPGs, online video games, or virtual worlds may potentially lead to mental and behavioral disorder in the brains and the neurological reward systems of these players. The ways in which this happens, we seminally outline, are similar to how harmful chemical substances such as alcohol or drugs infiltrate the brain. The process of evolution, in our view, takes place in five phases: (1) casual play, (2) immersion, (3) engagement, (4) flow, and (5) addiction. The sequence is a series of gateways and stepping stones towards a near-deterministic climax, followed by a state of entropy of the fragments of the mind.

The first phase: casual play

If not a primordial or pre-modern experience, learning to play an MMORPG or any other online game can be likened to the early-modern experience of learning to be a painter. Now, as then, there is no school or university in which to learn by rote how to become a master of one's art. Before having rights to private audience with the master, it is important that the apprentice learns elementary skills of the art in question. Insight develops on the basis of developing elementary skills into more refined ones. Learning in the first instance takes place by doing, by a gradual process of casual interest, by the development of the interest into a true hobby. Only after much practice, much in the same way as in an Academy of Art in the time of the Renaissance, does an apprentice have any legitimate right to talk 'one-on-one' with a master.

Like the novice or even apprentice painter, novice players first train in practical terms on their own, on the fringes of virtual worlds or at the bottom of MMORPGs, before being recognized as legitimate by more experienced master-players. Thus, any player begins his or her journey into virtual worlds and video games typically as a 'casual' player, at first of a typical role-playing game (RPG), such as the classic and originally pre-digital Dungeons & Dragons. This kind of player will typically be happy at first to observe what more experienced players are doing in this new world. These persons will take the naïve pleasure and delight of innocent newborns in being able to 'read' in an elementary way the architecture of this virtual world. They will delight in the ways this new world unfolds in their senses and fools them. They will learn to converse a little, in elementary ways, in this world. Then, they will notice that there is also an MMORPG version of Dungeons & Dragons called 'Dungeons & Dragons Online: Stormreach', and that there are also many other MMORPGs that immerse each player to lead a fantasy character on a life of combat and adventure that may last for months or even years of play. They may occasionally appear to be engaged in critical talk about the MMORPG. They will also talk about it with their friends in the real world outside. To the true aficionados, the latter will be a sign that they must remain an outsider to the essence of what the MMORPG is about. They do not take the MMORPGs sufficiently seriously. For them, the virtual world is only a pastime or a technological artifact peripheral to what really matters in everyday life. They do not show virtual character as yet.

Then, however, one day, they may have a fleeting passion, a fling, really, in trying out an MMORPG or some other online game. When this relationship does not last, they may then develop the right kind of passion with another MMORPG or other online game. This is precisely how they get sucked in. They pass through an important gateway and stepping stone towards becoming dependent and – over time – addicted.

The second phase: immersion

Games are designed to plug into our deep human desire to learn, so the games can indeed provide neurological 'highs' similar to consuming alcohol or sugar. We believe four basic motives drive playing video games, spending time in virtual worlds, or both. These four motivations are: (a) killer instinct, (b) adventure, (c) exploration, and (d) socialization. In or across each of these four motivations, players will experience a strange mix of freedom and constraint. A player will spend time explaining why the fluid sense of identity that the gaming experience offers is worth the expense of money, time, or both, playing ever-demanding roles and games to the extent that playing begins to compete with activities in the boring everyday life of the real world.

A virtual world is a space where one's identity is entirely composed of one's words and actions. There are obvious benefits to being able simply to circumvent any kind of prejudice; such benefits are potentially huge.

All of a sudden, one can be in any optimal social category one fancies at that point. One can, say, be attractive and aged between 20 and 35, when in the real world one is 13, or an old man. Besides age, a virtual world is also a tremendous leveler in terms of wealth, appearance, education, and race. The tip of this increasingly disturbing iceberg of video game abuse and addiction is that the playing experience in a video game or a virtual world will tend to appear to 'magnify' the player's personality. In 2007, an American Medical Association's study found that as many as five million Americans (ages 8–18) might be addicted to gaming, including, but not limited to, MMORPGs.

One of the first signals of immersion having gone too far in developing one's false or provisional self is ever-deeper dives into the ways of inhabiting a virtual world. Dedicated players have in more than one study been found to spend between 21 and 40 hours a week playing MMORPGs, while players of other games report playing under six hours week. Many, as a result of being more and more accustomed to virtual space and the assumptions of an emerging 3D internet as a fully artificial life and correspondingly less and less used to everyday carnality, begin to think of avatars and the virtual world as 'more real' than the less-imagined real people of what other real people consider the real world. In their virtual reality, what kind of 'real' matters is a question answered on the basis of what is for them, personally, the most 'real' affects. They will know the social cues, codes, and roles that one is expected to know in a virtual world but lose touch of what is expected of them in the real world, and how to behave there.

Another signal of emergent addiction is resorting to consumption of one or another of the many higher-order 'value-added services' that are cropping up in virtual games. These services are designed for players who begin to lack time to play the game and develop their virtual identity, provisional self, or habitus as much as they would like. Some of them resort to the services of 'gold farmers' who play online games such as World of Warcraft and then sell the loot and/or level acquired in the game to them for real-world dollars. New York journalist Julian Dibbell even spent a year documenting how he made a living simply by playing games and selling off his virtual rewards. In 2010, the going rate for 100 Warcraft gold coins was about $3, and those 100 gold coins were then resold by international brokers for as much as $20. To some of us, the idea of spending real money on pretend money or loot may seem absurd, but the demand for what 'gold farmers' provide exists, even if it goes against the End User License Agreement (EULA) that most games have.

Many consider that virtual worlds are also the future of education and, by extension, of social change. Games for Change, a New York-based company, promotes the use of video games as tools for raising political and social awareness, considering words such as 'engaging', 'challenge and reward', and 'balance' most apt to describe its offering. While immersion is thus a good thing in terms of developing a casual form of recreation into a hobby that provides significance and meaning, it can go too far. A psyche that is overly immersed will lose any sense of distinction between the virtual and real worlds. When immersed in a world, perceptions, reactions, and interactions all take place according to the cues, codes, and role-play and in the landscape of the virtual world. The virtual world in itself usually suggests a single worldview, with few alternative understandings or interpretations of the significance and meaning of that landscape or views of any other landscape. The understanding will be purely 'intra-world' (Douglas and Hargadon, 2000), characterized by closure.

The third phase: engagement

Emerging criticism and evidence suggest that there is a dire need to become more critical regarding MMORPGs, video games, and virtual worlds. What is called for is what can be termed 'engagement'. It can also be called 'a critical stance', the players' perceptions, reactions, and interactions assuming an extra-textual perspective of the virtual world itself as well as other landscapes that have shaped it and meanings and significances operating within it. The understanding includes 'inter-world' understandings or an ability to juggle multiple worldviews that, in turn, will help to reconcile the psychological differences between the real world and one or several virtual worlds. Clearly, both immersion and engagement represent the ideals or goals of affective experience, when the goal is a sustained recreational and fun experience. A horror movie is fun when seen as an escape from the boredom of everyday life, not as a nightmare come permanently true day after night and night after day. One example of the productive interplay of immersion and engagement is Stardoll, a highly successful Swedish–Finnish virtual world (*Helsingin Sanomat*, 2010). The background of this success story is that a Finnish-born girl by the name of Liisa drew paper dolls from a young age and dreamed of becoming a fashion designer. She was very immersed in this pastime even when the tools at her disposal were pre-modern, consisting of only water colors and paper. Passion and immersion in her art kept Liisa going, drawing paper dolls and designing clothes to dress them up. However, it was only when her son created a business corporation for her – Paperdoll Heaven – that things started happening. An increasingly growing user base showed potential for venture funding, and a new CEO with a proven track record in online business was recruited to manage the company.

The fourth phase: flow

It can be proposed on the basis of the Stardoll case that the engagement of professionals with immersed creatives can result in new framings and a flow experience for all those concerned. In other words, the case of Stardoll, we believe, is proof of the emerging modernization of MMORPGs and other online games and virtual worlds. More conceptually, we believe Stardoll is an example of how an online game can result in an optimal flow experience in MMORPGs, at least in passing.

Like others, we define 'flow' as an optimal, extremely enjoyable experience when an individual engages in an activity with total involvement, concentration, and enjoyment and experiences an intrinsic interest and sense of time distortion during his/her engagement. When in the flow state, people become absorbed in their activity, and the focus of awareness is narrowed down to the activity itself. The concentration is so intense that there is no attention left over. Irrelevant perceptions and thoughts are screened out and worries about problems disappear. In short, the term flow was given to describe the best feeling and the most enjoyable experience possible in human lives as 'the bottom line of existence' (Csikszentmihalyi, quoted in Chen et al., 2000).

Flow seems to be the engine of evolution, propelling human beings to a higher level of complexity and to improved psychological well-being. When an activity stimulates an individual's enjoyment and peak experience, this engagement frequently promotes psychological growth and increased personal skills. Studies have found that time spent in adolescent life in a state of flow contributes to experiencing student life, later, as a time that is cheerful, friendly, sociable, and happy. Thus, not surprisingly, the optimal combination of immersion and engagement in flow has had many implications in terms of marketing, neurosciences, literature research, art, and virtual-worlds research.

In flow, the activity in which a person is engaged becomes autotelic, or intrinsically rewarding, because the activity itself, which is fun and enjoyable, already provides enough motivation to do it. In order to duplicate the experience of exhilaration, an individual must slightly increase the challenge level and also develop his/her skill level to meet the increased challenges. This continual process guides human beings into a world of slight complexity and slight uncertainty, which in turn drives human beings to evolve. Many behavioral disorders are the result of boredom. One recent study found that the self-esteem of women is significantly higher when the challenges and skills are higher than average and they are in a state of flow.

Certainly flow can help even a man achieve peak performance, promote psychological growth, and increase personal skills. However, just like any phenomenon, flow in its essence is a neutral experience that can result in positive and negative effects in its application. Since flow experience is enjoyable, people like to duplicate their experience as much as possible. Under certain situations, people may abuse their time and indulge themselves. In any situation when the process of experiencing flow is not employed to create positive activity that is beneficial to people or society as a whole, the situation can generate harmful and negative results. Thus, in more ways than one, the flow experience is similar to addiction, which turns an experience of intensive involvement and immersion into a destructive force in personal life. Below, we look at addiction in more detail.

The fifth and final phase: addiction

In ways formerly believed to belong only to science fiction (Gibbons, 1984), there is now an emerging understanding of video games and virtual worlds as being similar to substances such as alcohol and drugs; that is, one can become dependent on having more of the same, or at least a more or less constant supply of the same. As one proof of the face-validity of the emerging understanding, 'detox centers' for World of Warcraft can now be found, acknowledging the fact that a MMORPG is like a psychoactive, mind-altering chemical substance. As proof that there is no quick and easy cure for addiction to MMORPGs, or the internet more generally, cures tend to be available in the first stages only on the internet (e.g., *WoWdetox*, 2011). Re-emerging from a virtual world and back to the behavioral order that functions in the real world has been proposed to demand up to 14 steps and phases (*WikiHow*, 2011).

Internet addiction has been identified as a pathological behavior, but its symptoms may be found in normal populations, placing it within the scope of conventional theories of media attendance. Conceptualizations of gratifications specific to the internet that are emerging appear to uncover seven kinds of gratification factors (Song et al.,

2004): (1) virtual community membership, (2) seeking and finding information, (3) aesthetic experience, (4) monetary compensation, (5) diversion (i.e., recreation, entertainment, having fun), (6) personal status, and (7) relationship maintenance.

Four of the above seven gratification factors (virtual community membership, monetary compensation, diversion, and personal status) appear to account for more than a quarter (28 per cent, to be exact) of the variance in internet addiction tendency. With no parallel in prior research, the first of these (i.e., virtual community membership) might be termed a 'new' gratification. Besides online games and virtual worlds, the relationship between internet addiction and gratifications has been identified in the context of formation of media habits and the distinction between content and process gratifications. The American Society of Addiction Medicine has the following definition of addiction:

> Addiction is a primary, chronic disease of brain reward, motivation, memory and related circuitry. Dysfunction in these circuits leads to characteristic biological, psychological, social and spiritual manifestations. This is reflected in the individual pursuing reward and/or relief by substance use and other behaviors. The addiction is characterized by impairment in behavioral control, craving, inability to consistently abstain, and diminished recognition of significant problems with one's behaviors and interpersonal relationships. Like other chronic diseases, addiction can involve cycles of relapse and remission.

Still, at the time of writing this chapter, there is as yet no formal medical category for MMORPG addiction or related addiction in other forms of gaming, virtual worlds, or both. However, the American Psychiatric Association (APA) is currently renewing its *Disease Classification Manual*, which it plans to release in 2013. The DSM, this almost universal 'bible' to diagnose behavioral-health problems, will include a new disease category: 'addiction-like behavioral disorders'. Within that new category, one of the drafted subcategories is 'Internet addiction'. In the DSM, there are ten behavioral criteria for addiction, two of which have traditionally been considered core items: increased tolerance and withdrawal symptoms.

The fact is that almost any kind of behavior can develop into a dependency, and any dependency can develop into an addiction. The majority of video game and virtual world aficionados and supporters tend to be overly vocal, short-sighted, and ineffective in their defenses of their beloved pastime. Short-term fun for the player, or rapid growth of revenue for the successful game owner, turns into its opposite. Unless the player is able to stop immersing himself or herself and devoting an ever-increasing share of his or her time and resources to playing, or there is a successful intervention, the addictive personality will suffer such behavioral disorder until the end.

Heed this warning, call for help

Beginning as an innocent pastime, the inhabitancy of a virtual world can habitualize, lead into first occasional and then regular immersion, and finally evolve into addiction. Standing apart from such immersion, with critical distance and a period of trial engagement rather than rushing into real life-long inhabitancy, can, for a time, maintain a healthy balance between inhabitancy in one world and inhabitancy in another. The critical forms of cognition, typically cognizance of one's playing, can even evolve into a temporary state of flow and feelings of a healthy distance in one's amount of gaming and inhabitancy of MMORPGs and other virtual worlds. With growing tolerance of the effects of playing, and with ever-worsening withdrawal symptoms, even an apparently critical and detached stance towards online play environments can evolve into a loss of distinction between one's psyche and the external world. A critical stance of engagement before giving one's heart away for good is not a permanent solution. Rather, engagement is a solution whose valence tends to degenerate over time. Over time, the engaged individual often loses touch with the real world despite temporary solace from a critical stance. The player who believes engagement will keep immersion in check, when it really does not, deceives him or herself.

This chapter is a word of warning for all players 'in there', whether in a MMORPG or another virtual world. Beware of losing yourself. Join us in a call for research on addiction of ourselves and those out there, to develop an understanding of how to prevent or overcome our addiction to an MMORPG or a similar online game, and we and other potential addicts can learn from each other how to keep the requisite control. Finally, this chapter is a call for those who are the in-betweens – counselors, teachers, and psychiatrists – to help bring back human minds that are at one with a virtual world. Please help those who already need help, as well as those, even more numerous, who will need help in years to come.

References

Chatfield, T. (2010) *Fun Inc.: Why Gaming Will Dominate the Twenty-First Century*. New York: Pegasus Books.

Chen, H., Wigand, R. T., and Nilan, M. (2000) 'Exploring Web Users' Optimal Flow Experiences', *Information Technology & People*, 13, 4, pp. 263–81.

Dibbell, J. (2007) 'The Life of the Chinese Gold Farmer', *New York Times Magazine*, 17 June 2007.

Douglas, Y. and Hargadon, A. B. (2000) 'The Pleasure Principle: Immersion, Engagement, Flow', *Paper Presented at the Conference on Hypertext and Hypermedia*, San Antonio, TX. USA, 30 May–3 June, pp. 153–60.

Gibbons, W. (1984) *Neuromancer*. New York: Ace Books.

Helsingin Sanomat (2010) 'Liisa Wrang: The Rags-to-Riches Story behind Stardoll', *Helsingin Sanomat*, 7 December 2010. Accessed 15 January 2011, http://www.hs.fi/english

Song, I., Larose, R., Eastin, M. S., and Lin, C. A. (2004) 'Internet Gratifications and Internet Addiction: On the Uses and Abuses of New Media', *Cyberpsychology & Behavior*, 7, 4, pp. 384–94.

WikiHow (2011) 'How to Break a World of Warcraft Addiction', *WikiHow*. Accessed 30 June 2011, http://www.wikihow.com/Break-a-Worldof-Warcraft-Addiction

WoWdetox (2011) 'WoWdetox is a Volunteer-Run Web Site Aimed at Helping People with Gaming Addiction to the World of Warcraft. Here Gamers and Ex-gamers Can Share Their Testimonies Freely and Anonymously', *WoWdetox*. Accessed 30 June 2011, http://www.wowdetox.com

15
Relationships, Community, and Networked Individuals

Rhonda McEwen and Barry Wellman

The 'I' in community

The internet and mobile phones are intertwined with social relationships. In this chapter, we focus on relationships with neighbors, strangers, Twitter-folk, romantic interests – and in particular we emphasize relationships with friends. Friendships function as a social glue of contemporary Western society. Friends and friendships are a popular choice for song titles from as far back as Joseph Scriven's 1855 hit 'What a Friend We Have in Jesus' to Kate Nash's 2010 release of 'My Best Friend Is You'.

As people increasingly use both online and in-person means to connect with each other, a recurring theme emerges both in the popular press and in academic discourse on whether technology is making us better or worse off as communities; this is also known as the 'community question' and persists even today. We maintain that, while community has never been lost, there is a need to understand what kinds of community flourish, what communities do – and do not do – for people, and how communities operate in different social systems. As the internet and mobile phones have infiltrated contemporary life, analysts have had to move from seeing these technologies as providing alternative or external worlds for people to seeing how they have become integrated into the complexity of everyday life (Rainie and Wellman, 2012).

Relationships in personal communities

Personal community research invokes a certain understanding of 'community'. Instead of regarding communities as bound up with organized institutions such as family, neighborhood, work, or voluntary organizations, personal community research treats communities as the network of personal relationships to which a given individual belongs and that he or she manages. When we think of relationships in the everyday sense, we initially think about the people in our personal communities who are close to us – those people with whom we are intimate and share deep affection, those with whom in the vernacular sense we are *in a relationship*, like our boyfriends, girlfriends, spouses, and partners. We recall persons with whom we have a longer history and memory, such as our *relations*, including parents, siblings, and in many societies extended family, who may not be blood relatives but whom we still call 'aunt' or 'uncle' as markers of the role that they play in our family life. And we may think of some people who have shared specific and significant experiences with us so that we are associated with each other in *relation* to something, like sorority sisters, hockey team members, or work colleagues.

Authenticity of online relationships

Along with the rise of the internet and mobile communication in relationships (including social networking software applications), some have questioned whether online relationships are authentic; that is, how do they measure up to the gold standard of face-to-face interaction which is the 'real' thing? Even the Pope (Benedict XVI) expressed his viewpoint in his World Communications Day message 2009 when he recognized the power of the internet for spreading information but cautioned that people need to get away from their computers and meet in person. In the Philippines, the Catholic Church sends text messages to community members to keep the flames of the parishioner–church relationship going while at the same time encouraging parishioners to attend services.

For a while, many viewed the internet as a realm separate from the concreteness and realness of the physical world. For example, some pundits imagined the internet as a sacred forum of interaction that would make socio-economic status markers arcane and time constraints irrelevant while simultaneously bringing together diverse people with shared interests (Rheingold, 2000; Turkle, 2005; Wellman and Hogan, 2004). Although we still deal with media queries about the supposedly isolating nature of the media (Anderson, 2006), consistently research has made it clear that the internet is in fact seamlessly integrated with personal communities and is rarely a separate second life in itself.

While much of the effort involved in forming, maintaining, and even terminating relationships takes place in the offline spaces of school cafeterias, shopping malls, and homes, virtual places assembled by information and communication technologies (ICTs) increasingly provide fertile ground for sociality. Virtual places are constructed via instant messaging, text messaging, wikis, blogs, social networking software (e.g., Facebook, MySpace), massively multiplayer online role-playing games (MMORPGs), and other social media like Twitter. They offer unstructured environments for 'hanging out', and the content of social life enacted virtually mirrors that of the offline world. This is particularly true of young people, who 'gather in networked publics to negotiate identity, gossip, support one another, flirt, joke and goof-off' (boyd, 2008, p. 170).

Increasingly, people do not generally differentiate between offline and virtual places in an overtly conscious way. Expressions such as, 'See you later', or references to conversations like, 'He told me that...' could as easily refer to face-to-face encounters as they could an instant message (IM) exchange or a turn in the game World of Warcraft (WoW). These places are just alternate spaces for people of all ages to connect with their friends and peers; technology-enabled interaction fits seamlessly into their everyday lives and complements other practices (Abbott, 1998; boyd, 2008; McEwen, 2010; Osgerby, 2004).

These online interactions are perceived to be as real to people as their offline contacts and are valued as authentic. Socializing using communication technology and socializing face-to-face result in an altered conceptualization of 'community' especially relevant to young people. Relationships are created, maintained, terminated, and recalled in both sets of places. The rapid emergence of computer-mediated communications means that relations in cyberspaces are combining with relations on the ground (McEwen, 2010; Wellman, 2001). These different forms of interaction should be considered as complementary, and taken together they represent the channels selected by an individual for sociality. For the networked individual, 'community' is not geospecific but is defined as networks of personal communities that provide sociability, support, information, a sense of belonging, and social identity, managed on and offline using ICTs (Rainie and Wellman, 2012).

Forming relationships online

This leads us to briefly consider the ways in which relationships are formed online. The current body of internet research indicates that the internet has not caused a widespread flourishing of new relationships that are disembodied, existing only in the realm of an immersive online world. In reality, only a relatively small proportion of internet users have ever met someone new online. Two large-scale national surveys conducted in 1995 and 2000 indicate that only about 10 per cent of internet users have ever met someone new online (Katz and Aspden, 1997; Katz and Rice, 2002). It is probably safe to assume that at least some of these relationships were short-lived, fizzling over time. Many of the relationships that do continue to exist for a longer duration tend to migrate offline. Evidence for this has been found in two studies of relationships formed through online newsgroups, showing that the desire to meet internet friends in person is common among those who make new friends online (McKenna et al., 2002; Parks and Floyd, 1996).

This is not to deny that an online forum might be important to making new friends, especially when physical or psychological barriers make in-person meetings difficult. Research indicates that people who felt physically isolated or dissatisfied with their own self-image were more prone to use an online forum for making friends. Nevertheless, once the friendship was established, there was a common desire to meet in person, implying that people wanted a broader range of interactions than online communication could easily supply (Boase and Wellman, 2005).

These findings can be summarized as follows. First, a relatively small minority of internet users actually use the internet to communicate with people whom they do not already know from their everyday lives. Second, of the minority who do form relationships online, those relationships often become incorporated into offline life. In other words, it is not the case that the internet has immersed people in a new world of social relationships with others whom they never see in the flesh. While the internet does create a new venue through which people may form new relationships, at present, this venue represents only one small aspect of the internet's role in personal relationships for the majority of its users.

In many parts of the world, social networking software such as Facebook and MySpace has often superseded email and instant messaging as the main way for students and young adults to keep track and stay connected to their personal communities (boyd, 2008; Lenhart et al., 2005; McEwen, 2010). In Canada, Facebook adoption within urban centers is especially high. Twenty-two per cent of Toronto's population (aged 18+), 16 per cent of Montreal's population, 32 per cent of Vancouver's population, and 54 per cent of Halifax's population have a Facebook profile (Zinc Research and Dufferin Research, 2009). By contrast, in the US at the same time, 80 per cent of visits to all social networking sites were to MySpace (Zinc Research and Dufferin Research, 2009), while elsewhere in the world Bebo, Hi5, Orkut, Cyworld, and Friendster were also popular.

The evidence demonstrates that romantic, kinship, and friendship relationships continue to exist and flourish with new forms of media to facilitate communicative exchanges. Absolutely you may still see distant cousins over a Thanksgiving weekend, but you may also be sending photos of the turkey dinner on Pinterest, Instagtam, or Flickr to Aunt Judy working abroad in Kenya. Teens may still be surly and monosyllabic on the telephone with granny, but she can still keep up with their more lively moments on Facebook. The focus is no longer, or should no longer be, on whether or not relationships are rising or falling in a hyperconnected world, but on the interplay of online and offline relationships for the networked individual.

Multiplexity: when your neighbor is more than a neighbor

Creating relationship categories such as friend, family, coworker, and neighbor is not only helpful in considering network structures and analyzing forms of interaction but is part of the way we make sense of our everyday lives. In the transition from place-based to person-centered networks, in a certain sense there is a broadening of definitions that in the past have held location-specific meanings. A prime example of this is the term *neighbor*, which conjures up images of people chatting casually over a backyard fence in the style of Tim Allen of the TV series *Home Improvement*. However, for many of the relationships that we have with others there is more than one category that could simultaneously characterize a single individual, and this is especially so in the age of the triple revolution, where a neighbor may be more than a neighbor. Your boss may be someone with whom you socialize on a regular basis, your spouse may be your closest confidant, and your neighbor could be your archrival in the online fantasy hockey pool. When in a relationship with someone who takes on multiple roles in different social arenas of your life, we say that the relationship is multiplexed.

Relationships, both on and offline, exhibit multiplexity. For networked individuals, significant amounts of communication with another person over a period certainly contribute to the broadening of the relationship, so that the weekly chats over the fence with the neighbor can grow into a friendship. Increased interaction also strengthens the relationship so that it becomes a natural progression to invite the neighbor over for a coffee or take his dog for a walk when he, now your friend, is ill.

Communicative intensity across multiplexed media drives us to share more of ourselves with overlapping audiences. Apologies for multiple cross-postings are sympathetically accepted as the cognitive load of remembering who is in which groups or who is on only some lists becomes too much to manage. The networked individual finds some relief in using social media aggregators like TweetDeck, Flipboard, or Glossi. Yet the pressing urge to connect with all groups while reducing the number of communicative transactions to maintain your sanity, leads to a glomming together of groups and media types that may be less than you were hoping for.

When the networked individual manages relationships through a wide variety of media, such as email, landline telephone, instant messaging, Facebook, Twitter, mobile phone, and so on, we describe both the relationship and the media as being multiplexed. Multiplexity is very often a good thing; however, there are sometimes good reasons why you don't want your rabbi to be your MySpace friend or your stepmother to start texting you daily. Some relationships are better when confined to a specific arena.

One of the complications of the networked society is the growing difficulty of intentionally keeping people in separate roles. A significant part of the problem is that the networked individual is publicly accessible from many different media routes, is searchable via browsers, and often does not know how to delicately navigate requests from persons in their lives who wish to extend the relationship by virtue of being part of another media group. While it is true that we use different media to communicate with the same individual, there is evidence that we associate certain types of relationship roles with certain media. For example, while mobile phones are predominantly used in communications with strong, personal, and intimate relationships, email is associated with more formal and work-related relationships. So, when an undergraduate student asks for a professor's mobile phone number, a small butterfly takes flight.

Demultiplexing relationships is complicated and often technically impossible given system design. Some systems remember too much, and really erasing the memory of an individual in a specific role requires a major effort. After developing a relationship based on reciprocal messaging, it is difficult to delete your brother from your Twitter feed while trying to keep your sibling relationship intact. People know when you have deleted their number from your mobile phone contact list or blocked their forwards on email. And then it becomes an all-or-nothing scenario as the relationship hits a socio-technical bump.

Ephemerality: here today, unfriended tomorrow

The triple revolution is accompanied by new ways of expressing relationships and relations. The use of the word *friend* expanded significantly in this decade. The proliferation of social networking software such as Facebook, where the word 'friend' is used as a way to indicate a count of the numbers of people associated within the application, reflects a shift in the meaning of the word among the general population. For example, Oxford University Press chose Facebook's 'unfriend' as the word of the year for 2009.[1] It is a way to express a relationship change in a way that previously did not exist in a single word. 'I broke it off with Frank', 'I dumped Belinda', 'I got rid of Terri' are now simply represented by a status change from 'in a relationship' to 'single' and a missing person in the friend list. Gone, dismissed, simply – unfriended.

In a comedic ditty, Garrison Keillor strums the following verse on his YouTube video rendition of 'Unfriended': 'the hourly updates on your activities, Your joys, your pain, your sensitivities, All of the parties you have attended, No, I've been unfriended' (*Unfriended* by Garrison Keillor, 2009).

In a few keystrokes, it is possible to rid oneself of a former friend and announce this to everyone else in the group. Of course, it is more complicated than that. When relationships break down, whether and how the connection is severed depends on multiple factors. Also, for close relationships, unfriending someone at the technological level does not necessarily cauterize the emotional process of dealing with the loss. No matter how good it feels to slam the Facebook door on them, it is still a relationship damaged. Having a fight and deciding not to deal with someone in the future can now take place on a stage that is an order of magnitude more public than before social media.

Unfriending is a public statement that the relationship has been compromised, and communicates volumes not just to the unfriended but to the networked audience as well. An unfriending kicks off a wave of support, queries, and interest from the network. Also, since the unfriended person more likely than not knows others on the list, they witness first-hand some of the spectacle via the connections of other network members. Depending on the centrality of the unfriender, this information may flow quite quickly to even far-flung networks. What we find curious is that, although applications such as Facebook model the real world by creating a system for both parties in a relationship to consent to being connected, there is no system-generated way for both parties to communicate a mutual unfriending. There is no proxy for 'we decided it was better for both of us to go our separate ways'.

The transitory nature of many relationships implies that social relationships are not only being lost, they are also being formed. High turnover creates a demand for the internet as a means both to form new relationships and to build upon existing relationships. For example, Hampton and Wellman found that people moving to a suburb in Toronto, given the pseudonym 'Netville', used the internet to maintain ties with former neighbors (Hampton and Wellman, 2002). As the research discussed above indicates, it appears that the internet is being used for both purposes, although more often for the latter. Although online forums are not particularly common ways to meet new people, they nevertheless aid those who might have trouble forming relationships by typical means offline. For the rest of the population, internet use provides a way to maintain new relationships by 'keeping in touch' and arranging times to meet in person. The Netville project also indicates that the internet can be used to form new relationships among neighbors. Moreover, we theorize that computer-mediated communication might also be particularly useful in ending relationships, as it may be emotionally easier to ignore digital messages than to ignore people in face-to-face situations.

Virtuality: the person behind the avatar

Relationships for the contemporary networked individual include those with persons to whom we feel close as well as to those persons considered more distant, and they cover the range from those whom we see face-to-face daily to those with whom we primarily interact online. Relationships with persons whom we have never met are called virtual, distinguishing them from, for example, those with persons with whom we have previously had face-to-face contact but who are now geographically far away. These are not *virtual*, just physically removed.

By applying the term *virtual* to a relationship type, we introduce some bias about the substantiveness of the connection. Virtual speaks to something or someone that exists in essence or effect though not in actual fact (Boellstorff, 2009). The term conjures up a feeling that there

is something imaginary about the connection, that it is a more insignif-
icant form of relation, and is somewhat artificial. This likely stems from
the use of the word virtual in other fields to reference the building of
artifacts that simulate animate objects, such as FooPets[2] that wag their
tails and pant with their paws on the screen, or the advances in the technologies that construct virtual realities complete with faux landscapes
and science fiction imaginary.

Chris Shorow, a senior pastor at a First Christian Church in
Edmonton, Canada, said, '... apparently, many people in our society are
longing for a community, even if it means being a virtual community
online. At the same time, many of us long for meaningful, face-to-face
relationships.'[3] Shorow echoes what has become a dominant perspective for many North Americans, particularly those in the 40+ age range.
The assertion is clear – there are the meaningful face-to-face relationships and the... well, less meaningful virtual ones. Supposedly, virtual
relationships are the poor stepsisters to the real deal that we all really
want to have – the physical connection.

Yet, if you ask persons who regularly engage with communities of
others who have never met each other in person but engage in online
activities, often they do not consider these people or themselves to
be artificial approximates of the real thing. Virtual relationships may
be distinguished from virtual FooPets in the sense that there actually
are real people behind the avatars. And because there are real hearts,
minds, and hands on the other end of the connection, for all parties in
the virtual community it is as much a relationship as any other – with
some differences. Teens online do not distinguish between relationships
on and offline, but see them all as relationships perhaps bounded by
activity types, such as online gaming or school sports.

There are hundreds of massively MMORPGs, such as WoW and Dungeons & Dragons. The players are located around the world and range in
age from 7 to 70, although most are in their twenties. Most MMORPGs
are highly structured environments with distinct roles and goals. The
players interact over online terrains and communicate by chat, text,
voice, and email. Nardi and Harris reported that, in their participant
observation in a WoW guild, leaders and their guild members formed
cohesive and close-knit communities (Nardi and Harris, 2006).

As in the real world, much of the communication in virtual communities is about creating and maintaining feelings of connection between
people rather than trying to convey specific messages. Virtual community members are often a mix of people whom the networked individual
knows offline as well as people whom he or she may never meet

outside the virtual environment. Affinity, commitment, and attention are aspects of virtual relationships. According to Nardi and Harris,

> they are active fields of connection between dyads that are constantly negotiated and monitored. These fields 'decay' or grow inert without interaction. While face to face interaction is especially rich in ways to establish connection (touching, eating together, making eye contact, sharing common space, informal chitchat), people also establish connection through mediated communication.
>
> (Nardi and Harris, 2006)

One aspect in which virtual relationships are different from other more tangible forms is that, because the interaction is mediated and abstracted away from the physical person, people may experiment with different aspects of their personas in a manner not easily executed in face-to-face interaction. For example, there are instances of gender inversion, whereby a man may use a female avatar to participate in an online community and vice versa (Cooper, 2007). Also, depending on the application or game, age, weight, skin color, and other phenotypes can be altered so that the player may try out a different look and see how he or she is accepted by the community. Although there is evidence that many people will adapt their virtual selves to look a lot like themselves offline, there is an understanding among those in the virtual community that it is acceptable practice to experiment.

Thus, virtual communities provide spaces for some networked individuals to connect, interact, play, and experiment, and for their participants they are a source of meaningful interaction and purposeful relationships.

Conclusion

The internet revolution has opened up and renewed ways of communicating and finding information. The power of knowledge is no longer the monopoly of professionals, since common folk can now engage the internet and compare research notes with their healthcare and financial experts. This internet revolution is bound up with the mobile revolution which allows individuals to communicate and gather information while on the move. With greater connectivity all around, people can engage their networks and access information regardless of their physical location. Home bases are still important as sources of ideas and inspiration, but the mobile revolution ensures that people never lose touch with

either home base or their other important social worlds. These technological changes are in reciprocal acceleration with the social network
revolution. While social networks have always been with us, the internet and mobile revolutions are both weakening group boundaries and
expanding the reach, number, and velocity of interpersonal ties. Modern individuals have become networked individualists managing their
personal communities with the help of communication technologies as
social affordances. Taken together, the personal community approach
accurately reflects the habits of modern people, who are profoundly and
individually mobile and networked.

Changing social connectivity is, after all, neither a dystopian loss
nor a utopian gain but an intricate, multifaceted, fundamental social
transformation.

Notes

1. *Globe and Mail*, Josh Wingrove, 24 November 2009.
2. http://www.foopets.com/
3. Shorow quoted in *The Edmonton Sun*, 25 November 2009.

References

Abbott, C. (1998) 'Making Connections: Young People and the Internet', in
Sefton-Green, J. (ed.) *Digital Diversions: Youth Culture in the Age of Multimedia*.
London: UCL Press, pp. 84–105.
Anderson, A. (2006) 'Are iPods Shrinking the British Vocabulary?', *Ars Technica*,
http://arstechnica.com/apple/news/2006/12/8431.ars
Boase, J. and Wellman, B. (2005) 'Personal relationships: on and off the internet',
in Perlman, D. and Vangelisti, AL. (eds), *Handbook of personal relations*. Oxford:
Blackwell.
Boellstorff, T. (2009). 'Coming of Age in Second Life: An Anthropologist Explores
the Virtually Human', Princeton, NJ: Princeton University Press.
boyd, d. (2008) *Taken Out of Context: American Teen Sociality in Networked Publics*.
Unpublished doctoral dissertation, Berkeley: University of California.
Cooper, R. (2007) *Alter Ego: Avatars and Their Creators*. London, UK: Chris Boot.
Hampton, K. N., and Wellman, B. (2002) 'The not so global village of Netville',
in Wellman, B. and Haythornthwaite, C. (eds), The Internet in everyday life,
pp. 345–71. Oxford: Blackwell.
Katz, J. E. and Aspden, P. (1997) 'Motives, Hurdles, and Dropouts: Who Is On and
Off the Internet, and Why', *Communications of the ACM*, 40, 4, pp. 97–102.
Katz, J. E. and Rice, R. E. (2002) 'Project Syntopia: Social Consequences of Internet
Use', *IT & Society*, 1, 1, pp. 166–79.
Keillor, G. (2009) *Unfriended* (song), last viewed June 2012 on YouTube http://
www.youtube.com/watch?v=CXsorPbcSgo
Lenhart, A., Madden, M., and Hitlin, P. (2005) 'Teens and Technology:
You Are Leading the Transition to a Fully Wired and Mobile Nation'.

Retrieved 12 October 2005, www.pewInternet.org/pdfs/PIP_Teens_Tech_July2005web.pdf

McEwen, R. (2010) *A World More Intimate: Exploring the Role of Mobile Phones in Maintaining and Extending Social Networks*. Unpublished doctoral dissertation, Toronto: Faculty of Information, University of Toronto.

McKenna, K. Y. A., Green, A., and Gleason, M. (2002) 'Relationship Formation on the Internet: What's the Big Attraction?', *Journal of Social Issues*, 58, pp. 9–31.

Nardi, B. and Harris, J. (2006) 'Strangers and Friends: Collaborative Play in World of Warcraft', in J. Hunsinger, Klastrup, L., and Allen, M. (eds) *Human Factors*, pp. 149–58.

Osgerby, B. (2004) 'Brave New World – Youth Media, Business Conglomeration and post-Fordism', in *Youth Media*. Abingdon: Routledge, pp. 37–58.

Parks, M. R. and Floyd, K. (1996) 'Making Friends in Cyberspace', *Journal of Communication*, 46, pp. 80–97.

Princeton University (2010) 'About WordNet', WordNet. Princeton University, http://wordnet.princeton.edu

Rainie, L. and Wellman, B. (2012) *Networked: The New Social Operating System*, Cambridge: MIT Press.

Rheingold, H. (2000) *The Virtual Community: Homesteading on the Electronic Frontier* (Revised ed.). Cambridge: MA, MIT University Press.

Turkle, S. (2005) *The Second Self: Computers and the Human Spirit*, Cambridge, MA: MIT Press. Available at http://www.loc.gov/catdir/toc/fy0601/2004064980.html

Wellman, B. (2001) 'Physical Place and Cyber Place: The Rise of Networked Individualism', *International Journal of Urban and Regional Research* 25, 2, pp. 227–52.

Wellman, B. and Hogan, B. (2004) 'The Immanent Internet', in J. McKay (ed.) *Netting Citizens: Exploring Citizenship in a Digital Age*. Edinburgh: St. Andrew Press, pp. 54–80.

Zinc Research and Dufferin Research (2009) *Canadians and Social Networking Sites*. Accessed June 2012, http://www.zincresearch.com/include/get.php?no deid=23

16
Gemeinschaft Identity in a Gesellschaft Metaverse

Cynthia Calongne, Peggy Sheehy, and Andrew Stricker

Introduction

For the first time in history, it is possible to use a digital device to rapidly connect, publish, and exchange ideas with people from around the world. Everyone has a voice in this global marketplace of thought, and, as digital citizens, we have an opportunity to step through the looking glass (Carroll, 1865) and to become architects of the future. The 21st century has introduced the dawn of global democratization driven by the convergence of mobile IT with emerging media. In paradoxical ways, however, people can be increasingly mobile and socially connected in public spaces on a global scale, yet feel isolated from community, family, and friends due to a lack of private places that bridge or blend physical and virtual spaces. There is much promise in how the metaverse can help to harmonize the tensions between the need for gemeinschaft (community, family, and private blended places) with gesellschaft (society and public blended spaces). Informal and formal learning environments, blended across physical and virtual locations, can be designed to better harmonize gemeinschaft places with gesellschaft spaces. Innovation through technology in this context is mostly about obtaining strategic value from harmonizing gemeinschaft and gesellschaft with ingenious thinking and courageous will to design and use blended physical and virtual locations in ways unforeseen or unimagined from tactical perspectives on instrumental uses of the metaverse. Escaping these tactical instrumental uses is made possible by supporting how people learn, regardless of location, in harmonious ways across the gemeinschaft places and gesellschaft spaces in the metaverse.

The metaverse both facilitates the opportunity to build community and social identity and allows educators to focus greater attention on fostering affective learning experiences and transcend social and identity barriers towards self-affirmation and relational unity grounded on shared purposes and inspired values. With a focus on identity, this chapter examines the dramatic new ways in which individuals and communities will learn and benefit due to these social, global interactions.

As a social context for multidimensional engagement, fostering familial relationships as a virtual gemeinschaft, an organic social relationship, and a sense of community in society that forms around respect and trust as a virtual gesellschaft, the metaverse offers a melting pot of ideas that blend the diverse cultures and genders to shape an evolving global perspective. These terms, gemeinschaft and gesellschaft, were defined by Ferdinand Tönnies in 1887 (De Cindio and Ripamonti, 2010; Deflem, 1999) to define the sociological differences between societal identity and individual identity within self-selected communities. While gemeinschaft focuses on a person's actual role in society and social strata, gesellschaft centers on the individual, building a community beyond the family ties.

As a world metropolis continues to evolve, the gemeinschaft-like life involving the family, village, and town, which centered on the established roles and professions inherited from generation to generation, gives way to gesellschaft-like living, shifting from a role defined by society to the choices that individuals make to participate in a community. While gemeinschaft represents an organic sense of community as defined by the family and its values, gesellschaft offers relational unity and kinship that are not based on a relationship by birth with others, and it is this self-selected, natural union forming across the metaverse that characterizes a social identity within a global community. These connections to the global community are informal yet quite compelling within the metaverse.

The rise of social communities and the conversations within them as noted in popular social media sites are of great interest to educators, and these informal networks not only bring people together in gesellschaft communities but also offer opportunities for understanding the role of affect in learning and the development of a global identity within the metaverse.

Social identity and affective learning

The shift from traditional familial relationships to the establishment of a global community requires more than technology. The metaverse is an online space where communities form and gather to share ideas, socialize, create content, and develop a social identity that defines their behaviors within the group. Extrapolating this notion of community and social identity, individuals within the metaverse who join learning communities develop a social identity that strengthens as they participate, explore, and learn, and these learning experiences are enhanced by the opportunity to benefit from the community. This social participation offers distinct benefits for learning beyond the convenience of online access and tools that reduce the burden on cognition.

Affective learning extends beyond cognition and the memorization of basic facts and rules, recognizing the benefits of context, discussion, and meaning as expressed through socialization, discussion, and the influence of changing emotional states on the learning process (Kort, 2008; Picard et al., 2004). Blending thoughts and feelings with how people learn, affective learning recognizes the opportunities that social learning environments and virtual worlds present for exploring and sharing diverse perspectives while constructing knowledge (Stricker, 2009). (Several examples of affective learning through the use of virtual worlds are included in this chapter's appendix.) Learners who are geographically distant benefit from studying in the metaverse as it offers 3D educational spaces where they can share their perspectives amid visual stimuli and kinesthetic learning activities.

Mirror identity is the means by which we can perceive how others see themselves through the reflection of their avatars in 3D spaces. Bridging the social capital in a marketplace of ideas with our mirror identity is one of the benefits of these diverse learning spaces. The next set of near and long-term forecasts examines the future of the metaverse and the implications for virtual world education, affective learning, and social identity.

Future technology

What lies on the horizon for the metaverse in the next five years and what are the implications for social identity and affective learning? The five and ten-year forecasts noted in Table 16.1 are derived from current trends in emerging technology and a review of the 2011 Horizon Report, produced by the New Media Consortium (Johnson et al., 2011), Gartner's Hype Cycle for Emerging Technologies, 2010 (Gartner, 2010), and Gartner's Hype Cycle for Cloud Computing, 2011 (Columbus, 2011; Gartner, 2011).

Table 16.1 Future technologies in the metaverse

In one to five years	In six to ten years
Virtual world education grids with portable 3D content	One integrated, open source 3D virtual world with rich media
Open source 3D content and virtual world educational repositories	Student-configurable learning content, intelligent educational agents
Game-based learning and educational games	Educational MMORPGs and quest-based non-linear games
Video phone calls and video social spaces	Interactive 3D video and high-res images projected anywhere
Graphics-intensive handheld and mobile devices	Location-independent, auto-synchronized devices
Augmented reality applications for blending virtual data in a real world	Augmented reality with holographic 3D content in real-world spaces
Gesture-based computing for software interaction	Natural gestures for navigation and avatar animation
Artificial intelligence and voice recognition	Natural voice interaction AI agents supporting affect

Table 16.1 illustrates the projections for the next five years on the left and extends their capabilities to project the technological advances for the next ten years on the right. These technologies promise a bright future in which an integrated virtual world grid may be accessed over a mobile device, integrating 3D content with video and social media using voice and gesture-based interfaces to reduce the cognitive load, thus making it easy for learners to interact, socialize, and conduct holographic and virtual activities. The addition of artificially intelligent agents affords new ways of mentoring and providing feedback during the learning process to support emotional engagement.

The future promises enhanced synchronization, data integration across cloud-based repositories, new methods of navigation and avatar animation, and the integration of real-world spaces with virtual world content. Among the challenges, however, are the technological breakthroughs needed in holographic projections, the affordability of flexible, synchronized displays that allow users to auto-synchronize their data, and displays with any location and display device. For intelligent agents to interact seamlessly and support emotional engagement, their level of sophistication requires improvements in natural language processing, culture, idiomatic expressions, and the ever-elusive understanding of humor. It is quite possible that there will be breakthroughs in this area, but not quite at the level needed for intelligent agents to fully understand and support emotion and affective learning. Even so, we will see progress in this area within the next ten years, and these early efforts will help to support the assessment of affective learning.

From today to the future

Today's capabilities feature technological advances that have stimulated a heady mix of mobile devices, cloud computing services (Buyya et al., 2011), 3D virtual worlds, sophisticated massive multiplayer online role-playing games (MMORPGs), non-linear games, and collaborative learning environments to offer a bright future for community development, social identity, and affective learning in the metaverse.

What do these new capabilities and technologies offer for social identity and affective learning? The projected increases in access and bandwidth, coupled with the technological advances forecast in Table 16.1, will make it easier for learners to interact naturally and to socialize, express ideas, conduct activity-based learning activities in real and virtual spaces, and share these experiences ubiquitously.

Popular handheld digital devices are primitive windows to the metaverse when compared with those envisioned for the future. Their benefit is that they provide access from any location that has cellular or internet access, and the future is bright for improvements in internet access and increases in bandwidth. The ability to easily access the metaverse, coupled with ubiquitous cloud computing services, powerful free browser-based applications and low-cost mobile apps, long battery life, and customizable features, makes it natural for learners to stay connected and to be able to communicate frequently.

Current research in virtual worlds for educational use includes grid development using open source software solutions (e.g., Open Simulator) and grassroots efforts by educators (Jokaydia), open source platform solutions (OSGrid), commercial efforts (Second Life, Inworldz, ReactionGrid with JIBE), and research conducted by the Military Open Simulator Enterprise Strategy (MOSES) project (MOSES, 2011), sponsored by the United States Army's Simulation and Training Technology Center in conjunction with researchers, educators, and 3D content designers.

In addition to more than 200 virtual environment solutions, cloud computing services (Buyya et al., 2011) make it easy to archive and access data from any location and to publish, manage, and store rich media and educational content from digital, handheld devices. Many of these services offer free and low-cost opportunities that make them attractive for educational use.

Artificial intelligence, advances in mobile technology, and new ways of interfacing with these systems will make it possible for users to interact easily and ubiquitously while receiving useful feedback from an intelligent tutor, mentor, or agent. While gesellschaft often refers to communities comprised of real people, and, in this context, those who are distributed across the metaverse, interaction with artificially intelligent tutors that reflect the community's knowledge and social identity will leverage the affordances of ubiquitous learning. The metaverse is more than a virtual space and far greater than the collective thought of its membership. It is a place of self-discovery and empowerment, a realm where the mind and body connect, where the virtual and real intersect, and where we can thrive through concentrated unity. It provides the means for illuminating how the notion of self can become more powerful through relational and transformational experiences and how the identities may be mirrored through the perspectives of others to support the realization of a more meaningful future.

Social identity, gender diversity, and culture

One advantage of the metaverse is the anonymity afforded individuals and the community while sharing opinions. While the context in this chapter on social identity is not focused solely on women, this is one of the benefits that may be strengthened by affective learning and social identity within the metaverse. In a series of educational materials, the National Center for Women & Information Technology (NCWIT) states that, over the past decade, there has been a decline in the statistics regarding the involvement of women in technological degree programs and careers (NCWIT, 2011). Not enough women, and especially women from diverse cultural backgrounds, are entering the computer science and information technology fields.

- There was a 79 per cent decline in the number of Computer Science majors entering undergraduate degree programs between 2000 and 2008.
- In 2008, women received 18 per cent of the degrees awarded to computer and information sciences graduates.

• According to the Department of Labor Bureau of Labor Statistics in 2008, females comprised 28 per cent of the computer scientists, and, of that number, 3 per cent were African–American, 3 per cent were Asian, and 1 per cent were Hispanic.

A balance of female to male technology professionals with ethnic diversity is needed to facilitate the exploration of diverse cultural perspectives and approaches to creativity and innovation. Females are needed to express their unique perspectives, offer deeper interaction, foster significant relationships, and delve into a better understanding of how to apply science, mathematics, and technology. Women identify with the contextualized experiences that the metaverse offers and can form social connections that strengthen technological development through affective learning.

In contrast to the concern over the decline in women in technology in the USA, the evolution of communities and their subcultures is very bright. A global culture is developing out of the social interactions across the World Wide Web as well as a multitude of subcultures, and, with the increase in online communities, the metaverse may be considered a virtual world metropolis as it nurtures and sustains communities that share a familial sense of fellowship, shared purpose, and values.

Conclusion and areas of future research

Fostering learning communities that define and enhance the social identity of learners provides opportunities for supporting affective learning. The technological advances proposed in Table 16.1 leverage these opportunities to offer increased capabilities and usability via natural interaction styles such as voice and gesture. Increases in access, bandwidth, artificial intelligence, mobile technologies, holographic technologies, and rich media may strengthen the development of a global gesellschaft and its social identity, which will promote new ways of thinking and affective learning.

Future work in this area includes the development of 3D educational content and scenes for inclusion in a repository of learning artifacts that leverage emotional engagement (Kort, 2008) and analyze the forecast technologies for their effect on social identity. Studies in affective learning are needed to understand the requirements and potential benefits that may be achieved through the development and use of 3D content, non-linear learning games, virtual world simulations, and holographic content to stimulate emotional experiences even as they enhance skill and competency development across the metaverse.

Appendix: affect and social identity

The following stories offer poignant examples that illustrate the benefits of social identity and community within the metaverse. These examples highlight transformational learning experiences and illustrate the benefits of affective learning as experienced by over 400 13-year-old students who study at Ramapo, a virtual educational community hosted by Suffern Middle School in Suffern, New York. The topics range from a learning activity that examines perceptions and cultural values and how they can change during an affective learning activity to a learning activity that focuses on media beauty and identity. The last tale examines personal integrity and cultural values as they are challenged during a digital storytelling session.

Exploring gesellschaft and values

In February 2006, 400 middle school students from Suffern Middle School read the John Steinbeck novel, *Of Mice and Men* (Steinbeck, 1937). The students enacted a hypothetical courtroom scene that might have occurred at the end of the story and asked themselves the question, *Was George guilty of killing his mentally disabled friend, Lennie*?

In preparation for the role-play, the students were asked to read the book and to reflect on the legal consequences of murder and manslaughter. They put the book aside and entered the virtual world to enact a courtroom scene. During four days of courtroom testimony and deliberations, the students struggled to discover what might have happened if George had been brought to court for the murder of his friend, Lennie.

The students then portrayed all of the courtroom roles, such as the judge, jury, attorneys, witnesses, the defendant, and the court reporter (Calongne, 2009) with the exception of the two bailiffs, who were portrayed by the Ramapo coordinator (Peggy Sheehy) and a mentor (Cynthia Calongne). Before the trials began, when asked about their findings, the students said that they were not going to convict George for killing his friend, Lennie. After all, he meant well and had killed him to save him from torture murder. For four days, eight court sessions were conducted each day, and during the proceedings the students were engrossed in the story. Sheehy noted that they did not type their lines from their books but instead put the books aside to discuss their roles during the court proceedings within the virtual world environment (Sheehy, 2007).

In contrast to their previous plan to acquit George, after four days of courtroom testimony and jury deliberations, the students returned a verdict of guilty (Calongne and Hiles, 2007, p. 77). When asked what changed their minds, they replied that the law did not ask whether he meant well but whether George was guilty beyond reasonable doubt of killing Lennie. They recommended a lighter sentence, for, in the end, they found that he had meant well.

Other insights included the court reporter who enforced the use of proper English for the court records as noted in the courtroom proceedings (Sheehy, 2007). When a witness used l33t (pronounced leet) speak and text messaging acronyms, such as *l8tr* (later) and *lol* (laughing out loud), the court reporter admonished them to speak correctly for the court record. In a subsequent year, an instructor posted a video that demonstrated how the learning activity flows from the school's lab and classroom into the virtual world (TeachertubeMS, 2009).

Discovery of self

On the fifth day, at the end of the trials, Sheehy removed the benches and transformed one of the courthouses into a conference center. A nearby school was scheduled to visit and tour the conference center, and the Ramapo students wrote biographies of famous people and hung photos of them on the walls of this virtual museum. When touched, each photo showed a copy of a famous person's biography, written by the middle school students for display in Ramapo's 3D virtual classroom.

During a last-minute survey of the content, a large portrait of a young girl was displayed. After asking the students about the photo, a 13-year-old girl noted that it was her portrait, and that one day she would be famous and accomplish great things. This was a great surprise, as it was both unexpected and evidence that the students were visualizing the future in a natural way, without encouragement, assignment, or direction.

Moments like this one are an epiphany and an inspiration for educators. The student's complete confidence in her future and simple acceptance of it were exciting. All the 13-year-old students learned so much through their online virtual world activities via role-play, discussion, and reflection that words do not adequately express the significance of these learning experiences.

Mirror identity

To explore their identity in the metaverse, each new class of 400 eighth grade students at Ramapo creates a series of avatars to serve as a context for discussion, and, after reviewing their avatars, they meet in small groups to share how they feel about themselves and the avatars of their classmates. Their first avatar is a self-portrait that reflects how they see themselves, mirroring their real-life identity. As they form groups with random or selected group assignments, they examine one another and discuss how they feel amid light-hearted jesting and teenage banter.

The second avatar that they create relates to how the media perceives beauty. The students change the appearance of their avatars to look attractive from the popular media viewpoint and discuss how they feel about it. The discussion is lively as their physical features resemble celebrities, and some of them have notable physical features, similar to Dolly Parton and Arnold Schwarzenegger. The third day, they come into the virtual library and conduct the same activity, but this time for the opposite gender. At this point, the discussion is sometimes heated as the students object to the exaggerated physical features, supermodel and rock star physiques.

On the fourth day they are asked to return to the avatar that was most comfortable to them, and most of them return to a look that resembles their self-portrait image. As they discuss their rationales, they discuss their issues with weight, and support networks form, offering positive support for improving their self-image and to help them feel better about themselves. The students concluded that we should rethink how beauty is defined, noting that it is more about what is inside and not based on outer appearance.

The road not taken: facing tough choices

While striving to master the course competencies, students in the metaverse develop their social skills and learn what it means to be a good digital citizen as they explore the consequences of good and bad decisions. After reading the poem *The Road Not Taken* by Robert Frost (Frost, 2002), students from Suffern Middle School in Suffern, New York designed and filmed a digital storytelling simulation set in Second Life in collaboration with Bernajean Porter's 3D StoryWorlds project (Porter, 2010). Machinima is a video set in a virtual world, and it was featured at the 2008 International Society for Technology in Education (ISTE) conference.

The class worked in groups to design a collection of stories but only had the resources to produce and film one story. In their machinima, a 13-year-old girl steps into a school bathroom as her friend places a hand inside her mouth and coughs, emptying the contents of her stomach into the lavatory (Julie, 2008). As she hears her friend enter the restroom, the girl in the restroom sobs, 'Please don't tell! Oh, please don't tell!' Our protagonist faces a big decision, as whispered voices and a text chat narrative express the inner conflict that plays inside her head, 'What will happen if I tell? What if I do not tell?' Should she tell and get help for her friend? Bulimia is a serious condition and she may die from it, yet her friendship may end if she tells.

The consequences of her decision unfold as she chooses her path, amid a set design rich in symbol and metaphor. As she chooses to tell and steps through the door, her friend collapses and an ambulance comes to take her to the hospital. If she does not tell and moves through the second door, a hearse arrives to take her friend to the graveyard. The brutal consequence of failing to help a friend is death. The story closes with the newspaper headline, 'Teenage Eating Disorders on the Rise'. From the Wiki project journal (Julie, 2008), the student notes in her lessons learned that, 'The most important decisions are also the hardest ones.' Another student (Porter, 2010) observed, 'Well, for an old dead guy, Frost really *got* how hard it is to be a teenager these days.'

References

Buyya, R., Broberg, J., and Goscinski, A. M. (eds) (2011) *Cloud Computing: Principles and Paradigms*. New Jersey: John Wiley & Sons, pp. 3–37.

Calongne, C. and Hiles, J. (2007) 'Blended Realities: A Virtual Tour of Education in Second Life', TCC 2007 Worldwide Conference Proceedings. Accessed 23 April 2012, http://etec.hawaii.edu/proceedings/2007/calongne.pdf

Calongne, C. (2009) 'Teaching in an Avatar World'. GameTech 2009. Accessed 25 May 2012, http://www.slideshare.net/lyrlobo/gametechteaching-in-an-avatar-world

Carroll, L. (1865) *Alice's Adventures in Wonderland, 1920*. New York publication, Project Gutenberg. Accessed 25 May 2012, http://www.gutenberg.org/ebooks/19033

Columbus, L. (2011) Gartner Releases Their Hype Cycle for Cloud Computing, 2011. A Passion for Research: Focusing on the Intersection of Technology and Trust. Accessed 25 May 2012, http://softwarestrategiesblog.com/2011/07/27/gartner-releases-their-hype-cycle-for-cloud-computing-2011/

De Cindio, F. and Ripamonti, L. (2010) 'Nature and Roles for Community Networks in the Information Society', *AI & Society*, 25, 3, pp. 265–78.

Deflem, M. (1999) 'Ferdinand Tönnies on Crime and Society: An Unexplored Contribution to Criminological Sociology', *History of the Human Sciences*, 12, 3, pp. 87–116.

Frost, R. (2002) *The Road Not Taken: A Selection of Robert Frost's Poems*. New York: Holt Paperback.

Gartner (2010) Gartner's 2010 Hype Cycle Special Report Evaluates Maturity of 1,800 Technologies. Accessed 25 May 2012, http://www.gartner.com/it/page.jsp?id=1447613

Gartner (2011) 'Hype Cycle for Cloud Computing 2011', David Mitchell Smith Publication, 27 July 2011.

Johnson, L., Smith, R., Willis, H., Levine, A., and Haywood, K. (2011) *The 2011 Horizon Report*. Austin, Texas: The New Media Consortium, http://net.educause.edu/ir/library/pdf/HR2011.pdf

Julie (2008) Julie's Journal, RamapoProject. Accessed 25 May 2012, http://ramapoproject.wikispaces.com/Julie%27s+Journal

Kort, B. (2008) 'Cognition, Affect and Learning: The Role of Emotions in Learning'. Accessed 25 May 2012, https://sites.google.com/site/barrykort/home/cognition-affect-and-learning#Basic_Concepts_and_Terms

MOSES (2011) Military Open Simulator Enterprise Strategy, US Army Simulation and Training Technology Center (STTC), http://fvwc.army.mil/moses/

NCWIT (2011) 'By the Numbers: Statistics about Women & IT. Revolutionizing the Face of Technology', *National Center for Women & Information Technology*, http://ncwit.org/pdf/BytheNumbers09.pdf

Picard, R. W., Papert, S., Bender, W., Blumberg, B., Breazeal, C., Cavallo, D., Machover, T., Resnick, M., Roy, D., and Strohecker, C. (2004) 'Affective Learning – A Manifesto', *BT Technology Journal*, 22, 4, pp. 253–9.

Porter, B. (2010) 'Digital Storytelling in Second Life, Learning Connections, Learning & Leading with Technology, Learning Connection', ISTE. Accessed 25 May 2012, http://kti2010.wikispaces.com/file/view/PorterStoryWorld.pdf

Sheehy, P. (2007) 'Of Mice and Men. A Running Account of Ramapo Islands: The Virtual Presence for Education at Suffern Middle School, Suffern, NY'. Accessed 25 May 2012, http://rampoislands.blogspot.com/2007_02_01_archive.html

Steinbeck, J. (1937) *Of Mice and Men*. New York: Penguin Putnam, Inc.

Stricker, A. (2009) 'Why Affective Learning in a Situated Place Matters for the Millennial Generation', A4/6I Innovations & Integrations Division. Accessed 25 May 2012, http://myauinnovate.com/documents/WhyAffectiveLearninginSituatedPlace.pdf

TeachertubeMS (2009) *Of Mice and Men. Teacher and Student Responses to Using Second Life for Education*. Accessed 25 May 2012, http://www.youtube.com/watch?v=zsghYT4Idw8

17
Sorting Out the Metaverse and How the Metaverse Is Sorting Us Out

Isto Huvila

The idea of virtual realities and the metaverse as an ultimate form of information carrier is as old as the idea of immersive technologically mediated experience. The consequences of a cognitively unlimited access to information and enhanced capability to know and experience our surroundings have been perceived in both utopian and dystopian terms, but the basic capacity of virtual realities and of the broader metaversal reality to integrate man with information has often been cited as a plain practical fact (Bouchlaghem et al., 1996; Soon et al., 1999). This essentially instrumental point of view has been suggested to reduce the metaverse to a tool (or a medium) and the act of integrating human beings with information to an essentially solvable technical problem.

Besides generic references to authors like Marshall McLuhan, Geoffrey Bowker and Susan Star, there has been conspicuously little explicit discussion about the precise social, cognitive, and cultural processes of how the metaverse is functioning as a carrier and category of information and experiences, and even less on how the convergence that directs us towards a virtually enhanced reality links back to the two converging worlds. Is it that the virtual ceases to be virtual and the physical will be no more physical? Or does the physical become more than physical and the virtual more than virtual? Are my friends in virtual worlds farther away or closer to me than my physical friends? Does a photograph become different if it is used as a visual overlay in an augmented reality setting? Are virtual worlds closer to my physical home than my neighbors? What is a non-metaversal reality (or does it exist)?

This chapter discusses a phenomenon that may be called double-immersion. It is the process of how cyberspatial presence changes our experience of non-metaversal aspects of reality. Immersion in an enhanced reality is affecting the ways we are present in timespace, how we categorize and structure the world, and how we are informed and become knowledgeable. Information is not something we can observe per se. Similarly, we may be unable to know and make sense of reality *as is*. Reality becomes a metaversal reality that is structured according to a set of metaversal categories. The aim of this chapter is to look critically into how metaverse is both a category and a classification system and how it may affect our capabilities and perspectives of knowing how things are related to each other, what these things are, and how the metaverse changes how we see them. The problem, as it is seen, is that we are easily fascinated by the utopian possibilities of the metaverse (i.e., how the metaverse can help us) and at the same time incapable of adapting ourselves to the new environment (i.e., how we have to change our behavior to adapt to the metaverse).

Categories and their consequences

Citing the words of Eviatar Zerubavel, the social order and the way in which we gestalt the world are based on drawing 'fine lines' (Zerubavel, 1991). The act of making distinctions between kin and non-kin, allowed and forbidden, or here and there is a fundamental part of human experience. It makes very fundamental sense to make a distinction between young and old, male and female, the ethnicity of people, or the color of your socks and those of your brother. Categories and categorizing have a propensity to turn into hierarchies and become instruments of power, but the various consequences of classifications do not negate their fundamental function to help us to make sense (in both passive and active meanings) of the world. Further, again using a wording by Zerubavel, we need to create 'insular' entities of things in order to make sense of the reality. In terms of Johan Huizinga, these small worlds that are delineated from the rest of the experienced reality have a capability to form 'magic circles' that keep individuals within a particular frame of reference (Huizinga, 1949). The insular categories can overlap in a sense that different aspects of life are often framed on specific islands of meaning. The appreciations of certain phenomena in the context of work or leisure, here or there, or us or them may be entirely different from each other. The distinctions of virtual and actual, or virtual and real, digital and analog, or metaverse and physically based reality are not different from the general pattern of classifying the reality. They are attempts to frame and understand the aspects of reality we are experiencing in our everyday life and imagination. The act of drawing these lines protects us from anomalies, things that do not fit into our understanding of the reality. Even if the metaverse is seemingly quite remote from the traditional ideas of taboos, the acts of drawing fine lines between virtual, metaversal, and physically based realities are highly similar to the processes described by Mary Douglas in her classical study of the conceptions of pollution and taboo (Douglas, 1966).

Besides functioning as contexts of understanding the reality, the islands of meaning are shaping it as well. Each individual 'island of meaning' (Zerubavel, 1991) incorporates its own mode of experiencing the reality, its own rules and context of understanding how things are related to each other and what their fundamental meaning and role are as a part of our experiences. This division of reality is not only an act of rendering visible some existing lines of distinction but also of drawing new lines. This is true of every attempt to label things and organize them in categories, as Geoffrey Bowker and Susan Star have described in their account of three widely different case studies of classification and its consequences (Bowker and Star, 2000). Classifications change the way in which we perceive the reality, but, at the same time, the drawing of a line makes a difference in the reality. Feminist scholars have placed frequent emphasis on how traditional male-dominated social and intellectual categorizations have marginalized women (Olson, 2002) and other non-dominant groups in society. The categorization of men's and women's duties at home and in society has had a considerable effect on the possibility for women to educate themselves and choose a career of their liking. In a similar manner, categorizations have changed the digital sphere. One of the longest-standing disputes pertains to the labeling of things as 'only games' and related belittling connotations attached to the notion of gameplay. The contrasting viewpoints emphasize, on the one hand, the seriousness and relevance of games and the predominance of gameplay in all human activity, and, on the other, the impropriety of labeling certain phenomena such as 'social virtual worlds' as games (Bell et al., 2010). Both interpretations may be contested, but it is apparent that 'game' or 'metaverse' is not especially useful as merely an evaluative, non-analytical, or descriptive category.

Another example of the power of categorization is how the classification of web services similar to certain others has had a major, in some cases fatal, effect on their popularity. For instance, in the case of the late Google Lively, the early popular expectations seeing the service as a Second Life 'killer' were an obvious factor that contributed to negative reviews and the eventual closing of the service. Similarly, the positive reputation of individual companies can help services and technologies to be categorized as useful and successful, and, consequently, to flourish beyond their technical or social excellence.

The active role of categorizations in the processes of shaping reality is coupled with the influence of the premises of classification. Not only is the act of labeling something of a game, but so is the system of categories, which includes a particular notion affecting the formation of the archipelago of the islands of meaning. Formal semantics-based, universalist classification systems have a tendency to highlight a rigid all-embracing categorization of things (Almeida et al., 2011), while faceted systems tend to prioritize a more complex view of categories and the relatedness of individual entities. Seeing the metaverse as a faceted system of various related aspects leads to a very different idea of the phenomenon than a bipolar division of things as either belonging to the sphere of the metaverse or not. Complexity can be an asset in the context of such a multidimensional concept as the metaverse (as with the notion of game; Mäyrä, 2008) and a way to retain a certain productive cacophony of viewpoints instead of simplifying the notion by assuming a single master theory. However, in the end, all categorizations are a question of drawing a supposedly uncontroversial line that demarcates the borders between individual islands of meaning. The major difference between the two approaches is, however, the difference in how the shaping of a border and defining the anomalous are performed.

The final consequence of the assumption of the prescriptiveness of categorizations is an ultimate denial of absolute miscellaneity. David Weinberger has argued that in the age of digital information everything is miscellaneous (Weinberger, 2007). He is undoubtedly correct in principle. Digital systems give us opportunities to make and support an endless variety of different types of the order of things. At the same time, however, the possibility of infinity does not equate to a practical equality of every categorization. Even if the digital system allowed us to demarcate according to our own will, the practice of drawing fine lines is related to preferences that are stronger than the opportunity of miscellaneity. The physical reality and order of things has an impact on the digital reality and the outlines of the metaverse. Even if the social reality may be very different in virtual worlds than in the physically based reality, they are not completely detached (Huvila et al., 2010).

Metaverse as a category

The majority of the metaverse-related literature has followed a close-to-Baudrillardian (Baudrillard, 1996) logic of perceiving the notion of virtual and its manifestation as a metaverse as something 'different'. Not all, however, have shared his or Neal Stephenson's dystopian visions of the outcomes of digital realities. In contrast, the metaverse may be claimed to be a predominately positive species of a virtual form of reality. Distinguishing the metaverse is a necessary precondition to creating and maintaining such a category and demarcating it from other forms of digital and analog spheres.

As a distinct category, metaverse has its own set of rules and references. Metaverse transforms its participants into characters that are not fictional as in a fictional theatre piece, but individuals very fundamentally different from their physical representations. In the scholarly and popular discourse, metaverse forms its own peculiar island of meaning in the sense described in the work of Zerubavel. A metaphorical sea separates it from other islands, and especially from the contrasting part of reality outside the digital sphere.

As a category, metaverse is an attempt to bring order into the anomalous field of digital forms of reality. Besides referring to a particular service based on a certain data communications protocol known as HTTP, the World Wide Web and the more recent and by far less unanimous concepts of Web 2.0, 'social media', virtual reality, and virtual worlds are similar categories to the metaverse. The metaverse has emerged as a meta-category within which wildly different digital contexts are not apparently anomalous to each other, and, consequently, they can be less dangerous to our individual and collective self-understanding. In the sense of Douglas, the notion of metaverse creates a taboo against traversing the boundaries of this new form of insular reality that attempts to bring homogeneity to the heterogeneity of the virtual sphere (Douglas, 1966). Metaverse is a unifying category that brings together virtual worlds and other types of web services to form a thesis of a coherent whole.

Metaverse as a classification system

Even if metaverse clearly forms a (relatively) distinct category within social reality, its insularity is not monolithic. A closer look at the different contexts of metaverse, from three-dimensional worlds to text-based metaversal realities, reveals a sophisticated web of partly similar but at the same time quite distinct islands of meaning. As we look even more closely at the web of metaversal context, more and more islands become visible. The concurrence of the metaphor of islands in an archipelago used in the virtual world of Second Life and the idea of insularity of social reality discussed by Zerubavel is probably quite unintentional. Interestingly enough, it is capable of shedding light on the order of things in the metaverse.

The heterogeneity of the metaverse reveals an obvious fact, that it is not only a category. It is simultaneously a classification system, an archipelago of the islands of meaning, and, in a sense, very similar to Second Life, which is an archipelago of simultaneously somehow similar but very distinct islands (simulators) with their own explicit and implicit rules and norms. A Second Life version of Berlin in the 1920s (http://1920sberlin.com/) is part of the virtual world, both technically as an island in the Second Life archipelago and, in more abstract terms, by sharing characteristics of the 'generic' Second Life experience. At the same time, it presents residents with a distinct set of rules and categories that are very different from an average Second Life experience and sets the stage for an entirely different shaping and reshaping of meanings. A similar kind of synthesis of the general and the particular applies to most of the contexts in Second Life. Some projects place more emphasis on particularity, while others aim at 'going native' in the virtual world.

The rules and categories of metaversal realities represent distinct modes of expression in these contexts. They function in a largely similar manner to the categories in other types of classification systems. Lev Manovich discerned and described the ascent of a peculiar language of the cinema in the early 20th century and proposed the emergence of a novel language of new media based on the informationalization and databasification of media (Manovich, 2001). Similarly to his work on earlier forms of media, it is possible to conceive that the metaverse produces its own language that shares some characteristics of the new media described by Manovich, but incorporates things that have emerged during the decade following the publication of his work and have become distinct for the particular context of metaverse.

A Manovichian theorization of the metaverse seems to suggest that the classificatory and categorical language of metaverse is a language of what metaverse is, how it functions, and how it is perceived. The language stems from the general and the particular in the metaversal landscape. Places within individual contexts such as Second Life are compared with other places within the same virtual world. At the same time, Second Life is compared with other virtual worlds, and vice versa. Even if it is only a single metaversal context, Second Life is in many ways central to the notion of metaverse. Due to its relative popularity at the time and a capability to capture the public imagination as one of the first widely popular 'generic' virtual worlds, it has become and remained a benchmark of colloquial metaversal conjecture at the time of this writing. The possibility and relative ease of constructing three-dimensional artifacts in Second Life has become a metaversal assumption. The same functionality is assumed of other quasi-similar virtual worlds, and, if the particular functionality is missing, it is a distinct feature of the particular environment. As Pearce notes, however, Second Life is a very artificial benchmark. Even if it has captured the imagination of the media and researchers, it is not the largest virtual world or the only approach to operationalizing the notion of metaverse. A metaverse according to Second Life becomes a 'tyranny of majority' (Pearce and Artemesia, 2010), or, even if Second Life did not represent the majority, a simplification of the metaversal diversity. Even if simplifications are inevitable and, as discussed earlier, a fundamental aspect of human existence, a language of metaverse defined according to a particular system is counterproductive to the intrinsic emphasis of complexity of the very notion.

Considering the diverse and often rather inconclusive definitions of the metaverse, it is not an entirely uncontroversial concept. Metaversal [sic!] definitions of the metaverse tend to underline the convergence of the virtual and augmented realities and the internet, and place specific emphasis on embodiment, sociality, communication, and interaction (Forte and Kurillo, 2010). Metaverse is also attached to ideals of enhanced visual production and reproduction of entities, contextualization, and social presence (Lombardi and Lombardi, 2010), and an aspiration to see metaverse as a context for (Manovichian) language of social and cognitive enhancement with an attempt to realize the cybernetic vision of the convergence of technological and human systems (Vita-More, 2010). It is apparent that metaverse is difficult to describe, to say nothing of defining the term. The fluidity of the language of metaverse is not, however, necessarily a significant problem. The analytical relevance of acknowledging that metaverse has an implicit and explicit classificatory potential is a more significant observation than a futile attempt to seize upon a possibly relevant master theory.

Becoming double-immersed?

It sounds like a grand understatement to call the metaverse just an ordinary medium or tool. Yet the instrumentalist viewpoint is essentially correct, in that the metaverse is as ordinary as a medium or tool can be. The challenge is that nothing is ordinary until it has made us perceive it as a commonplace. Books were once truly extraordinary objects. Mobile telephones were similarly peculiar only a few decades ago. In this sense, like any other mediator of information and experiences, the metaverse is a tool. But, similarly to all tools, including books and telephones, the metaverse has consequences for how we perceive things and how we make things to be. If we learn things in the metaverse, we learn them in a metaverse way. If we are informed, the metaverse *is* the way we are being informed. If we are participating in the metaverse, metaverse becomes a category that influences how we perceive the reality and how the different aspects of reality are related to each other when it is appropriated (in a quasi-Heideggerian sense; Heidegger, 2001) as an instrument of social life.

The metaverse is hardly going to be the single frame of reference for the human experience, but, precisely because of that, it is very easy to get lost in the metaversal illusion. We might think that an observation is clear and information is what we were looking for without realizing the presence and consequences of a metaversal intervention. Besides being descriptive of the perceived similarities between various forms of virtual worlds, augmented reality and internet services, the notion of metaverse makes us assume and perceive further resemblance. At the same time, the convergence of categories affects our expectations of the functioning of the non-augmented forms of reality when the digital and physical realms do not converge. Yet the utopian (or dystopian) tendencies related to the notion of metaverse do not revoke its capability to penetrate into the world of that which is expected. Metaverse does not have to be fully realized to have an impact on our experience of the ordinary.

The evolution of the internet and transition of services from physical desks and telephone lines to the web has not only opened up new opportunities to interact with information in the context of various public and commercial services. At the same time, the emergence of new services has led to phasing out older modes of communication and interaction. A significant issue in the development of virtual worlds has been the lack of physical world affordances in the virtual milieu. In practice, virtual worlds have been interpreted within the frame of the category of physically based reality, or at least as a category that resides on an island of meaning that is not quite distinct from the physical world. In virtual worlds, the fine line was drawn far beyond the capabilities of contemporary technologies to make the desired kind of distinction.

In contrast to the intuitive and fierce attempts to define metaverse as related and unrelated to the physically based reality, and the aspirations to develop classifications of virtual worlds and to describe the phenomenon of virtuality, it is not a given that a fine line will be drawn between the metaverse and the physically based reality at all. Raine Koskimaa observed that the notion of 'digital culture' was becoming extinct already a decade ago (Koskimaa, 2002). Digitality was on the verge of turning into a self-evident part of social life and making 'digital' into a gratuitous attribute in conjunction with the notion of culture. Similarly, at present, the metaverse (as an intersection of virtual and augmented spheres) is becoming an organic part of the structures and practices of everyday life. However, the fact that both 'digitality' and 'metaverse' are becoming notions too colloquial to mention demonstrates their significance in contemporary culture. Precisely because the convergence of the metaversal and non-metaversal parts of reality makes them difficult to distinguish from each other, a closer look at the metaverse as a category and a classificatory principle can provide insights into the changes in the contemporary techno-social landscape.

The effect of the emergence of metaversal categories and islands of meaning that are induced by the colloquiality of metaversal categories in everyday life can be described as *double immersion*. We become immersed not only in the context of metaversal reality (in the convergent reality formed by digital contexts) but also in the representations and projections of metaverse in the physical reality. One of the early examples of digital double immersion was the effect of personal GPS navigators. Inexperienced yachtsmen wrecked their boats on clearly visible rocks and shores when they trusted their navigator more than their own capability to navigate properly. Possessing a portable navigator transferred an individual into an exact position in a virtual world defined by a global map. When technology functions, people are able to transverse physically based reality in a metaverse without being especially observant of their physical surroundings. When technology fails, an individual is thrown back into an unknown physical reality without a capability to navigate to the target. When the virtual world differs from the physically based reality, a poor yachtsman runs into rocks that are in a different position in a virtual world than in the physically based reality.

Celia Pearce describes another case of double immersion (Pearce and Artemesia, 2009). The members of the Gathering of Uru gaming community joined together at a physically based meeting of the community and began to reproduce their in-game collective behavioral patterns in the physical environment. The community members transformed a hotel lobby into a play space and began to play together a game usually played in their virtual world. The partiality of the translation became evident in that, in the physically based reality, the context did not provide automated tools for keeping track of scores in the game. In the absence of automatic scorekeeping, the functionality of the metaversal reality was replaced by a proxy, the husband of one of the players. The result may be described as a physical immersion in the digital context, a double immersion in the metaverse. Patterns of being together in a digital environment affected social intercourse in the physical reality, which was in the end augmented by a physical replica of a digital affordance. The translations of the practices and gestures stretched the social texture over metaversal boundaries.

Double immersion is also present in the partly playful comments on the inconvenience of being incapable of teleporting between two locations in physically based reality in a similar manner to what is done in many virtual worlds. Even if the contemporary impossibility of teleporting in the physical reality is acknowledged as a 'fact', the concept of teleporting is a similar fact that underlines our limitations to act freely. The 'why not' is a consequence of a double immersion in the metaverse and back in the physically based reality. Finally, a similar sense of powerlessness can be felt in the sense of the difficulty of communicating outside the reach of an internet connection. The lack of access to customary social networks and email has become a handicap. Even if the consequences of not being online would be minimal, it is easily sensed as impairment.

The effect of double immersion is twofold. First, it is an indication that a category is becoming dominant in the sphere of colloquial experiences and it has begun to lose its significance as a particular island of meaning in contemporary society. At the same time, double immersion means that a category has become a classification system in its own right. The convergence of the bipolar effect provides a practicable context and a language for discussing and describing the phenomena of everyday life. It is an instrument for drawing fine lines to shape new islands of meaning. Metaverse does not end the existence of the categories of virtual or physical. In a sense, it makes them both something else, albeit hardly 'more', than they are at the present.

Double immersion is undoubtedly a real phenomenon, but it is equally apparent that there is no absolute form of a twofold presence in two categories of reality. For part of the discourse, metaverse remains a category that separates it from other categories, but at the same time it can be used consciously to pinpoint the essence and structures of both inside and outside that which is assumed to be metaversal. The new language forms islands of meaning by drawing fine lines that traverse both metaverse and non-metaverse. The translation is not direct, but the language seems to be capable of assuming forms that function to bring together aspects from the different contexts of human experience. Double immersion may perhaps be seen both as a cause and a consequence of something that Celia Pearce describes as the increasing difficulty of socializing in the physically based reality (Pearce and Artemesia, 2009, p. 191). The category of metaverse exists as a meaningful entity, but at the same time the twofold translation complicates any attempt to make a real distinction. There is still a metaverse and a non-metaverse. The transformation is not translation or reflection, and, indeed, a photograph or a gesture becomes different when it is mediated to the metaverse and back. It is impossible to make sense of things and know separately in the metaverse and outside its boundaries. The outcome is not an emergence of the two realities. Rather, double immersion has made it easier to socialize and categorize reality according to an entire new set of insular realities that are convergent outcomes of the interlinking of the metaverse and physically based reality.

References

Almeida, M., Souza, R., and Fonseca, F. (2011) 'Semantics in the Semantic Web: A Critical Evaluation', *Knowledge Organization*, 38, 3, pp. 187–203.

Baudrillard, J. (1996) 'Disney World Company', *Ctheory, Event-Scenes: E025*. Original French version published in Liberation, 4 March 1996, translated by Francois Debrix.

Bell, M. W., Smith-Robbins, S., and Withnail, G. (2010) 'This is Not a Game: Social Virtual Worlds, Fun, and Learning', in Peachey, A., Gillen, J., Livingstone, D., and Smith-Robbins, S. (eds) *Researching Learning in Virtual Worlds*, London: Springer, pp. 177–91.

Bouchlaghem, N., Thorpe, A., and Liyanage, I. G. (1996) 'Virtual Reality Applications in the UK's Construction Industry', in Turk, Z. (ed.) *Construction on the Information Highway. CIB Proceedings*, May 1996, Slovenia: University of Ljubljana.

Bowker, G. C. and Star, S. L. (2000) *Sorting Things Out: Classification and its Consequences*. Cambridge, MA, USA: MIT Press.

Douglas, M. (1966) *Purity and Danger: An Analysis of Concepts of Pollution and Taboo*. New York: Praeger.

Forte, M. and Kurillo, G. (2010) 'Cyber-archaeology and Metaverse Collaborative Systems', *Metaverse Creativity*, 1, 1, pp. 7–19.

Heidegger, M. (2001) *Poetry, Language, Thought*. New York: Perennical Classics.

Huizinga, J. (1949) *Homo Ludens: A Study of the Play-element in Culture*. London: Routledge.

Huvila, I., Holmberg, K., Ek, S., and Widén-Wulff, G. (2010) 'Social Capital in Second Life', *Online Information Review*, 34, 3, pp. 295–316.

Koskimaa, R. (2002) 'Digitaalinen Kulttuuri', *Agricolan Tietosanomat*, 1. Available from http://agricola.utu.fi/tietosanomat/numero1-02/digikulttuuri.html

Lombardi, J. and Lombardi, M. (2010) 'Opening the Metaverse', in Bainbridge, W. (ed) *Online Worlds: Convergence of the Real and the Virtual*, New York: Springer-Verlag, pp. 111–22.

Manovich, L. (2001) *The Language of New Media*. Cambridge, MA and London: MIT Press.

Mäyrä, F. (2008) *An Introduction to Game Studies: Games in Culture*. London: Sage.

Olson, H. A. (2002) *The Power to Name: Locating the Limits of Subject Representation in Libraries*. Dordrecht and Boston: Kluwer.

Pearce, C. and Artemesia. (2009) *Communities of Play Emergent Cultures in Multiplayer Games and Virtual Worlds*. Cambridge, MA: MIT Press.

Pearce, C. and Artemesia (2010) 'The Diasporic Game Community: Trans-ludic Cultures and Latitudinal Research across Multiple Games and Virtual Worlds', in *Online Worlds: Convergence of the Real and the Virtual*. London: Springer, pp. 43–56.

Soon, T. H., Hong, L. K., and Kuen, K. K. (1999) 'VR Telerobot System', *Proceedings of the 5th International Conference on Manufacturing Technology (ICMT1999)*.

Vita-More, N. (2010) 'Epoch of Plasticity: The Metaverse as a Vehicle for Cognitive Enhancement', *Metaverse Creativity*, 1, 1, pp. 69–80.

Weinberger, D. (2007) *Everything is Miscellaneous*. New York: Times Books.

Zerubavel, E. (1991) *The Fine Line: Making Distinctions in Everyday Life*. Chicago: University of Chicago Press.

18
On the Shoulders of Giants: Understanding Internet-based Generative Platforms

Jonny Holmström

'Standing on the shoulders of giants' is a common metaphor for scientific progress. It is depicted on the Google Scholar website as a reminder of the ways in which a scholar must climb the body of the giant, that is, the accumulated knowledge of previous generations, in order to position his or her research contribution. Building on the published work of other scientists is a fundamental activity that we perform as scholars. The evolving character of science also works well as a metaphor for how internet-based products and services evolve. Indeed, the ubiquity of digitalization is one of the primary forces behind innovations across a wide range of product and service categories, and the so-called 'generativity' of new products and services – the ways in which they continuously evolve and spur future innovations – is evident throughout society (Zittrain, 2006). Each new innovation must 'stand on giants' shoulders' – stand on a generative platform – in order to build something new.

Researchers have long recognized how technology discontinuities present incumbent firms with a set of challenges that are different from the challenges of technology management within continuous regimes. In studying technological discontinuities, we have arguably seen no technology as potentially disruptive as generative internet-based platforms. This chapter is motivated by the power of this disruption and by the simple observation that we are surrounded by technological artifacts of astonishing complexity – from the phones in our pockets to the control systems used in nuclear plants. Amazing feats of coordination are required to produce these objects and make sure they run smoothly in their environments. What is even more amazing is that these artifacts are only the most tangible elements of a global network of interconnected flows of information. They are all integral parts of generative internet-based platforms.

I suggest that these things are not just feats to be marveled at, but rather something that demands a systematic explanation. In what follows, I will explore how the emerging 'Immersive Internet' is increasingly the platform underpinning everyday life and how we need to better understand internet-based generative platforms and their consequences.

The generative internet

Since their introduction, information systems have substantially changed the way business is conducted. This is particularly true for business in the shape and form of cooperation between firms that involves an integration of value chains across multiple units. The resulting networks do not only span the business units of a single firm but typically also include multiple units from different firms. As a consequence, firms do not only need to consider their internal organization in order to ensure sustainable business performance; they also need to take into account the entire ecosystem of units surrounding them. In order to allow these different units to cooperate successfully, the existence of a common platform is crucial.

Many industries use platforms to build derivative products tailored to customer needs. With his well-known Model T, Henry Ford successfully introduced the platform concept into the automotive industry (Alizon et al., 2009). Based on Ford's seminal work, the platform approach has been further developed in the automotive industry (Womack et al., 1990). Platforms are more recently defined by Tiwana et al. as an 'extensible codebase of a software-based system that provides core functionality shared by the modules that interoperate with it and the interfaces through which they interoperate' (Tiwana et al., 2010, p. 676).

Platforms typically consist of multiple layers, such as the hardware layer, the system software layer, the middleware layer, and the application software layer. Moreover, platforms can be established within firms or as a market offering shared services to multiple firms. In addition, different roles need to be distinguished, such as the platform operator, module provider, and module consumer. Platforms can build on different module provider participation models, complemented by specific governance approaches, such as the open model, the proprietary model, or the exclusive model (Economides and Katsamakas, 2006).

Platforms and ecosystems are tightly interrelated. Cusumano and Gawer define the platform and the modules specific to the platform as the platform's ecosystem (Cusumano and Gawer, 2002). Following this notion, the concept of platform-based ecosystems is rapidly becoming the dominant model for software development and software-based services (Tiwana et al., 2010). Well-known examples are the Firefox add-ons and Apple's iPhone apps. Business ecosystems can be defined as an economic community supported by a foundation of interacting organizations and individuals (Moore, 1993). Firms participating in such ecosystems typically co-evolve their capabilities and roles and tend to align themselves with the directions set by one or more focal firms. Tiwana et al. argue that the evolutionary dynamics of platform-based ecosystems and their modules is influenced by the coevolution of the choices of the platform owners endogenous to the ecosystem (e.g., platform architecture and governance) and the environmental dynamics exogenous to the ecosystem (Tiwana et al., 2010).

Generativity is key for internet-based platforms. Jonathan Zittrain uses the term generativity to describe the internet as a generative system which 'might grow or change over time as the uses of a technology by one group are shared with other individuals, thereby extending the generative platform' (Zittrain, 2008, p. 70). The emerging digital innovation landscape rests on an emergent nature of innovation processes in line with processes described by scholars pointing at the social shaping of technology (e.g., Bijker et al., 1987; Leonardi and Barley, 2010). It should be noted, however, that the stabilizing of the meaning of an artifact like a bicycle (Bijker, 1995) or a key (Latour, 1991) or a speed bump (Callon and Latour, 1992) is replaced with more generative mechanisms. Indeed, innovation processes can be characterized by heterogeneity, generativity, locus of innovation, and pace (Yoo et al., 2010). For instance, internet-based generative platforms such as Apple's iPhone operating system and its 140,000 apps are emerging as a dominant model for software development and software-based services. Apple's success with the iPhone illustrates how a well-working platform ecosystem (open or restricted) consisting of the platform and the modules specific to that platform is a key for innovation success in today's digital landscape (Cusumano and Gawer, 2002).

I find generativity to be a key concept in relation to the evolution of ecosystems, as it expresses the ability of a self-organizing system to create and generate independently, with little or no input from the system's originator. The strength of a generative system, Zittrain argues, is its ability to trigger unanticipated change ('innovative output') and to allow for the inclusion of large and varied audiences ('participatory input'). In this chapter I explore the impact of internet-based generative platforms on innovation processes. In particular, I argue that these platforms, when employed mindfully, will lead to an emergence of increasingly new innovations. Indeed, there are many accounts of the growth and success of the internet as a generative communication network. Zittrain traces the internet's success to its generative capacity, that is, 'a technology's overall capacity to produce unprompted change driven by large, varied, and uncoordinated audiences' (Zittrain, 2006, p. 1980). In Zittrain's work, it is the openness of the internet to a wide variety of audiences that is emphasized. In particular, generative technologies generally come with a capacity to leverage, ease of mastery, adaptability, and accessibility.

Generativity denotes a technology's overall capacity to produce unprompted change driven by large, varied, and uncoordinated audiences. As noted by Zittrain, *'Generativity is a system's capacity to produce unanticipated change through unfiltered contributions from broad and varied audiences'* (p. 70; emphasis in original). He lists five elements of generativity:

(1) how extensively a system or technology leverages a set of possible tasks;
(2) how well it can be adapted to a range of tasks;
(3) how easily new contributors can master it;
(4) how accessible it is to those ready and able to build on it; and
(5) how transferable any changes are to others – including (and perhaps especially) non-experts.

In their analysis of the evolutionary dynamics of platform-based ecosystems and their modules, Tiwana et al. note the ways in which the evolution of these ecosystems is immersed in a complex socio-technical system where success or failure depends on a large set of variables (Tiwana et al., 2010). Benkler proposes a three-layer model to discuss how the potential for wider creativity to be unleashed by the internet may be in conflict with the ways in which incumbent media giants can exert content control (Benkler, 2000, 2006). In this model the physical layer infrastructure includes the networks of cables, computing hardware, and radio frequency spectrum. The non-digital physical layer infrastructures include books and magazines, LPs and CDs, video tapes, and so on. The logical infrastructure (or code) layer is the logic that drives the physical infrastructure, for example, data protocols and the software that implements them, as well as services logics embedded in phone networks. Finally, the content layer represents what is sent across the infrastructure, for example, images, text, speech, music, or movies. As noted by Tilson et al., such layers can be stable for long periods (e.g., socio-technical infrastructures built around analog technologies), but gradual changes in one layer impact others and occasionally reach an inflection point that brings about radical change (e.g., unleashing of digital flexibility) (Tilson et al., 2010). These sorts of non-linear interactions across layers can lead to punctuated equilibria in the evolution within and across the socio-technical ecologies. This, in turn, presents any media producer with a complex set of challenges.

Platforms and generative challenges

Platforms redefine the way in which software is produced and distributed, thus fundamentally changing not only the business paradigms of the software industry but also the industries in which platforms are immersed. Thus, emerging platform models have to be evaluated regarding efficiency and effectiveness, and the creation of complementary service models needs critical scrutiny.

As the discussion of platform evolution shows, innovations in the digital age are rapidly transforming the landscape for contemporary business. Rapid advancements in digital computing and digital convergence are modifying business and organizations and disrupting their traditional boundaries and associated ways of operating (Yoo et al., 2010). As a result, my own research has shown how physical artifacts are now being intertwined with digital components that give them digital capabilities in traditional production business processes, such as the mining industry (Jonsson et al., 2009). This in turn raises complex issues regarding the social consequences of such technological advancements, such as the importance of trust in socio-technical settings (Westergren and Holmström, 2012) or even how technological advancements can trigger undesired responses in communities, such as racism (Hsieh et al., 2012). To this end the focus on platforms is a useful approach to address the challenge for researchers to understand the nature of socio-technical reality and the entanglement of humans and technology in practice (Orlikowski, 2007; Orlikowski and Scott, 2008). As we understand the intimate tangle of Information Technology (IT) and organizations, the 'conceptual bubble' of the social/material duality must be burst (Woolgar, 2002) if we are to understand generative platforms, their co-emergence, co-production, and socio-technical consequences.

It is thus safe to say that the digital convergence of applications, devices, networks, and artifacts presents both challenges and opportunities for firms (Yoo et al., 2010). In analyzing the impact of internet-based generative platforms on innovation processes, I argue that these platforms will lead to an emergence of increasingly new digital services. This, in turn, presents us with a number of challenges, which I detail below.

First, the 'triggers' for digital innovation are increasingly difficult to predict and control. The non-linear interactions across layers – physical layer infrastructure, logical infrastructure (or code) layer, and content layer – lead to punctuated equilibria in the evolution within and across the socio-technical ecologies. Such complexity lies at the heart of generativity as defined by Zittrain. This is a challenge for any actor in the realm of digital innovations. In particular, it is a standardization challenge, as the platform paradigm represents a standardization problem that not only consists of competing standards (e.g., battle of platforms such as Android and iOS) but also consists of multiple levels of interdependent standards (e.g., standards on different layers). Moreover, as platforms are highly dynamic, the underlying technologies are very volatile as well, which makes 'platform standards' challenging, or 'morphing' as Tiwana et al. suggest (Tiwana et al., 2010).

Second, the internet-based generative platforms represent a major challenge to firms that want to engage in digital innovations (Yoo et al., 2010). These firms are likely to face never-ending and unbounded innovation challenge in order to keep up with the generative nature of digital innovations. This requires them to organize themselves in new ways. Clearly, the design of the platform architecture and of the corresponding governance has a substantial influence on the decisions of the different ecosystem participants and will thus influence the ecosystem dynamics. Since the ecosystem consists of at least platform provider, module providers, and module consumers – but also increasingly of added-value providers – these interdependencies represent a highly complex and important research topic.

Third, there is a particular challenge in understanding the dynamics behind the coevolution of endogenous choices by platform owners and the dynamics of an ecosystem's exogenous environment. Clearly, when understanding the influence on evolutionary dynamics of such ecosystems there is a tendency to underestimate the exogenous environment and overestimate the role of the endogenous environment.

Fourth, there is a clear tendency towards the free/open option for content. While this may be welcomed by many, it also presents many incumbent firms with challenges. Incumbent firms in many different industries are currently challenged by the ways in which digital content is increasingly free of charge (Holmström and Boudreau, 2006; Holmström et al., 2010).

There is no reason to believe that the waves of digitization are finished. In fact, what we have witnessed to date may well be just the early phases. Cloud computing, web services, and related approaches will arguably result in infrastructures operating at higher layers of the stack than current networking protocols, which could again be catalysts for new radical platform-based innovations (Arthur, 2009; Rönnbäck et al., 2007). Against this backdrop it is clear that we need to better understand not only the opportunities but also the challenges associated with platform-based innovation. The complexity of the 'dual aspect' of such innovation must be better understood. Compared with traditional, non-platform-based markets, platform-based markets must be understood as dual or two-sided, as platform providers must get both consumers and developers of complementary applications on board in order to succeed. An example is the video game console market, where the platform providers (such as Sony, Nintendo, and Microsoft) produce game consoles, with each console having its own associated developer and player communities. In addition, developers and users of modules do not only decide for a certain platform because of the benefits delivered but also because of the opportunities of getting involved in shaping the services deployed on the platform. Therefore, the platform itself becomes a function of the involved entities' decision behavior. An investigation of how value is constituted is thus critical to better understand the success of different platforms. Such an understanding might help platform and module providers to design better offerings and attract and retain more customers.

Conclusion

An important motivation for writing this chapter is to explore generative platforms as legitimate strategic choices for both scholars and managers to consider as they seek to understand key aspects of the Immersive Internet. While scholars have developed a deep understanding regarding the broad patterns in technology life cycles (e.g., Abernathy and Utterback, 1978; Henderson, 1995; Klepper, 1996) and the dynamics of technology emergence (e.g., Adner and Levinthal, 2001; Basalla, 1988; Sahal, 1985), far less attention has been focused on generative platforms, their evolution, and their consequences.

Innovation is critical, but it is not trivial for firms to determine which kind of innovation to choose, as innovation challenges existing capabilities in different ways. In any case, architectural competencies play an important role in the design of platform architecture. However, the development of such competencies is in itself full of dilemmas. The key ambition in this chapter was to draw attention to the neglected problem of how the 'generativity' of new products and services – the ways in which they continuously evolve and spur future innovations – presents us with some very specific challenges. As noted in the Introduction, the literature on generative platforms is still in its early stages. Further rigorous analysis is needed on issues such as the impact of generative platforms on innovation among ecosystem actors. In this chapter, I argued for the importance of better understanding internet-based generative platforms. Indeed, the ubiquity of digitalization is one of the primary forces behind innovations across a wide range of product and service categories, and it is becoming increasingly clear how new innovation must 'stand on the shoulders of giants' – stand on a generative platform – in order to build something new. As a consequence, the information systems field must discard the notion of the information systems artifact as the center of activity that builds identity and legitimacy for the field and replace it with generative platforms at the core.

References

Abernathy, W. J. and Utterback, J. M. (1978) 'Patterns of Innovation in Industry', *Technology Review*, 80, pp. 40–7.

Adner, R. and Levinthal, D. (2001) 'Demand Heterogeneity and Technology Evolution: Implications for Product and Process Innovation', *Management Science*, 47, pp. 611–28.

Alizon, F., Shooter, S. B., and Simpson, T. W. (2009) 'Henry Ford and the Model T: Lessons for Product Platforming and Mass Customization', *Design Studies*, 30, pp. 588–605.

Arthur, W. B. (2009) *The Nature of Technology: What It Is and How It Evolves*. New York: Free Press.

Basalla, G. (1988) *The Evolution of Technology*. Cambridge: Cambridge University Press.

Benkler, Y. (2000) 'From Consumers to Users: Shifting the Deeper Structures of Regulation Toward Sustainable Commons', *Federal Communications Law Journal*, 52, p. 561.

Benkler, Y. (2006) *The Wealth of Networks: How Social Production Transforms Markets and Freedom*. New Haven: Yale University Press.

Bijker, W. E. (1995) *Of Bicycles, Bakelites, and Bulbs: Toward a Theory of Sociotechnical Change*. Cambridge: MIT Press.

Bijker, W. E., Hughes, T. P., and Pinch, T. (1987) *The Social Construction of Technological Systems: New Directions in the Sociology and History of Technology.* Cambridge: MIT Press.

Callon, M. and Latour, B. (1992) 'Do Not Throw Out the Baby with the Bath School', in Pickering, A. (ed.) *Science as Practice and Culture.* Chicago: Chicago University Press, pp. 343–68.

Cusumano, M. and Gawer, A. (2002) 'The Elements of Platform Leadership', *Sloan Management Review*, 43, 3, pp. 51–8.

Economides, N. and Katsamakas, E. (2006) 'Two-sided Competition of Proprietary Vs. Open Source Technology Platforms and the Implications for the Software Industry', *Management Science*, 52, 7, pp. 1057–71.

Henderson, R. M. (1995) 'Of Life Cycles Real and Imaginary: The Unexpectedly Long Old Age of Optical Lithography', *Research Policy*, 24, pp. 631–43.

Holmström, J. and Boudreau, M.-C. (2006) 'Communicating and Coordinating: Occasions for Information Technology in Loosely Coupled Organizations', *Information Resources Management Journal*, 19, 4, pp. 23–38.

Holmström, J., Wiberg, M., and Lund, A. (2010) *Industrial Informatics Design, Use and Innovation.* Hershey, PA: IGI Global.

Hsieh, J. J., Keil, M., Holmström, J., and Kvasny, L. (2012) 'The Bumpy Road to Universal Access: An Actor-network Analysis of a US Municipal Broadband Internet Initiative', *The Information Society*, 28, 4, pp. 264–83.

Jonsson, K., Holmström, J., and Lyytinen, K. (2009) 'Turn to the Material: Remote Diagnostics Systems and New Forms of Boundary Spanning', *Information and Organization*, 19, pp. 233–52.

Klepper, S. (1996) 'Entry, Exit, Growth and Innovation Over the Product Life Cycle', *The American Economic Review*, 86, pp. 526–83.

Latour, B. (1991) 'Technology Is Society Made Durable', in Law, J. (ed.) *A Sociology of Monsters. Essays on Power, Technology and Domination.* Routledge, pp. 103–31.

Leonardi, P. M. and Barley, S. R. (2010) 'What's Under Construction Here? Social Action, Materiality, and Power in Constructivist Studies of Technology and Organizing', *The Academy of Management Annals*, 4, 1, pp. 1–51.

Moore, J. F. (1993) 'Predators and Prey: A New Ecology of Competition', *Harvard Business Review*, 71, 3, pp. 75–86.

Orlikowski, W. J. (2007) 'Sociomaterial Practices: Exploring Technology at Work', *Organization Studies*, 28, 9, pp. 1435–48.

Orlikowski, W. J. and Scott, S. V. (2008) 'Sociomateriality: Challenging the Separation of Technology, Work and Organization', *The Academy of Management Annals*, 2, 1, pp. 433–74.

Rönnbäck, L., Holmström, J., and Hanseth, O. (2007) 'IT-adaptation Challenges in the Process Industry: An Exploratory Case Study', *Industrial Management & Data Systems*, 107, 9, pp. 1276–89.

Sahal, D. (1985) 'Technological Guideposts and Innovation Avenues', *Research Policy*, 14, pp. 61–82.

Tilson, D., Lyytinen, K., and Sørensen, C. (2010) 'Digital Infrastructures: The Missing IS Research Agenda', *Information Systems Research*, 21, 4, pp. 748–59.

Tiwana, A., Konsynsky, B., and Bush, A. A. (2010) 'Platform Evolution: Coevolution of Platform Architecture, Governance, and Environmental Dynamics', *Information Systems Research*, 21, 4, pp. 675–87.

Westergren, U. and Holmström, J. (2012) 'Exploring Preconditions for Open Innovation: Value Networks in Industrial Firms', *Information and Organization*, 22, pp. 209–26.

Womack, J. P., Jones, D. T., and Roos, D. (1990) *The Machine that Changed the World*. New York: Rawson Associates.

Woolgar, S. (2002) 'After Word? On Some Dynamics of Duality Interrogation', *Theory, Culture & Society*, 19, 5/6, pp. 261–70.

Yoo, Y., Henfridsson, O., and Lyytinen, K. (2010) 'The New Organizing Logic of Digital Innovation: An Agenda for Information Systems Research', *Information Systems Research*, 21, 4, pp. 724–35.

Zittrain, J. (2006) 'The Generative Internet', *Harvard Law Review*, 119, pp. 1974–2040.

Zittrain, J. (2008) *The Future of the Internet – And How to Stop It*. New Haven and London: Yale University Press.

19
Social Norms, Regulatory Policies, and Virtual Behavior

Andrew Harrison, Brian E. Mennecke, and William N. Dilla

Introduction

Where do virtual worlds end and the real world begin? Many consider the boundary between virtual worlds and real-world phenomena to be quite distinct, with the delineation drawn based on criteria such as representations (e.g., avatar appearance, behavior), functions and capabilities (e.g., communication through voice, movement, and gestures; flying or teleporting), social dynamics (e.g., the social system, norms, social structures, and composition), and artifacts (e.g., electronically generated objects). There are many problems with relying on these criteria alone or in combination. Chief among these problems is that the criteria for drawing these boundaries are often chosen based on preconceptions involving the social construction of what defines value to the user (e.g., a physical chair is more valuable than a virtual chair) or the limited frame of reference used to define differences (e.g., in many virtual environments, an avatar can fly or carry out other superhuman feats; however, with proper technology support, one could also fly in the 'real world'). Given this, we conclude that these commonly applied criteria for establishing boundaries are arbitrary, ill-defined, and ultimately unstable.

We argue that the three most important criteria for comparing and contrasting the 'real world' and virtual worlds are based on behaviors, normative structures, and regulatory systems. However, these three domains are not of equal importance, because these domains possess asymmetric rates of convergence between the virtual and real worlds. Physical and virtual worlds each have their own distinct behavioral forms, social norms, and regulatory policies, and yet interactions between virtual and physical systems produce pressures towards conformity for each dimension in both settings. The processes through which behaviors, social norms, and regulatory policies overlap, shift, expand, and contract in relation to each other creates confusion about how to apply laws and policies for actions occurring within virtual worlds and how to arbitrate justice within virtual environments. Confusion over jurisdictional issues and the definitions of crimes like harassment, assault, theft, and fraud emerges from the interaction between these systems (Brewer, 2008; Carli, 2007; Lazarus, 2010). Examining behavior with respect to the alignment of relevant social norms and regulatory policies in both the virtual and physical environments offers a more consistent framework for understanding the relationship between virtual worlds and the physical world. In this chapter, we examine these relationships with the goal of identifying a framework for understanding and classifying the boundaries between what may be considered real and virtual. We do so by proposing a socio-regulatory framework and then applying this framework by examining how virtual-world and real-world socio-regulatory systems evolve and converge. We conclude the chapter with a discussion of the model and its implications for understanding the dynamic interplay of behaviors, norms, and policy in both virtual and real-world settings.

A socio-regulatory model of virtual worlds

A thorough examination of the regulatory policies and social norms applicable to actions occurring within virtual worlds requires a dynamic socio-regulatory model. The social and legal motivations occurring in the context of corporate social responsibility (CSR) research provide such a framework and represent the foundation for the model we propose in this chapter. Specifically, when viewed through the lens of CSR, economic, legal, and ethical motivations combine to create a set of domains that overlap and define the relationship between economic self-interest, normative social influences, and regulatory compliance (Carroll, 1991; Schwartz and Carroll, 2003). Figure 19.1 presents this perspective, which we have adapted to examine specific behaviors, norms, and policies that are manifest in virtual worlds.

In our socio-regulatory model, behavior is chiefly motivated by self-interest and examined with respect to the regulatory policies and predominant social norms of the virtual world where the actions occurred. Most 'law-abiding' individuals will act within the domain of these norms and policies, with the result that for most individuals these

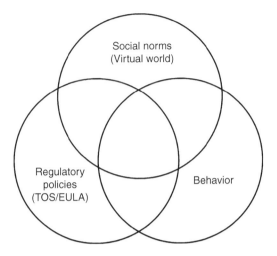

Figure 19.1   Virtual world socio-regulatory model

three domains will principally coincide. These individual behaviors put pressure on the other two domain boundaries, with the result that an equilibrium position is reached where social norms and regulatory policies largely overlap. Individual behaviors and norms are developed through interaction and the interpretation of societal behaviors and norms. A single individual has an array of actions in which they can potentially engage; however, a single person is unlikely to participate in every potential behavior in a virtual world. Some individuals may choose to behave in ways they perceive to be advantageous, even if those actions deviate from applicable social norms and regulations. Thus, for a society with a diverse population, the norms of individual groups and subcultures may also diverge from the norms and regulations held by the broader society.

Given this, we would want to analyze behaviors within virtual worlds at an aggregated level, because the variance in norms and behaviors from regulatory policies is most evident. As a result, our model addresses virtual environments at an aggregate level of behavior, which allows us to apply our model to the spectrum of behaviors exhibited in virtual worlds. This societal view also allows us to understand how social norms and regulatory policies are related to the array of actions taken within these environments. An aggregated level of analysis provides a parsimonious representation that is useful in defining the contextual environment of each virtual world, while maintaining the ability to be applied to study a variety of individual behaviors within virtual worlds. Furthermore, from this perspective the dynamic interactions between social norms, regulatory policies, and behaviors and the mechanisms through which real-world characteristics are absorbed into virtual worlds become more evident. Finally, at this level of analysis we can examine both how behaviors, social norms, and regulatory policies change and evolve in virtual worlds and how these changes influence the real world.

Dynamism within worlds

The increased dynamism and diversity found within virtual worlds fosters the perception that virtual environments are somehow 'different' from the real world. Islands in the virtual world of 'Second Life' are called 'sims', which is short for simulators, and many users have taken this concept to heart when they apply the technology to simulate real-world behaviors or to explore new behaviors. Because these explorations and their consequences often play out in 'internet time', observers may perceive that this diversity and dynamism are themselves unique to virtual worlds. We would argue that, in fact, this diversity and dynamism are not really unique; rather, virtual worlds merely condense what are 'normal' behavioral and societal evolutionary phenomena into more proximate venues and more constrained temporal frames. Virtual worlds give us a unique lens through which we can observe real human behavior and group dynamics (Castronova, 2004; Bloomfield and Rennekamp, 2009; Bloomfield and Cho, 2010). The point is that behaviors in virtual worlds are carried out by real people and are driven by similar motivations, attitudes, and desires to those that drive behaviors that take place in the real world.

In this context, our model accounts for the important factors influencing these diverse and dynamic venues. Because regulatory policies and social norms influence behavior within the virtual world, each domain shifts, overlaps, expands, contracts, and pressures the others. For instance, when social norms are not closely aligned with regulatory policies, there is an incentive to resist legal authority (Sutinen and Kuperin, 1999; Tyler, 1990). Social norms are often derivatives of routinized regulatory policies, but regulatory policies can also result from the institutionalization of predominant social norms (Edelman and Suchman, 1997). Figure 19.2 represents how pressures of compliance and conformity coerce behavior within acceptable boundaries in accordance with regulatory policies and social norms, while motivation and

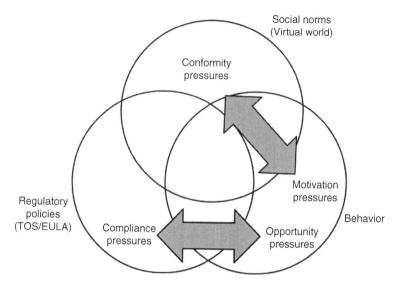

Figure 19.2 Social and regulatory pressures and behavior

opportunities provide an incentive to behave outside the bounds of rules or social norms. The elements of the dynamic socio-regulatory model have an asymmetrical influence on one another and change at idiosyncratic rates. The social norms and regulatory policies of a world can strongly influence behaviors, but behavior has a more muted and slower effect in changing norms and policies because the latter require social consensus.

Most behavior that occurs in virtual worlds is within the regulatory policies of the virtual world and within the social norms of that world's community, but the shifting boundaries between the three domains and discrepancies between these boundaries in the game compared with the boundaries in the real world create a context where much confusion exists about what types of actions are legal or ethical. It is at these boundaries where rules are often ambiguous, unclear, or unrecorded. For example, in a virtual world like EVE Online, the 'wild west' nature of the environment, combined with social and normative pressures, encourages players to engage in increasingly outlandish or unprecedented forms of deception that might be considered to be illegal or fraudulent acts in the real world (Drain, 2010). In such a context, the game developers purposefully design the dynamic nature of the environment with fluid boundaries between the three socio-regulatory domains because it serves to make the game more challenging and engaging (Evelopedia, 2011).

In the model we propose, behaviors are the most likely dimension to shift in response to changes in other dimensions in the model because individual and, by extension, social behavior is more flexible than either social norms or regulatory policy. Behavior is typically guided by a bounded rational self-interest. An individual will be tempted by self-interest to violate social norms when potential actions have associated economic rewards that are outside the bounds of socially accepted behavior. Simultaneously, that individual is motivated to conform to social pressure and abandon purely self-interested behavior for the sake of upholding responsibilities and maintaining relationships. These same counter-valances occur as individuals weigh their economic self-interest against regulatory policies. Many economically beneficial actions occur within the bounds of regulatory policies, and individuals have strong incentives to comply; however, actions outside rules or laws can put strong opportunity pressures on an individual's decision-making processes.

In order to understand behavior in virtual worlds as well as the real world, one must understand the dynamic relationships between social norms, regulatory policies, and behavior. The social norms and regulatory policies that influence behavior are constantly shifting, and there are strong motivational pressures for both adherence to and deviation from social norms and regulatory policies. When deviation does occur, it can result in actions that may be considered illegal, immoral, or both. Although social norms and regulatory policies shift, these shifts involve the collective assent of larger groups of individuals and the shifts tend to be more gradual in comparison to changes in individual behavior, which may occur rapidly and often represent much more dramatic deviations.

The most obvious of these shifts is the tendency for legislative rules to follow social norms. In contrast to behavior, regulations are slow to change and generally require social consensus. As consistent behavior is rationalized, it can become embedded within deeper normative responses. In this manner, behavior tends to be the most malleable element of the proposed model, while regulatory policies are the most static. As a result, rules instituted by a governing institution will only occasionally strongly influence the norms and beliefs of a society, while stronger pressures will exist to adjust regulatory policies to approximately match socially prescribed concepts of justified behavior.

In addition to shifts in social norms, regulatory policies, and behavior, individuals may attempt to portray these factors in an interpretive manner that is in their best interest. Portraying shifts in regulatory policies or social norms is fundamentally different from actually shifting those factors, which would require a more prolonged social process. Nevertheless, an individual may, intentionally or unintentionally, deviate in behaviors based on his or her personal interpretation of regulatory policies and social norms. These individuals may engage in an attempt to persuade others to adopt their perspective, but may also attempt to portray deviations as socially acceptable behavior or within legal confines. After committing an act that is outside norms or legal strictures, individuals often rationalize their behavior by attempting to reduce the obvious gap between the personal norms that guided their actions and conventional social norms or legal constraints. Additionally, a person may attempt to portray his or her actions as more closely aligned with regulatory policy after committing an 'out of bounds' behavior such as fraud. This can also occur when an individual misinterprets, or feigns a misinterpretation of, norms or laws.

Examining the shifting interactions between social norms, regulatory policies, and behavior is a useful way to understand how, for example, fraudulent behavior occurs and why it is considered to be unethical and illegal in most circumstances. This perspective provides a conceptually clear model of how the misalignment between social norms, regulatory policies, and behavior caused by economic pressures of self-interest can result in illegal or unethical actions, and it can also be expanded to model differences in societies that rely on strong social pressures for governance versus those that rely on strong regulatory institutions. Figure 19.3 indicates an environment with strong social controls and

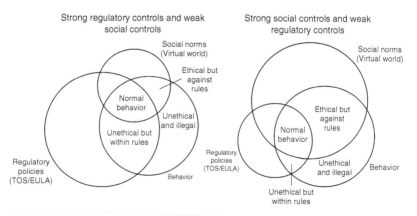

Figure 19.3   Contrasting socio-regulatory systems

weak regulatory controls, which encourages a preponderance of behavior that is ethical but either illegal or unregulated. In this representation, the sizes of the areas displayed are generally not measured in Euclidean distance; rather, the differences in the sizes of the components describe the relative magnitude of each component. In contrast, strongly regulated environments with weak social controls have a higher rate of unethical, but legal, behavior. Virtual worlds, with a wide variety of social and regulatory mechanisms, provide useful tools for developing a more precise understanding of these systems, without risking strong social or economic consequences.

Absorption between worlds

The community constructs social norms within a virtual world, but they are based on real-world social norms. In some virtual worlds, like Habbo Hotel, social norms are closely aligned with real-world social norms, while in other virtual worlds, like Eve Online, they deviate significantly (Evelopedia, 2011; Habbo Hotel, 2009) and appeal to a wide range of motivations to participate (Yee, 2006). As described in Figure 19.4, the virtual and real-world social environments pressure and affect each other, and traits of virtual communication can be manifested in subsequent real-world social interactions (Nardi et al., 2000). Regulatory policies are derived from social norms (Edelman and Suchman, 1997),

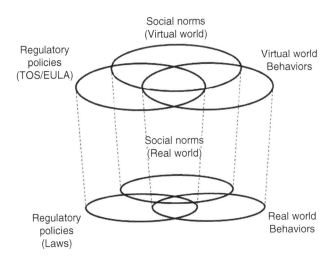

Figure 19.4 Absorption between real and virtual worlds

and, as a result, virtual-world and real-world regulatory policies are also indirectly affected by changes to social norms in each domain.

New or unanticipated actions occurring within a virtual world, or mediated through a virtual world, can result in real-world legal actions (Lazarus, 2010; Sophos, 2005, 2007). In some cases, actions occurring within a virtual world are perceived as violations of real-world laws (Knight, 2005), while some actions are considered to be outside the scope of real-world laws (Brewer, 2008; Finlayson, 2005). Some countries, such as Korea, tend to have very literal interpretations of virtual phenomena and prosecute the theft of virtual assets, while other countries, such as the US, have been more deliberate in addressing specific issues such as theft, taxation, and gambling within virtual worlds (Mennecke et al., 2010; Papagiannidis et al., 2008). Virtual world participants are not always governed by the same legal policies as a result of the geographically dispersed nature of virtual world participation, causing confusion in interpreting jurisdictional authority. Crimes may be perpetrated within a virtual world by a person living in one country against a victim living in a second country, and the servers supporting the virtual world may be located in a third country. As a result, virtual worlds absorb an assortment of international regulatory statutes into a unique melting pot of rules loosely based on regulatory concepts stemming from the real world but unbounded by many of the constraints that govern behaviors during real-world interactions. This conglomeration reflects the integration of a variety of social norms that form the bases of regulations.

Social norms in virtual worlds often appear to be distinctive relative to real-world social norms. For example, it is not unusual for a player in a competitive game such as 'World of Warcraft', 'EVE Online', or 'Star Wars Galaxies' to rob, threaten, or kill one of his or her opponent's characters. Similarly, in less competitive virtual worlds such as 'Second Life', behaviors that might violate real-world social norms, such as avatar infidelity or second marriages between virtual-world characters, are not uncommon. Such abnormal behavior occurs either because the nature of the virtual world is such that the behaviors represent a component of the character of the game or because they exceed the boundaries of situations for which there are predefined social expectations and obligations. When players rob, threaten, or kill other players' characters in competitive games, this is generally within both legal and socially acceptable boundaries because it is integral to the nature of the game, was ascribed as part of the game by the game designers, and was assented to by the players when they consented to the terms of service. In a way, such behavior is no different from taunting and 'beating' an opposing sports team or besting a rival business in a competitive marketplace.

Alternatively, when behaviors such as virtual infidelity occur, it is likely in part a consequence of moving beyond the boundaries where existing norms and laws offer clear guidance about what is proper or legal behavior. For example, a spouse who is discovered by his or her partner to have engaged in a virtual affair may rationalize the behavior by citing, 'It is just a game.' While a naïve spouse may accept such an explanation, attitudes will likely change as his or her understanding of the nature of the virtual relationship evolves. In other words, as the spouse learns more about the nature of the game, the virtual world relationship, and the effect on the real-world relationship, it is likely that the norms for playing the game will 'catch up' with the norms that exist for the relationship in the real world. These examples illustrate that, when new social circumstances evolve within virtual worlds for which normative conventions need to be developed, these circumstances may be considered deviations from real-world analogs in the short term. However, in the long term, virtual-world norms and rules will likely move towards conformance with real-world norms and regulations.

We argue that behaviors exhibited within virtual worlds are extensions of the user's behavioral tendencies and proclivities towards real-world behaviors. As a result, real-world behaviors often are absorbed into virtual world activities. We posit that the same principles of bounded rationality and self-interest also govern motivations within a virtual world and that behavior is guided by these principles in accordance with the regulatory and social characteristics of the virtual world. Thus, behaviors in a virtual world involve the same logical processes that motivate and rationalize behaviors in the real world, but the decision-making processes can result in drastically different conclusions for virtual-world actors due to the unique social and regulatory characteristics of the virtual world. In large part, perceptions about where and how virtual worlds differ from real worlds are rooted in these apparent discrepancies between how we see people act in these two venues, yet, while the form of behaviors may appear to be different, the motivations underlying these actions are quite comparable to those held by these same individuals when they engage in real-world behaviors. As noted, the rules and norms that motivate these behaviors are different. As we will elaborate below, norms and rules are slow to evolve and, as a result, actually represent a more useful way to demarcate the boundaries between real and virtual.

Misalignment between worlds

The shifting relationship between the characteristics of virtual worlds and the real world creates a variety of complexities. While virtual worlds are ultimately coupled to the real world in terms of the three domains in our model, a lag exists between these worlds, so that norms and regulations are often out of sync with real-world conventions and rules. This is due, at least in part, to the dynamic nature of behavior in virtual worlds and the ability of virtual world vendors to manipulate environments in unique and unanticipated ways. This can create an environment where actions and events within virtual worlds have real-world consequences for which there are no regulatory or social principles that effectively guide or restrict both virtual-world and real-world responses. This lack of precedent also creates confusion because individuals and groups may react differently to similar situations that occur within each venue. For example, in some jurisdictions the theft of virtual assets may be punished and those virtual assets may be taxed, while in other jurisdictions the theft of virtual assets or wealth accumulation would not trigger any real-world legal consequences (Brewer, 2008; Carli, 2007). We argue that some misalignments will always exist because the real world lags behind the frontier of behaviors in virtual worlds, but, in general, norms and rules within virtual worlds will move towards equilibrium with the real world.

The asymmetrical rates of absorption for regulatory policies and social norms play an important role in the prominence of misalignments. Most misalignments are ephemeral and occur as virtual worlds explore new frontiers for which no practical social norms or regulatory statutes already exist. Within the virtual world, we suggest that over time virtual world norms and rules that are truly out of sync with their counterparts in the real world will converge towards their real-world equivalents. Additionally, these misalignments may also become integrated into real-world social and regulatory structures as the real-world rules catch up with new phenomena that emerge within virtual worlds. For example, tax policies and regulations that have had to be re-examined in light of virtual-world economics and realized incomes illustrate this real-world feedback from virtual worlds (Terando et al., 2008). Because changes to regulatory policies generally require social consent, regulatory changes are absorbed at a slower rate than social norms. Accordingly, regulatory differences constitute the most practical and robust domain in which to delineate between virtual worlds and the real world, because laws and rules are the most persistent, least ambiguous, and easiest to document.

In contrast to the temporary misalignments caused by the exploratory nature of virtual worlds, some misalignments are more durable because they represent fundamental differences in the underlying conditions and structures of a virtual world. In these circumstances, the characteristics of the phenomena that govern the development of regulations and norms differ significantly from their real-world counterparts. In a virtual world, it is not uncommon for theft to be considered a greater crime than murder because the loss of a virtual asset may be a more significant and enduring loss than a temporary loss of a virtual character's life. Thus, the virtual world remains rooted in the notion that behaviors that cause the highest magnitude of loss should be the most aggressively deterred or punished. However, the magnitude of loss associated with specific behaviors can vary dramatically between virtual worlds and the real world. Under these conditions the absorption of real-world norms and rules is much less pronounced, and there is little pressure to align the characteristics of the virtual world with the real world. Thus, to understand the relevant context and predict behaviors within virtual worlds, it is necessary to understand both the current socio-regulatory state of a virtual world and the trajectory and rate of its absorption of real-world social norms and regulations.

Conclusion

The real world and virtual worlds affect each other, and the links between these environments and the misalignments that occur cause consequential confusion and misunderstandings (Lazarus, 2010). However, misalignment is not always bad; it can act as a guide for experimentation to explore behavior in environments that are not bounded by the same physical, regulatory, or social rules as the real world. We argue that these differences between the social and regulatory boundaries within virtual worlds and the real world constitute important and often overlooked distinctions that are necessary for understanding behavior within virtual worlds. For example, in many virtual environments the killing of another person's avatar is not viewed with the same type of social stigma as in the real world, whereas the theft of virtual assets is considered to be a serious form of misconduct. To adequately understand how people and organizations function within the context of a virtual world, it is critical to understand how these behaviors are shaped and linked to real-world analogs. Consequently, we posit that the social norms and regulatory policies within these worlds provide unique frames for behaviors motivated by self-interest and bounded rationality and offer an improved understanding of how social norms, regulatory policies, and behavior within a virtual world interact and evolve. Consequently, the differences in these domains represent the most persistent and relevant criteria for differentiating these worlds.

Additionally, we suggest that an understanding of how the various elements of the proposed socio-regulatory model interact is critical in anticipating how changes within virtual worlds and the real world are likely to affect each other. Reflecting on the normative and regulatory distinctions relevant to a virtual world provides a useful method for examining phenomena within these worlds while retaining critical relevant context. A clear understanding of the relevant social norms and regulatory environment within virtual worlds provides a critical foundation for utilizing virtual worlds as simulated settings for studying individual and group behaviors.

References

Bloomfield, R. and Cho, Y. (2010) 'Unregulated Stock Markets in Second Life'. Working paper, Cornell University, pp. 1–43. Available at http://papers.ssrn.com/sol3/papers.cfm?abstract_id=1695057

Bloomfield, R. and Rennekamp, K. (2009) 'Experimental Research in Financial Reporting: From the Laboratory to the Virtual World', *Foundations and Trends in Accounting*, 3, 1, pp. 1–85.

Brewer, J. (2008) 'When a Virtual Crook Struck this Gamer, He Called Real Cops', *St. Paul Pioneer Press*, 31 January. Available at http://www.lexisnexis.com

Carli, R. (2007) 'The Sword, the Thief, and the EULA: A Virtual Property Crisis in Online Videogames', *Ethics and Law on the Electronic Frontier*, Massachusetts Institute of Technology, Department of Electrical Engineering and Computer Science, 6.805.

Carroll, A. (1991) 'The Pyramid of Corporate Social Responsibility: Toward the Moral Management of Organizational Stakeholders', *Business Horizons*, 34, 4, pp. 39–48.

Castronova, E. (2004) 'The Right to Play', *New York Law School Law Review*, 49, 1, pp. 185–210.

Drain, B. (2010) 'EVE Evolved: Outlaws of EVE', *Massively: Daily News About MMOs*, 8 August. Available at http://www.massively.com/2010/08/08/eve-evolved-outlaws-of-eve/

Edelman, L. B. and Suchman, M. C. (1997) 'The Legal Environments of Organizations', *Annual Review of Sociology*, 23, pp. 479–515.

Evelopedia (2011) 'Corporation Management Guide'. Available at http://wiki.eveonline.com/en/wiki/Corporation_management_guide

Finlayson, A. (2005) 'Online Gamer Killed for Selling Virtual Weapon', *The Sydney Morning Herald*. 30 March. Available at http://www.smh.com.au/news/World/Online-gamer-killed-for-selling-virtual-weapon/2005/03/30/1111862440188.html

Habbo Hotel (2009) 'The Habbo Way'. Available at http://www.habbo.com/help/51

Knight, W. (2005) 'Computer Characters Mugged in Virtual Crime Spree', *New Scientist*, 18 August. Available at http://www.newscientist.com/article/dn7865

Lazarus, D. (2010) 'A Real-world Battle over Virtual-property Rights', *Los Angeles Times*, 30 April. Available at http://articles.latimes.com/2010/apr/30/business/la-fi-lazarus-20100430

Mennecke, B. E., Terando, W. D., Janvrin, D. J., and Dilla, W. N. (2010) 'It's Just a Game, or Is It? Real Money, Real Income, and Real Taxes in Virtual Worlds', *Communications of the Association for Information Systems*, 20, pp. 134–41.

Nardi, B. A., Whittaker, S., and Bradner, E. (2000) 'Interaction and Outeraction: Instant Messaging in Action', *Proceedings of the ACM Conference on Computer Supported Cooperative Work*, pp. 79–88.

Papagiannidis, S., Bourlakis, M., and Li, F. (2008) 'Making Real Money in Virtual Worlds: MMORPGs and Emerging Business Opportunities, Challenges, and Ethical Implications in Metaverses', *Technological Forecasting and Social Change*, 75, pp. 610–22.

Schwartz, M. S. and Carroll, A. B. (2003) 'Corporate Social Responsibility: A Three-Domain Approach', *Business Ethics Quarterly*, 13, 4, pp. 503–30.

Sophos (2005) 'Suspected Gang Who Stole from Online Game Players Arrested in Korea', 8 July. Available at http://www.sophos.com/pressoffice/news/articles/2005/07/va_krarrests.html

Sophos (2007) 'Habbo Hotel Sounds Alarm on Real Theft of Virtual Furniture', 15 November. Available at http://www.sophos.com/pressoffice/news/articles/2007/11/habbo-hotel.html

Sutinen, J. G. and Kuperan, K. (1999) 'A Socio-economic Theory of Regulatory Compliance', *International Journal of Social Economics*, 2, 6, pp. 174–93.

Terando, W. D., Dilla, W. N., Mennecke, B. E., and Janvrin, D. J. (2008) 'Tax Policy in Virtual Worlds: Issues Raised by Second Life and Other Unstructured Games', *Journal of Legal Taxation*, 6, pp. 94–107.

Tyler, T. (1990) *Why People Obey the Law*. New Haven and London: Yale University Press.

Yee, N. (2006) 'The Psychology of Massively Multi-user Online Role-playing Games: Motivations, Emotional Investment, Relationships and Problematic Usage', in Schroeder, R. and Axelsson, A. (eds) *Avatars at Work and Play: Collaboration and Interaction in Shared Virtual Environments. Computer Supported Cooperative Work*, 34, pp. 187–207.

20
Self-organizing Virtuality

Rick Oller

Self-organization is a foundational characteristic of nearly everything within our purview. The cosmos is self-organizing: it grew from a singular point to an estimated 150 billion light-years in diameter in the span of approximately 13.7 billion years. Life is self-organizing: in the presumed absence of divine intervention, the first living cells emerged 700 million years after the Earth formed. Life and the planet have coevolved in the ensuing 3.8 billion years, giving rise to a third major self-organizing entity: mind. Mind has spawned a fourth major domain that is on the threshold of becoming self-organizing: technology. Complexity theorist Stuart Kauffman argues convincingly that cells, organisms, and even the various components that constitute markets and economies all exhibit self-organization, or what he terms 'spontaneous order' in tandem with natural selection, in their development processes (Kauffman, 1995).

Human technology cannot yet be characterized as self-organizing – it is largely driven by authorship, design, and determinism. This approach has served us well but is giving way to new paradigms across many disciplines. Semi-autonomous robots that utilize swarming algorithms have exhibited a degree of emergent behavior not possible in prior generations of robots that embodied top-down design principles. Genetic algorithms that emulate evolutionary principles are used today in bioinformatics, engineering, economics, chemistry, and manufacturing (Wikipedia, 2011). Advances in robotics and software design have pointed towards wisdom that the universe has always possessed: optimal existence results from evolution and self-organization. Evolutionary computation, machine learning, artificial life, complexity theory, and swarm computing all borrow heavily from the foundational characteristics of the universe, life, and mind.

One of the more compelling paradigms to arise from the computing revolution is virtuality. This is not a new concept, as the arts and literature have a legacy of created worlds within the pages of a book, the proscenium arch of the theater, and the frame of a canvas. Computational virtuality, however, takes the paradigm much further. Immersion is the hallmark of this arena. It can be all-encompassing, as with the head-mounted displays of virtual reality, or more modestly (yet, arguably, of near-equal effect) with the widespread adaptation of massively multiplayer online role-playing games (MMORPGs) and virtual worlds for common personal and mobile computing platforms. Computational virtuality is also open-ended: games can be scripted (to a degree) but virtual worlds are largely stochastic, with elements of free will and non-determinism that roughly parallel real life.

Virtuality can be thought of as a mode of being. We speak of being 'in-world' when we are immersed. Actions such as unassisted flying and teleporting are 'not possible in real life' or 'NPIRL'. An uncanny fusing of one's identity with the avatar occurs: for example, witness when our avatar suddenly loses its clothes in the company of others – it is almost impossible not to feel embarrassment and turn away. We project our personalities into virtuality, but we also undergo a degree of transformation. Social reticence may ease, allowing more free-flowing interaction and forthrightness. Phobias may lessen, as much more is possible without fear of injury. Real life disabilities can be overcome in-world in ways not possible before the onset of virtuality. Some of us who have spent significant amounts of time in-world may have found ourselves invested in virtuality in ways that surprise us and which have led to rich and meaningful experiences, albeit of an other-worldly nature.

Yet, for many, virtuality falls short of offering a full-blown mode of being and comes to resemble a game without goals or a chat room with a 3D engine bolted on. It may be the specific designs of virtual worlds that are responsible for this disenchanted reaction, or then again it may run more deeply. Perhaps it is not the specific designs that are the problem, but the very fact that these worlds are designed at all. A designer or a team of designers could never think of everything that would keep a vast diversity of minds engaged enough to keep returning, month after month, year after year. And so we see the shift in mass participation from virtuality to social networking that has occurred, and begin to look for root causes.

As our knowledge-modeling tools evolved from myth, scripture, and philosophy to the scientific method, our models of the universe also evolved. Leading-edge theoretical physics takes us beyond the twin 20th-century revolutions of quantum mechanics and relativity to string theory, m-theory, and other models that will inevitably arise in the search for a unified theory of all of creation. The trajectory of this evolution has brought the Newtonian 'background' universe into the foreground, relativizing and quantizing its myriad components into a seamless fabric of reality. Our bodies are made of the same quantum stuff as stars and planets; our minds and consciousness emerge from that self-same substrate. If we map the progress of virtual worlds to this trajectory, virtuality remains in a Newtonian universe. The virtual world is a passive background to us, the 'players'. Worse, it is more stage set than city street, more painted backdrop than landscape, more prop than tool. Granted, it is a social environment that dissolves geographic distance and has tremendous potential for teaching and learning – but the environment itself does not evolve; it does not surprise us with emergent wonders; it does not *live*.

What if the 'world' in virtual worlds could borrow from the playbook of our world? What if it could evolve, self-organize, and spawn life and mind? Algorithms that facilitate these principles (albeit imperfectly) exist and enjoy a level of relative maturity in the domain of artificial intelligence (AI). And what are virtual worlds, if not code? Apart from the inputs of its human participants, a virtual world is code and data and subject to the same manipulations and innovations as any other code base. If code can predict stock market trends, win at chess and jeopardy, drive a car or a Mars rover, model global weather and more, can it not be coaxed to apply existing self-organizational and evolutionary algorithms to the creation and ongoing development of a virtual world?

In cybernetics, dynamical systems have been shown to advance towards a state of equilibrium which chaos theory now calls an 'attractor'. This is a form of self-organization in which various parts of a system are mutually adapted by no other means or agency than the interrelationships of the system's components (Heylighen, 2001). In a multitude of disciplines over the last hundred years, trends in leading-edge thought have gravitated towards the eclipse of centralized command-and-control in favor of distributed models that borrow heavily from natural systems. These a priori systems are all, without exception, self-organizing. They tend to inhabit the interzone between stasis and chaos, seeking stable attractors about which to cycle. Non-dynamical ecosystems, like deserts, yield little in the way of significant biological innovation. Dynamical systems, like coral reefs, attract and multiply combinations and possibilities, creating oases of complexity and fecundity where innovation can prosper.

Language, arguably the most important component of human consciousness and culture, is largely self-organizing. Defying efforts at central planning and control, language evolves and mutates, spawning new words and phrases as it renders others obsolete, forms dialects, specializations, and slang. Poet Gary Snyder calls systems that self-organize and evolve 'wild systems'. Nature, as well as all natural human languages, is shown to be a wild system, deemed by Snyder 'too complex to master simply in intellectual or mathematical terms' (Snyder, 1999, p. 329). Imagination can also be classified as wild in this sense (ibid.).

The feedback mechanisms of cybernetics, the distributed low-level intelligence of modern robotics, machine learning, evolutionary computing, swarm intelligence, and artificial life algorithms are all technological outgrowths of this trend towards wild systems that have relinquished determinism in favor of self-organization and evolutionary models. Similarly to models and theories of the universe, life and mind have evolved from deterministic, top-down theistic or pantheistic scenarios to non-deterministic, bottom-up, self-organizing and evolutionary scenarios, and pedagogical theories have evolved from teacher-centric, one-way transmission of knowledge to learner-centric, networked exchange and creation of knowledge (Sawyer, 2006a, b; Scardamalia and Bereiter, 2003).

Personal learning environments and personal learning networks are concepts that have gained traction in the wake of these trends in learning theory and the proliferation of digital networks and tools. These approaches to learning place the individual in the center, connected to an ever-expanding and changing cloud of tools, knowledge repositories, and peers, many of which arise through serendipitous chains of association rather than as the result of a concerted, centrally designed initiative (Downes, 2005; Siemens, 2005).

Just as the internet has proliferated as a kudzu-like web of nodes and connectors encircling the planet via high-speed telecommunication networks, submarine cables and communication satellites, so have myriad networks of teachers and learners (many fulfilling both roles simultaneously), piggybacking on the capabilities and programs of the web, mobile computing, and communications, formed an intellectual superstructure, communicating, publishing, and subscribing to a burgeoning, dynamic body of knowledge. Communities of practice and communities in the service of education and knowledge creation (often one and the same) form spontaneously in this ecosystem. Attempts at wholesale design and engineering of these entities routinely fail. Communities evolve and self-organize, like living organisms, and as such can thrive independently of any particular member or task (Barab et al., 2004).

Virtual worlds such as Second Life provide fertile ground for teachers and learners to reach out and connect. Through presence embodied in avatars, participants can inhabit and traverse a symbolic landscape, interacting with other intelligences, both human and machine. Non-player characters (NPCs) are avatars with AI that can interact with participant avatars, much like the classic AI programs ELIZA (Weizenbaum, 1966) and Racter (Chamberlain, 1984), which conduct conversations by processing key words and phrases of input and constructing semi-intelligible sentences that appear to respond and converse. So far, NPCs provide the only measure of intelligence and interactivity at the level of software in virtual worlds today. NPCs are a breed of 'narrow AI' designed for a specific purpose and fairly useless outside the confines of their initial design. This is in contrast to general purpose AI, an elusive objective whose time has not yet arrived, which posits an autonomous intelligence, human-equivalent in cognitive ability, though not necessarily in design or behavior.

AI researcher Ben Goertzel posits a general purpose AI that inhabits a virtuality such as Second Life and learns from the human participants (avatars) via linguistic and behavioral interactions. The sheer number of avatars that could potentially be employed in teaching the AI would vastly augment the cognitive development and knowledge stores of the AI, rapidly accelerating its capabilities via distributed, non-deterministic means. Goertzel's AI follows a human developmental model augmented by the multiplying effect of a virtual community of minds. This is one vision of the power of virtuality combined with AI to foster emergent phenomena (Goertzel, 2007).

We suggest a different model, not based on human developmental lines but as the next stage in the progression of the great wild systems. The universe, life, mind, and technology are the systems that have brought us to the threshold on which we now stand. Computational virtuality, coupled with self-organizing and evolutionary algorithms, holds the possibility of humanity's offspring, technology, kick-starting the cycle (universe, life, mind, technology, virtuality) again, at an arguably higher level than the natural antecedents. Virtuality, as a mode of being, is the domain of minds freed from the material constraints of biological bodies, geographical distance, national boundaries, economics, and law. Yes, it can be argued that some or all of these play a role in how we approach virtuality, and yet, once there, these constraints fall away, and we are left with minds interacting with one another (usually in simulacra of familiar bodies and environments). It is precisely because of this freedom from constraint, coupled with the exponential multiplying effect of optimally interconnected minds, that we posit self-organizing virtuality as a higher-level substrate.

Billions of years of self-organization and evolution have resulted in minds that are capable of virtualizing the substrate from which they emerged. Mind now becomes the new substrate, from which emerges virtuality and the limitless growth and development possible therein – but this virtuality will not engender such myriad possibilities without itself becoming a wild system. It is not that no other model is possible – there are plenty of deterministic pathways that have created impressive cultural artifacts – but more that no other model is as powerful, efficient, and capable, or else it would have become the dominant driver for the universe, life, and mind.

What will self-organizing virtuality look like? How will it enhance our experience, our culture, and our lives? If it is employed first and foremost in the service of learning, it cannot help but richly augment and rapidly expand the capabilities of mind interacting with mind. No longer a painted backdrop to our simulated real-world movements, self-organizing virtuality, we predict, will exhibit the following traits.

It will grow from seeds. Initial parameters, combined with self-organizing algorithms and taught by participating minds à la Goertzel, will create an indeterminate, wild system that is completely unpredictable and open-ended. Such a system cannot arrive fully designed and built, like Athena sprung from the brow of Zeus, but must grow as all its antecedent wild systems have.

It will be shaped by its participants. Alongside shaping by evolutionary algorithms, self-organizing virtuality will receive continuous feedback from its participants. If its development takes it down pathways that are antithetical to the goals and sensibilities of its participants, they will reject it, voting 'with their feet'. Conversely, productive, innovative pathways will be rewarded as participation grows virally, spread by word of mouth and the internet. It is worth noting that this is exactly what has happened to commercial virtual worlds in recent years as participants have fled the static simulacra once so popular in favor of the arguably more connective and responsive (yet experientially narrower) domain of social networks.

It will be stable. Self-organizing systems evolve towards equilibrium, seeking stable attractors on the boundary between order and chaos. Lacking the enforcements of direct design, our virtuality will instead embody a living, morphing pattern system wherein the principles of the universe prevail – in this sense it will feel very familiar to us, yet it may also exhibit radically non-human versions of order.

It will reproduce. Virtualities will reproduce, spawning daughter worlds that retain some traits of their ancestors, yet deviate in ways that became impossible in their ancestors. For as virtual worlds grow from seeds, shaped by the feedback of their participants, they will naturally follow certain pathways while avoiding others and become constrained in their development. Reproduction will be a natural outgrowth of this, as continued innovation and evolution will only be possible in subsequent generations that retain favorable traits (ability to attract and retain human participants) but branch in unexpected ways because ultimately this kind of endless exploration of permutation and innovation is the only thing that will continue to engage the ever-increasing, restless, evolving minds that are its substrate.

It will enlighten its participants. Virtuality, where minds can embody anew, freed from the constraints of biology, geography, economics, and law, will prove irresistible to ever-increasing numbers of participants. For if it remains new, generating combinations and forms inconceivable to planners and designers, constantly incorporating the feedback of participants and changing and reproducing in order to survive, it will maximize connectivity and communication among its participants. This is why humanity has followed an exodus from virtual worlds to social networks. Social networks are designed to maximize interaction and engagement at the expense of everything else and have reaped the benefits of their design. Self-organizing virtualities will quickly learn this lesson based on the feedback of their participants and will 'sweeten the pot' of stickiness (participant loyalty) with an ever-accelerating phantasmagoria of immersive wonders unavailable to social networks with their flat, stripped-down interfaces. As participation in self-organizing virtualities grows and connections among participants grow, with virtualities quickly appropriating all the good parts of social networks, the scope of the 'adjacent possible' (to use another concept of Stuart Kauffman's) increases, and innovation and knowledge growth proliferate as a natural outcome (Johnson, 2010). In order to begin to bridge the divide between pure speculative theory and a practical, working self-organizing virtuality, we propose the concept of a rules engine that will help to bootstrap the nascent virtuality into existence.

The rules engine will not offer a set of hard and fast laws by which the virtuality will grow and function. Rather, it will present a scaffolding upon which the virtuality can accrete heuristic structure, much as crystalline growth proceeds from a seed crystal. The rules engine will be subject to the same evolutionary algorithms as the virtuality itself, its output being constantly challenged for fitness in a test harness consisting of model virtualities that are engendered for this purpose alone. Much as instructional scaffolding provides an ecosystem and armature for knowledge acquisition in children, the rules engine will present an analogous scaffolding for the virtuality to grow and learn.

An input to the rules engine could be a 'teaching world' – a legacy virtuality, possibly based on OpenSimulator or some other open source virtual world platform, that would feed all of its interactions with avatars into a repository. The rules engine could learn from the repository (machine learning) about avatar behaviors, interactions, and pathways and track key metrics about membership, affinity, chat content, and more over time.

There is perhaps room for human observers to influence the development of the rules engine, with the caveat that therein lies potential corruption of the model (self-organizing, evolutionary: universe, life, mind) but with the additional caveat that intervention may be necessary on a purely practical level for the purpose of, if nothing else, setting boundaries of reasonableness beyond which the rules engine attractors should not be permitted to cycle. Also, as the engine gathers its library of behaviors, interactions, and pathways from the teaching world, these human observers can act as counselors, guides, and teachers, imparting the benefit of 'soft' logic about human culture, language, history, and the like so that the engine and its pupil, the nascent virtuality, do not develop absurd patterns or behaviors that make sense to the machine but violate human conventions, mores, and cultural practices.

The next step in the training of the rules engine could be to gather empirical data from the internet and, by extension, from the greater culture and world of human affairs. Kevin Kelly characterizes the internet as a 'planetary electronic membrane' with 'three billion artificial eyes (phones and webcams)' (Kelly, 2010, p. 14). This membrane 'sees' the world, recording more and more of what occurs 'out there', and also absorbs increasing swaths of the culture as movies, books, essays, debates, emails (two million per second), and more flow through its networks and servers. Fed on the internet and guided by human counselors, the rules engine could gain a first class education in how a world works and translate this into baseline inputs and rules for the virtuality it instructs.

With these training and educational inputs, the rules engine will be optimally prepared to evolve a heuristic scaffolding upon which the self-organizing virtuality can base its bootstrap and development. As it self-organizes and evolves, the virtuality will feed its acquired knowledge back into the rules engine, the pupil instructing and optimizing the teacher in a virtuous circle that will enable increasingly intelligent virtualities to spawn and flourish.

All of the elements are in place for self-organizing virtualities to begin. The conceptual framework, as outlined above, rests on sound philosophic, artistic, and scientific thought propagated by some of the most innovative minds this planet has produced. The technological capabilities exist, albeit in somewhat siloed form, to begin to build the computational infrastructure. There is no lack of curious, intelligent, forward-thinking people to populate and help guide and teach the nascent self-organizing virtualities. Once a critical mass has formed, there will be no stopping the influx of minds that will grow and shape this novel domain that holds the potential for a new, untethered mode of existence that incorporates all the good parts of its ancestor domains while branching off in an infinite variety of fresh directions and possibilities. Having emerged from the same principles that engendered universe, life, and mind – the same principles that engendered humanity – self-organizing virtuality will, in a very real sense, become our peer, our partner in exploration and knowledge-seeking. As we teach it and it teaches us, as it self-organizes and evolves with our guidance, it is entirely possible that new orders of teaching and learning, interacting and exploring, and perhaps, ultimately, a new order of being will begin to emerge.

Acknowledgments

Many thanks to Jane Wilde (State University of New York at Albany) and Andrea Hodson (Marlboro College Graduate School) for their help and guidance.

References

Barab, S. A., MaKinster, J. G., and Scheckler, R. (2004) *Designing for Virtual Communities in the Service of Learning*. New York: Cambridge University Press.

Chamberlain, B. (1984) *The Policeman's Beard Is Half Constructed*. New York: Warner Books.

Downes, S. (2005) 'An Introduction to Connective Knowledge', *Stephen's Web*. Retrieved from http://www.downes.ca

Goertzel, B. (2007) 'AI Meets the Metaverse: Teachable AI Agents Living in Virtual Worlds', *Kurzweil Accelerating Intelligence*. Retrieved from http://www.kurzweilai.net

Heylighen, F. (2001) 'The Science of Self-organization and Adaptivity', in Kiel, L. D. (ed) *Knowledge Management, Organizational Intelligence and Learning, and Complexity* in *The Encyclopedia of Life Support Systems*. Oxford: Eolss Publishers, pp. 253–80.

Johnson, S. (2010) *Where Good Ideas Come From: The Natural History of Innovation*. New York: Penguin Group.

Kauffman, S. (1995) *At Home in the Universe: The Search for the Laws of Self Organization and Complexity*. New York: Oxford University Press.

Kelly, K. (2010) *What Technology Wants*. New York: Penguin Group.

Sawyer, R. K. (2006a) 'Introduction: The New Science of Learning', in Sawyer, R. K. (ed) *The Cambridge Handbook of the Learning Sciences*. New York: Cambridge University Press, pp. 1–16.

Sawyer, R. K. (2006b) 'Conclusion: Schools of the Future', in Sawyer, R. K. (ed) *Cambridge Handbook of the Learning Sciences*. New York: Cambridge University Press, pp. 567–580.

Scardamalia, M. and Bereiter, C. (2003) 'Knowledge Building', *Encyclopedia of Education* (2nd ed.). New York: Macmillan Reference.

Siemens, G. (2005) 'Connectivism: A Learning Theory for the Digital Age', *International Journal of Instructional Technology and Distance Learning*, 2, 1, pp. 3–10.

Snyder, G. (1999) *The Gary Snyder Reader*. New York: Counterpoint.

Weizenbaum, J. (1966) 'ELIZA – A Computer Program for the Study of Natural Language Communication between Man and Machine', *Communications of the ACM*, 9, 1, pp. 36–45.

Wikipedia (2011) *Genetic Algorithm*. Retrieved from http://en.wikipedia.org

21

Making Currency Personal: The Salutary Tale of the Downfall of the Domdrachma

Matthew Zook

When did it all begin? It is a question that I am tired of hearing, as there is no hard border between the time before and the slide into the age of personal commodification and currency. It really started with the crude computer billing systems of the 1950s that were followed by fits, jumps, and great gulps of data collection. And we were directly complicit with it, a grocery store membership card here, a blog post there, the earning of an elite airline status on one of the long-dead legacy airlines. Bits of information about your diet, your wit, your spending on the daily acts of living sucked up and mashed together by code and commercialism. Of course, the repudiation of the common currency project by Germany in 2015 and the win of the Santorum–Bachmann Tea Party ticket of 2016 'ripped the last freakin' lug nut off' the wheels of central banking before driving the global economy off a cliff. At least we all got to watch the pretty government buildings burn as sousveillance fanatics uploaded constant feeds of their own demise as the ultimate status update, 'The mob iz coming 2 kill me!!! brb!' Some people just don't know when to run.

But in the time after, when we all woke up and brushed off the ash of yesterday's fiat currency, it quickly became obvious that the small squares of plastic and paper that we had in our wallets didn't amount to much more than echoes of the past. I distinctly remember thinking, 'Shit! How am I going to pay for my sushi burrito now?' And, while the gold standard Paulinistas were convinced that their day had finally come, there just wasn't enough of the sparkly stuff to make the world economy go round. And besides, who wants to carry pounds of lucre when you want to throw some bling down in a club? That's when the techno-bank corporations made their play. Although MicrAppleSoft came to market first, their system of centrally verified iBanks badly misjudged both the competition and the mood of the populace, steeped in the Randian rhetoric of Fox News. The first lynching of executives with nooses made out of proprietary dongles and bloatware made MicrAppleSoft retreat faster than Clippy on a linux box. I hear all that is left of that corp(se)oration is the little Jobsian splinter sect and their blood stained iAlters.

Afterwards, in a clear masterstroke, GoogleBook rolled out the beta version of MyMoney, which clearly had been in the works for decades. We had revealed all our secrets – from Skylander preferences to our predilection for icanhascheezburger porn to the all-knowing algorithm. What little nuance and mystery was left, we voluntarily shared with the world with our updates to make us feel big and important. Even before MyMoney, advertisers were using the tera-crumb-bytes we were dropping to rank and judge our ability to consume. It was just a simple extension of the code to use this data to calculate the current and future worth of our capabilities and aspirations and how likely we were to achieve them. No wonder GoogleBook had been collecting all that data on us for years and years.

And at first it seemed like the perfect answer to the global money crisis. Rather than the stale systems of national currency (with all their issues of cross-subsidization and imperfect market feedback), MyMoney revolutionized and personalized the medium of exchange and value. GoogleBook invited each of us (or at least those of us with a high enough Klout score) to establish our own personal currency systems based on constantly updated, floating market values. I heard they were even passing out badges as they used game mechanics to inspire folks to get into the action. Of course, based on the exabytes of data they had collected, GoogleBook made sure that unqualified candidates for personal currencies were categorized into easily acquirable commercial units, freeing them up from the stuffy confines of citizenship. Just goes to show the kind of far-sightedness that went into the making of MyMoney.

In contrast to this vision, I was mainly preoccupied with coming up with a suitable name for my new currency. I toyed around with the obvious Dominic Dollar ($D) and briefly flirted with the Peseta of Power (Pts^2), but that seemed hackneyed. I ended up with the DomDrachma (D₫), which combined a sense of forceful assertiveness with the right blend of wealth and pizazz. Because, when your worth is being constantly calculated by the market, you need to appeal to both the cash and the flash (although a subtle promise of violence can work wonders as well). Of course, having more of the trashy trappings of materiality like real estate, jewels, and such mattered a lot at first, but it was within the intangible dimension of reputation, networks, and trendiness where the real money was to be made. And, damn, was it made.

Suddenly your network influence, your 'ability to drive action' as they said in the old days, was your worth and self-absorbed, navel-gazing about one's 'amplification' was the short path to riches. Luckily for me, this was an arena in which I excelled. Create a popular You&I-Tube feelie experience, LOLbratz meme, or integrate into the right social networks, and you'd see the value of your personal currency rise. Likewise, if you made a lame joke, delivered a poor presentation, or made unfortunate clothing choices, then your currency would tank. I remember several of my former academic colleagues destroying their net worth with a single lecture and having to fall back on eking out an existence in a boilerplate essay writing shop. Poor blokes, but at least I was able to salvage their publications (subject, of course, to my retroactive first-authorship) from disgrace. In the big picture, no one gave a damn about these articles anymore, but, since that had always been the case, I indulged my vanity a bit. I had acquired enough serious scratch to even change the name of my old discipline 'economic geography' to dominography, which had a much nicer ring to it anyway.

Of course, at first the geeks were all over it like Trekkies on Shatner as their hacker ethicists hailed MyMoney as the bright dawn of a new meritocracy. Finally the geeks would hackerbate their way to a world of endless silicon casual Fridays! Man, those nerds learned nothing in high school. Save for a few uber-geekoids, most ended up as code-monkeys in the _why-villes controlled by the new digiglitteratis. After all, it was the social networking, not the code, that drove value in MyMoney, and precious few techies had any meaningful chops in that area. And, once GoogleBook released MyMoney 3.0 (the natural artificial intelligence toolset) in 2018, any pretty face suddenly had the same coding abilities as the palest nerd herd in their mother's basement. Still, it must have been a shock to them that the skills of the coder-set were about as valuable and rare as a hipster in Portland. Thus, with the rise of the know-bots of AI making the software and the robots taking over the making of things in the factories of Asia, the only thing that the no-bots (formerly known as people) still had that was worth something was their network and what they could make of it.

As a result, most of the population were judged as 'high-risk' currencies and were strongly encouraged to join easily digestible work units that could be indentured to high value currencies' properties. Although a few radicals called this neo-slavery, it was more correctly termed the Strategic Alliance of Personalities (SAP) program and was designed to work in the interest of both parties. The sapped (as the debtor side was commonly referred to) got the security of three-month contracts and the promise of hard currency bailouts if they produced, and the merkels (the financially stable side) were able to show their benevolent nature (which was rumored to be a key variable in the MyMoney CurrencyRank algorithm) as well as pick up some material from the sapped to deploy across the social network markets. At the peak I had about 30,000 sappeds moving on and off contract at any time, and I loved being a job creator. More importantly, I knew that the sapped I employed loved me, as it was a clear contractual requirement outlined in Section 8, Paragraph 5.

To be frank, most of the stuff coming from the sapped was crap, but thankfully I had a layer of senior workers (known as sappers) who got the security of 12-month commitments (subject, of course, to meeting the usual metrics) to sort through and prioritize it. But still an occasional rough stone would surface that I was able to polish via some outsourced sapped public relations types into a good idea. For example, my line of designer and predigested breakfast cereals. Very popular in sub-Saharan Africa, Latin America, and Central Asia despite reports that it was less nutritious than dirt. Btw, this was completely wrong, as I know that at least 45 per cent of the mass of the cereal was formerly living carbon-based substances that logically had to increase the nutritional value of the sand that we were using as filler.

God, it was great. My twitter, feelie and smellie feeds went into international syndication and doors opened worldwide. Finally, I could live the dream of freedom – 'To ask nothing. To expect nothing. To depend on nothing' and stop asking 'who the freak' John Galt was. And the DomDrachma (D₄) did well. As a faceman with good teeth, a sense of how to dress, and the ability to banter across pop culture, fashion, and economic theory, I, or more correctly the DomDrachma (D₄), entered into a golden age of expanding influence, strong exchange rates, and easy credit. Of course I had jettisoned all of my former and increasingly exchange-of-payments-challenged friends, but least said, soonest mended. And besides, it was no trouble to leverage better-looking and more connected friends on a variety of one to six-month contracts in short order. With the market commodification of all social transactions – including friendship – everyone and everything was subject to the forces of international financial trading/speculation. People thought the dating scene was cut-throat in the old days; but better a meat market that left only a sense of shame and a rash the day after than the financial drubbing that a beer-goggled selection could inflict on your net worth in the new system. I once got some bad tequila in Chongqing and ended up in a hookup with someone with a concrete fetish that almost ruined me when the news hit the nets. Luckily, I was able to spin it into a morality tale of redemption that almost put me on the path to the presidency (not that it really matters much anymore) and served as the basis of my new religion, Domitology – talk about profit margins! But the important thing is that the experience solidified the creativity and inspirational value of the DomDrachma (D4) property. After all, a creative man is motivated by the desire to achieve, not by the desire to beat others.

Still, I must admit that everything wasn't perfect, especially since the old adage that 'time is money' was made very, very real. Choose the wrong morning to sleep in late and you could miss the latest meme and watch your currency fall relative to the latest Bieberlet. But anyone who couldn't successfully employ the sapped to track and respond to trends didn't have any business embodying a valuable currency. Hell, even Kevin Bacon was able to ride the 'let's make it only four degrees' meme successfully, and he was hamstrung by the old guard mentality of the Hollywood has-beens. Seriously, anyone who wasn't making it wasn't trying.

When things started to turn, I thought it was just one of the normal blips that any currency goes through from time to time. Granted, the 'non-chewed' movement put a ding in my predigested, mostly carbon-based, breakfast cereal trade, but I had hedged enough in currency swaps with several other currencies (personal friends of mine) to smooth the bump. Still, I should have been suspicious of this, since all social movements were astroturfed those days, but I never thought it would be the cat's paw into my world. Plus, I had more than enough reserves of the hardest currencies – Travoltas, Brins, and Zooks – to prevent a run. Sure, I had upped my rate of return (adjusted hourly on quarter-day loans) to get the capital needed for my foray into the cereal biz, but that was best practice in risk management and the potential expansion of my marketplace more than justified the inflow. I probably could have overseen the investment more closely, but what's the point of having senior sappers (I had picked up Ben Bernanke on the cheap from the ruins of the Fed) if not to have them worry about those details? Besides, I had to concentrate on the marketing side of things as well as work on my tan.

Still, it came as a shock when my 8:00 am bond offering (necessary for the marketing campaign titled 'Pre-chewed means half the work!') was only a third subscribed and I had to up the rate by half a point. Not really a big deal (stuff like that happens), but then the rumors started, I began hemorrhaging capital, and other currencies started to panic. Only later did I realize that it was an orchestrated attack by a contracted Rwandan hacker network; none of the standard metrics were pinging because apparently someone had paid off Bernanke just like they did with the Libor rate. I was falling into a classic Obamageddon. I took all the normal steps, activated the termination clauses for most of the sapped to cut my burn rate, went on a virtual road show to demonstrate my confidence, and sold off some excess contract friends that I was planning on ditching anyway (sorry, Mom). All tried and true techniques, but I just couldn't gain traction. It was getting worse than the Chongqing fallout. So I went back to my roots and did a live feelie feed to extoll the virtues of predigested breakfast slop, which is an undignified (at least for a property of my status) but reliable way to move product. But I had to meet my 2:00 pm note obligations and didn't really have a choice. Unfortunately, I'd never actually tried the stuff before and no one warned me that it tasted like concrete lunchmeat (in retrospect this was clearly again a Bernanke machination) and my reaction put the last bullet in the carcass of pre-chewed food.

Needless to say, I went into default to my creditors, and that guaranteed a complete flight of capital. Although it was antithetical to everything I stood for, I delisted myself from the New York and Dubai markets, pegged my value to a fixed conversion rate and shifted my exchange to Mumbai. God, did I get bad press on that one, but it was do that or suffer a currency collapse. Even then it was only a stop-gap measure. Due to the old-fashioned trading laws still in effect on the Indian subcontinent, Mumbai was the only exchange that didn't have 24/7 operations. I had bought myself 12 hours to reconstruct my value proposition. Of course I would take a major hit (I was already being hammered in the secondary markets in Tashkent), but if I played things right I could still emerge as a viable currency. But to do so I had to take a step I had vowed long ago never to take.

After caning the rest of my sapped and senior sappers, including Bernanke, who turned some quick coin by denouncing the crony capitalism of the DomDrachma (D4) (like that even makes sense for a personal currency!), I called my contact at a shadowy Asian currency syndicate known as Y.U.K.O. and arranged a meeting. No one sets up a sit-down with Y.U.K.O. unless it is their last choice, but it was going to be make or break for me. I needed a strong injection of confidence in the DomDrachma (D4) and that wasn't going to happen via the normal channels. Hell, it wasn't even going to happen via the back alley channels – I had headed straight into the seamy underwear of the global economy. But I still had my looks, charm, and wit, and I should have been able to make it out of the encounter without getting greeked. Oh, the naiveté. Little did I know then that Y.U.K.O. had been behind the whole run in the first place (something about payback for years of some kind of neo-colonial Marxist crap) and so my effort was doomed from the start.

The meet-up was scheduled for a Japanese–Italian fusion restaurant called Basta Pasta in the Flatiron district, which should have been no problem. But, since trading on my currency was suspended, I was running into an exchange problem. I had been counting on there being a few cached versions of the exchange rate tables on the Cincinnati servers (where everything seems to be about a day behind the rest of the world) but they were strangely up to date. Someone (turned out to be the Rwandan hackers earning coin from Y.U.K.O.) had put out a high-priority call. Bastards! This put me in a serious bind, since I was in LA and had been counting on chartering a flight. Luckily I found an old stash of BitCoin that I (and everyone else) had forgotten about, but I was able to trade it for enough to get me to New York. But get this, I had to fly commercial! In freakin' cattle class, no less, as my elite status guaranteeing upgrades had been suspended. I hadn't been in the seats in back since before MyMoney and I had forgotten that they were now charging for adequate oxygen levels in coach. Sure, you could skip the optional 'add on' (sapped don't need all their brain cells anyway) but I had to be pinging on all networks when I arrived at the sit-down.

But paying for the O_2 meant that when I arrived at Giuliani airport in New York I didn't have enough scratch left to book a seat on the shared shuttle to Manhattan. Instead I had to hoof it. I thought there used to be public transportation, but the sapped I asked just laughed and laughed. Apparently it had been right-made (what we used to call privatized) years ago. When I tried to buy a ticket, the system judged me a 'risk' and refused to allow me entrance. I tried to argue, but you can't charm a machine and my ass was sorted right out to the sidewalk. So I began walking – luckily I could afford the private toll sidewalks and didn't have to resort to the public ones – and tried to sort out my strategy for the sit-down. This actually calmed me down as it allowed me to get to the sweet spot of the DomDrachma (D₄), the creative process. I was going to blow the freakin' doors off the meeting with my destructive creation. Or was that the other way round? No matter.

By the time I arrived at Basta Pasta I had my elevator pitch down and was ready for the meet. But I couldn't make it through the freakin' door because it had classified me as risky and as a non-patron based on mode of arrival, heart rate, stance, eye movements, and scent. Jesus, Mary and Joseph! I had been coded a sapped or, even worse, a citizen (the pejorative we used for the uncontracted and uncontractable)! I had to bring out my currency ID to gain entrance (luckily the doorware only updated every 24 hours and so was not current on my situation). I have to admit it shook my confidence that I had been pushed so quickly out of my elite status, but you don't become a major MyMoney player by worrying about how the silicon sorted.

The restaurant was crowded, with an air of expectation. I learned later that a very marginal (but enterprising) currency – someone called it the Euro – had tapped my communications after I fired my security crew and learned about the sit-down. He/She/It had quickly set up this meeting as an event, marketed it as 'the Downfall of the DomDrachma (D4)', sold tickets and made a bundle. This meant that my fall was extremely well documented. This normally would have been very profitable for me, but since I ended up selling the rights to my likeness (along with everything else) I didn't see a dime. I'm told that the expletive that I let loose once I realized the game was up remains a popular ringtone for the tweener-boppers. In retrospect, I would have been better off cutting a deal with whoever was behind the Euro than continuing with my meeting with Y.U.K.O.

As I made my way over to the table, I realized that the Y.U.K.O. rep-resentative was McSkyping (one of the few successful spinouts from the MicrAppleSoft debacle) rather than being in meatspace. I should have walked right then but I was out of options. Besides, I was hungry and whatever came next would be better met on a full stomach. I ordered the Tonno Fresco Scottato (Tuna tataki with wasabi tartare sauce) as an appetizer and Spaghetti ai Ricci del Mare (pasta with sea urchin and jalapeños) as my main along with a bottle of Pinot Grigio. The Y.U.K.O. side (represented by a ballerina hippo avatar, of all things) said nothing, which was annoying as hell. In order for the DomDrachma (D4) magic to happen, I needed to establish a rapport. Clearly Y.U.K.O. knew this and was giving me as little to go on as possible. So I started out with my normal pitch, 'I have a deal that will make both of us rich.' The hippo barely moved and replied, 'Can you elaborate on that?' Damn, not even a snide remark about my current fortunes to give me something to work with. I'm great at faking regret and apologies but that wasn't going to work here.

So I continued, 'The smart money knows that you invest when every-one else is running out,' and the hippo shot back with 'Surely not everyone?' What? Y.U.K.O. had certainly done their due diligence on me and probably knew more about my prospects than I did. What was the game here? It seemed strangely familiar. So I replied, 'That's what they tell me, but you are smarter than that. You and I can reach an understanding that will work for us both.' Again the deadpan hippo replied with a cryptic, 'Why do you say that?' and suddenly I knew I was played. They had hooked up a freakin' Ask Eliza chatterbot for the meet! They hadn't even gone with one of the smarter Turing AIs! They wanted to deliberately insult me and I knew that my ass was fried. The Mumbai market opened in an hour and Y.U.K.O. was going to exercise its option to acquire the DomDrachma (D₫). My creditors would be happy to get out with anything so they'd dump and run as soon as the offer was made. I was merkeled well and good.

It has been about three months since that night, and things played out about as I expected as I moved from currency to sapped. I was surprised at first that the Y.U.K.O. actually kept the DomDrachma (D₫) running rather than shutting it down completely. But apparently the Chongqing incident had created a niche in the occidental fetish markets of the intertubes, and as a result there remained a bit of a cachet (granted, an exceedingly sordid one) to the DomDrachma (D₫). Still, it allowed me to maintain a little pride, which is destroyed every day (twice on Saturdays and Sundays) when I have to do my employer-mandated feelie broadcasts. Man, there are some sick, sick ideas about concrete out on the intertubes. Still as the advertising campaign says, 'Better sapped than citizen,' and I accepted my fate with a happy heart (as mandated by Section 13, paragraphs 2–7 of my contract).

An Afterword in Three Postcards

Tom Boellstorff

How do you reply to a postcard?

This book is comprised of postcards from the metaverse – reflective essays about online socialities. I agreed to write an afterword before reading any of these postcards: with all their fascinating insights they now lie scattered before me. What to do? I shall see where the path of analogy may lead.

Let us, then, truly regard these chapters as postcards from the metaverse. The metaphor suggests objects, practices, and subjectivities: it presumes temporalities and geographies. Let us thus treat these chapters not just as images but as two-sided artifacts with stamps, postmarks, and signatures that trace histories of social relation. Rarely does one send a postcard from home. Fragmented commentaries on travel, postcards imply that the sender is Elsewhere, in a strange and distant land, usually cosmopolitan (say, Paris) or exotic (say, a tropical island). Postcards from places like my home state of Nebraska in the American Midwest play off these tropes with their tongue-in-cheek images of skiers in cornfields, or giant jackrabbits. Brief records of fleeting encounters with the Other, postcards demand concision: one can only write a couple of sentences on their reverse sides. This shapes the striking fact that postcards do not demand a reply: it is typically assumed that the sender will have moved on (or returned home) by the time the receiver has the postcard in hand. They do not create a circuit of correspondence. Indeed, postcards usually do not even include a place for a return address.

So how do you reply to a postcard? It seems the most appropriate response is to violate the norms of one-way communication and exotic visitation the postcard genre implies, and send back three postcards of my own. Consider these not as postcards from the metaverse, or postcards from the 'real world' so often assumed to lie opposed to the metaverse, but postcards of the gap: postcards of the interchange between the online and offline, of the double move between virtual and actual that is not convergence, but the true reality of human existence.

First postcard

My first postcard shows two avatars sitting in a virtual Parisian park, enjoying the beauty of lush fields of blooms in a warm evening's glow. On the reverse I might write, 'went to the metaverse but didn't see anything unusual.'

There is a desperate need to banalize the metaverse, to question the idea that it lies at an exotic remove. It is this initial and deeply flawed gesture of estrangement that makes thinkable the equally flawed subsequent claim that the online and offline are 'blurring'. We must move beyond the hype of total social transformation but also the anti-hype of inevitable addiction and domination. We must move beyond, as well, obsessions with predicting the future: their utility is limited for the simple reason that we cannot study that which has not happened. We might consider speaking of unexpected developments and multiple paths of possibility. Those who present psyche or society in terms of discrete linear stages mask the diversity and contingency of reality, in the metaverse and the physical world.

The Immersive Internet can, of course, have good or bad consequences, and thinking about what comes next is useful for everyone from designers to science fiction authors. However, what is currently underemphasized is better understanding the less sexy (but no less valuable) everyday practices of online interaction. These everyday practices rarely appear on postcards but are noteworthy nonetheless. Photographs of a wedding say little about everyday married life: the important stuff is what happens between the big events. This everyday sociality is hard to grasp precisely because it is so taken for granted. It is contextual and emergent.

Second postcard

My second postcard shows an avatar on a tiny desert island, feet tucked into warm sand while considering how to obtain a coconut from the fronds of a tree above. Flip the postcard over and the short message might read, 'Could have used some help. Missing you.'

When it comes to the internet, what does it mean to be immersed? The question is best answered by examining the empirical realities of life online. With the rise of broadband internet connections and more powerful personal computers, we have seen the rise of more photorealistic online environments; these raise new possibilities for immersive experience. However, early visions of a future where we lie in warm baths of gelatin to be plugged into a system that hijacks our sensorium have not come to pass. While for a few specialized domains (flight simulators for novice pilots, for instance) systems approaching immersion in this totalizing sense may be of interest, overall the so-called 3D internet is only three-dimensional from the avatar's perspective. Most people neither want nor need sensory immersion: brilliant graphics and to a lesser extent sound suffice, limited to screen and speaker.

I intend my forlorn postcard to recall how, throughout the internet age, social immersion has been the true form of immersion. The 'stickiness' of a social networking site like Facebook has little to do with sensory excess and everything to do with social interaction, and this can include interaction with people we have never met (and will never meet) in the physical world. Even visually rich and three-dimensional online environments are rarely seen as immersive if there is no one else in them – one reason for the addition of sharing, chatting, and other social functions in more and more online environments, as well as the use of non-player characters (NPC) and other computer-controlled social interlocutors.

Third postcard

My final postcard is an avatar portrait: a head held in hand, gazing with clear eyes into an unseen distance. The reverse might read, 'I'll always be here for you.' Embodiment has always been a hallmark of the Immersive Internet, evoking strong reactions with regard to the key issue of the real. But this embodiment is always emplacement as well; if anything, what makes some aspects of online sociality seem 'immersive' is that it makes place, permitting things like synchronic social interaction and persistent content. And these selfhoods and socialities, these speech acts and commercial exchanges, these weapons and gardens, all are in their way real. The boundary between the virtual and the physical is not isomorphic with the boundary between the real and the unreal. Not only does the boundary lie in a different place: it is a different kind of boundary altogether.

Thus it is that the greatest conceptual error that continues to plague understandings of virtual worlds and the Immersive Internet more broadly is the idea that the virtual and the real are blurring or converging. This belief is mistaken on two counts. First, it is incorrect to oppose the virtual and the real. Such a dichotomy forces us into an analytic framework in which we decide ahead of time that the online is not real. Yet we make friends online we never meet in the physical world, or meet only after the reality of the friendship is well established. We spend real money online, some of it on virtual goods like a new shirt for that avatar gracing the front of our postcard. We take a math or history course online, and what we learn (and how we thus grow as individuals) is quite real. On the other hand, we play in the physical world, pretend to be something, lose all our money in a game of Monopoly.

The gap between the virtual and the actual is not the doing of a scholar, artist, or technology entrepreneur. It is a form of relation, like the relation between a postcard and the word 'postcard', or between the two sides of a postcard. In fact, what if we took the two sides of a postcard as one way to understand immersion – thinking of immersion not in terms of being 'inside' something but in terms of the surfaces that collectively delineate an object? Or, if we look to language for insight, the word is in no danger of becoming the thing, for it is the gap between them that makes language possible.

Alongside drawing from such possible alternative conceptual traditions, we badly need more careful empirical research exploring the constant movements between the virtual and actual that make the internet possible as a space of sociality. In this regard, one important arena for investigation is how it is not just that we enter the Immersive Internet to meet preexisting needs and desires (for friendship, fantasy, labor, etc.); new needs and desires can emerge through our engagements with the Immersive Internet itself.

Into the mail slot: mobile futures

So off I go to the post office with my three postcards to send back to you, dear reader. In turning the usual one-way communication of the postcard genre into a correspondence, I hope to build a research community, a shared conversation of inquiry. When it comes to the Immersive Internet, we can all say almost anything. We can point to legitimate examples of deception and malice. We can point as well to legitimate examples of creativity and kindness. In this, as in so many other ways, the online and the offline are not so different.

Indeed, a second reason I send these replies is, as noted earlier, to banalize or de-exoticize the Immersive Internet. The gap between virtual and actual is not a gap that divides. It is not a moat but a bridge – far less like the conceptual chasm between Self and Other or Same and Different, and far more like the productive zone of transaction between symbol and referent. It is a zone of connection, but not of blurring or convergence. It is the maintenance of the distinction – even with all the moving back and forth across it – that makes the virtual and actual possible, just as no laptop or gaming console could function without the gap between the zeroes and ones of digital computation.

This need to de-exoticize the Immersive Internet is of particular urgency because of our dire need for a theoretical language to address the co-occurrence of immersion and mobility. The rise of cloud computing and mobile devices like smartphones and tablets means that the Immersive Internet will increasingly be mobile in the physical world, and in real time. We now carry the Immersive Internet with us, and in specific places: in Germany or China, in a New York subway, or on a combine in rural Nebraska. In many cases this mobility of the Immersive Internet will thus vary according to physical world context: playing an online game while sitting on a bus versus in a darkened room at home, or holding up our smartphone to see information about local stores overlaid on our view of the street. In other cases, there may be surprising ways in which the Immersive Internet will not vary by physical world context, and could even provide threads of narrative and experiential continuity through those contexts and between dispersed localities.

We cannot know in advance what these futures will entail; even understanding the shifting present is a great challenge. But it is an exciting challenge that suggests new theories, new methods, and new research communities, even while suggesting renewed attention to classic theories, methods, and disciplines as well. It is precisely when everything seems to be so novel that it is crucial to engage deeply with histories of research practice and conceptual innovation; far too often what appears unprecedented is in fact powerfully predicated on what came before.

From their origins, forms of online sociality seen as 'immersive' have engendered concern. They can be regarded as places where people can lose themselves, become addicted, severed from reality. They can with equal validity be regarded as places where crafting, hacking, and making lead to forms of social engagement with real consequences for the physical world. So enough of postcards for now. They have done their valuable work of showing a range of realities and possibilities, online and offline. They have recalled important elements of the past, shown fascinating aspects of the present, and speculated on a range of possible futures. Now is the time for longer missives, products of sustained research and collaborative theoretical work. We need novels from the metaverse, diaries, even scholarly articles. Through such work we can strive for a more robust and multifaceted understanding of the promises and perils of the Immersive Internet, and seek to ensure that these worlds we make serve goals of social justice and true human flourishing, a flourishing which has always been virtual as well as physical.

Index